Welcome to the Wonderful World of JavaScript!

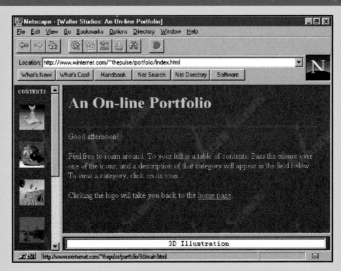

By adding a JavaScript script to your HTML web page, you can make your page do all sorts of things you never dreamed of before:

- ➤ Animate text or graphics
- ➤ Create interactive loan applications
- ➤ Beat others at Blackjack
- ➤ Program and fill out your tax forms
- ➤ Publish an online magazine with interactive links
- ➤ Calculate the reams of sports stats
- ➤ Change background colors or spew random phrases when you click a button
- ➤ Show off your artwork in an interactive portfolio
- ➤ Give automated tours to users without any clicking

The Bridge Between HTML and JavaScript: the <SCRIPT> Tag

```
<SCRIPT [LANGUAGE="JavaScript"] [SRC="scriptURL"]>
<!-- hide from non-Java browsers -->
<!-- JavaScript statements and functions go here -->
//-->
</SCRIPT>
```

JavaScript Objects

Objects are the building blocks of your JavaScript scripts. Here's a handy reference to some of the things you can manipulate with JavaScript's built-in objects.

The window Object

Properties	Methods	Events
frames[]	alert("*msg*")	onLoad
frames.length	confirm("*msg*")	onUnload
status	prompt("*msg*")	
self	open("*URL*", "*name*", "*characteristics*")	
parent	close()	
top		

The radio Object

Properties	Methods	Events
name	click()	onClick
length		
value		
checked		
defaultChecked		

The history Object

Properties	Methods	Events
	go(delta)	
	go("string")	
	back()	
length	forward()	

The document Object

Properties	Methods	Events
title	write("string")	onLoad
location	writeln("string")	onUnload
lastModified	clear()	
loadedDate	close()	
bgColor	open("*mimetype*")	
fgColor		
linkColor		
vlinkColor		
alinkColor		
forms[]		
forms.length		
links[]		
links.length		
anchors[]		
anchors.length		

The forms Object

Properties	Methods	Events
name	submit()	onSubmit
method		
action		
target		
elements[x]		

The text and textArea Objects

Properties	Methods	Events
name	focus()	onFocus
value	blur()	onBlur
defaultValue	select()	onSelect
		onChange

The checkbox Object

Properties	Methods	Events
name	click()	onClick
value		
status		
defaultStatus		
checked		

The select Object

Properties	Methods	Events
length		onFocus
name		onBlur
selectedIndex		onChange

options *which contain the subproperties:*

- index
- length
- name
- selected
- text
- value

The button Object

Properties	Methods	Events
value	click()	onClick
name		

The COMPLETE IDIOT'S GUIDE TO

JavaScript™

by Scott J. Walter and Aaron Weiss

A Division of Macmillan Computer Publishing
201 W. 103rd Street, Indianapolis, IN 46290

To my brother, best friend, and business partner, Matthew—S.W.

To family, friends, and groth!—A.W.

©1996 Que® Corporation

International Standard Book Number: 0-7897-0798-5
Library of Congress Catalog Card Number: 96-67566

98 97 96   8 7 6 5 4 3 2 1

Interpretation of the printing code: the rightmost number of the first series of numbers is the year of the book's printing; the rightmost number of the second series of numbers is the number of the book's printing. For example, a printing code of 96-1 shows that the first printing of the book occurred in 1996.

Screen reproductions in this book were created by means of the program Collage Complete from Inner Media, Inc., Hollis, NH.

Printed in the United States of America

Publisher
Roland Elgey

Vice President and Publisher
Marie Butler-Knight

Editorial Services Director
Elizabeth Keaffaber

Publishing Director
Lynn Zingraf

Managing Editor
Michael Cunningham

Development Editor
Lori Cates

Technical Editor
Martin Wyatt

Production Editor
Phil Kitchel

Copy Editor
San Dee Phillips

Cover Designers
Dan Armstrong, Barbara Kordesh

Designer
Kim Scott

Illustrations
Judd Winick

Technical Specialist
Nadeem Muhammed

Indexer
Craig Small

Production Team
*Stephen Adams, Claudia Bell, Anne Dickerson, Brad Dixon, Jenny Earhart,
Joan Evan, Trey Frank, Jason Hand, Damon Jordan, Bob LaRoche,
Julie Quinn, Bobbi Satterfield, Mike Thomas, Todd Wente, Paul Wilson*

Contents at a Glance

Contents

xvii

Introduction

Everybody's talking about it...everybody wants to do it: Killer Web pages. Animation, graphics, sound, changing information, reformatting text, nicely displayed documents—you want it all. Up to now, however, it was impossible to start doing the *really* fancy stuff unless you were a computer programmer and *intimately* familiar with the workings of the Web, CGI, HTML, and a slew of other jargon in the alphabet soup of the online world.

Things have changed.

The hot-shot companies in cyberspace have started to turn their attention toward the rest of us: the "idiot" user, the people who don't know COBOL from FORTRAN but still want our MTV. As an answer to the growing "We want to do it, too" cries coming from the Net, Java and JavaScript were born.

Welcome to The Complete Idiot's Guide to JavaScript

The Complete Idiot's Guide to JavaScript introduces you, gentle reader, to the hottest property in cyberspace today: JavaScript. With JavaScript, a normal, everyday, Internet-familiar person can create Web pages with the finesse of an experienced guru. No mantras, no strange languages, no expensive compilers—just a little common sense and an open mind.

This book explains what JavaScript is, how it works, what it's made of, and how you can use it. You'll discover the component parts that make up this language, understanding all the esoteric pieces in a language that don't require a Ph.D. You'll even find several examples of JavaScript scripts in action that you can rip apart, change, and enhance.

What about the title of this book—*The Complete* Idiot's *Guide*? Well, it assumes that you're no idiot on your own turf. You know your job, you know what you want, you know how to get things done. But there's one thing you don't know: how to use JavaScript.

This book assumes that you've done a little Web surfing and have created some of your own pages. However, as you've surfed, you've come across things others have put together and you want to learn how to do that, too. The underlying things (protocols, transmission layers, gateways, proxies) are of little concern to you—you want to get the job done. Quickly. Easily. And retaining as much of your hair as possible.

Here are some more assumptions:

➤ You know what the World Wide Web is.

➤ You know what a browser is.

➤ You're familiar with HTML, the language of the Web.

➤ You've created some of your own Web pages.

➤ You like chocolate.

If, however, you feel you want more background on any of these assumptions, check out *The Complete Idiot's Guide to the Internet* (Peter Kent), *The Complete Idiot's Guide to the Internet with Windows 95* (Peter Kent), *The Complete Idiot's Guide to Creating an HTML Web Page* (Paul McFedries), or *The Complete Idiot's Guide to the World Wide Web* (Peter Kent).

How Do You Use This Book?

You don't have to read this book from cover to cover. If you want to find out what makes up JavaScript, go to the JavaScript internals chapters, 6 through 14; if you want to dive right in and start creating script pages, go to the examples chapters, 15 through 19. Each chapter is a self-contained unit with the information you need to use and understand one aspect of JavaScript. If you require information that's covered elsewhere in the book, you'll find plenty of cross-references.

There are a couple of conventions in this book to make it easier to use. For example, when you need to type something, it will appear like this:

```
Type this
```

Just type what it says; it's as simple as that. If we don't know exactly what you'll have to type—because you have to supply some of the information— the unknown information appears in italics. For instance:

```
Type this filename
```

We don't know the filename, so you'll have to supply it.

Often it will be necessary to show longer examples of JavaScript. They will appear in a special typeface, arranged to mimic what appears on your screen:

```
Some of the lines will be in actual English.
Some of the lines will seem to be in a mutant dialect of English.
```

Again, don't panic.

If you want to understand more about the subject you are learning, you'll find some background information in boxes. Because this information is in boxes, you can quickly skip over the information if you want to avoid the gory details. Here are the special icons and boxes used in this book that help you learn just what you need:

Techno Nerd Teaches

Skip this background fodder (technical twaddle) unless you're truly interested.

Revue head
Tips, warnings, cautions, shortcuts, definitions, and that sort of information.

Acknowledgments

We, the authors, would like to thank a number of people for helping us with this book. Fighting for first position on the list are Martha O'Sullivan and Lori Cates, our editors, who put up with some, let us just say, "unusual" circumstances. Lori's technical savvy helped us greatly throughout the writing, and Martha's tolerance was truly amazing (considering she was expecting a child at any moment—Hi Megan Ann!). Barry Pruett also assisted in coordinating various phases.

Scotty would also like to offer spices and myrrh to his brother, Matthew Walter, who deserves special mention for letting him use his online site as a demonstration guinea pig during the creation of some of the examples. And to his coworkers, who silently dealt with a maniac who was writing at night and programming during the day. Last (and *definitely* not least) are his parents, whose support (as is the way with parents) was unwavering.

Aaron wants not to forget Phil Kitchel and San Dee Phillips, who helped smooth out the jagged edges. In addition, I'd like to give warm recognition to 2% milk, which was usually there for me when I needed it to wet down my cereal before each writing marathon. Lastly, to my Buoyier of Spirits, Angela.

Trademarks

All terms mentioned in this book that are known to be trademarks have been appropriately capitalized. Que Corporation cannot attest to the accuracy of this information. Use of a term in this book should not be regarded as affecting the validity of any trademark or service mark.

Netscape Communications, the Netscape Communications logo, Netscape, and Netscape Navigator are trademarks of Netscape Communications Corporation.

JavaScript and Java are trademarks of Sun Microsystems, Inc.

Part 1
What's It All About?

You've heard the jargon everywhere: Java, JavaScript, live Web pages. You've seen what the jargon does: animation, graphics, sound…in a word, it's multimedia for your Web page. You want it. But you've heard that Java is a programming language, and your heart sinks: you're not a programmer. Enter JavaScript, a way to get Java-powered pages with simple programming and without needing a computer science degree! Step-by-steps included.

Before you dive head-first into the world of JavaScript, learn a little background: what JavaScript is, what it does, and what it can do for you!

Chapter 1

The Top Ten Things You Need To Know

You can't turn on the television, open a magazine or newspaper, or listen to the radio without hearing about it. If your work involves computers (even if you're not a programmer), you might even have to deal with it. You may even find it creeping into the conversation at parties. It has become a force of its own, and it's gaining momentum: The World Wide Web is everywhere. More and more companies have *home pages*; they even advertise them on their commercials. In fact, "the Web" has gotten so big that a whole new occupation has popped up in the Sunday classifieds: Web Page Designer.

In the early days of the Web, you had to be a mainframe guru (those strange folks who prowl the company computer networks late at night, speaking a language unto themselves) to even begin to understand *how* to create beautiful pages. You had to use HTML, CGI, Perl, and other "computer-ese" languages.

The times they are a-changin'. And leading the pack is a new kid on the block. A language that's simple, yet powerful. Elegant, yet practical. Enter *JavaScript*: Web programming for the common man. That's what you're here to look at—what you're here to learn.

I know most of you never pictured yourself sitting down and reading a book on computers from cover to cover. I hope I can change your mind. Here's a quick look at some things you'll need to know to get started in the wonderful world of JavaScripting:

1. JavaScript Is New—I Mean New

Created by Sun Microsystems and Netscape, JavaScript isn't totally defined yet (some parts still need hashing out by the experts). The parts that *are* finished give you a great deal of power and control, but if you want to keep up with the language as it evolves, you'll need to stop by Sun's or Netscape's home pages from time to time. An excellent starting place would be:

```
http://home.netscape.com/comprod/products/navigator/version_2.0/script/
➥script_info/index.html
```

2. JavaScript Is Strictly for the World Wide Web

JavaScript was created in an effort to give Web authors more power and flexibility without driving them over the brink with programming syntax, language structure, and other dull things. To see how JavaScript fits into the Web scheme, check out Chapter 2.

With JavaScript, it's much easier to create a Web page that interacts with the user. For example, imagine a page where the user enters purchase orders. Using JavaScript, the page can easily make given calculations based on the customer's order and display an immediate on-screen invoice. Some experienced Web surfers may think, "Sure, I've seen that before JavaScript." It's true that this form of user interactivity has been possible before, but JavaScript makes it easier for everyone to implement—especially the novice or amateur Web page designer—and it requires fewer computing resources to do so.

3. JavaScript Is a "Scripting Language"

This is a fancy term for something that isn't quite a programming language but is more than the language currently used to create Web pages: HTML.

HTML is technically a "markup" language. It basically serves to mark out sections of text that should appear in a certain style. This is quite a bit different from a "programming" language, which is a set of grammatical statements and rules that can be combined to give instructions to the computer. A "scripting" language is something of a hybrid of the two, although it's closer to a programming language. In short, a scripting language serves the same purpose as a programming language (to provide a series of instructions to the computer), but its rules are less strict and less complex. Scripting languages are best suited for small programming tasks, such as those you would need in a Web page (as opposed to, say, creating a word processing program such as Microsoft Word).

4. To See the Magic That JavaScript Can Produce, You Need a Browser That Can Handle It: Netscape Navigator 2.0

Currently, there is only one browser available that takes advantage of JavaScript's power: Netscape Navigator 2.0. As time goes on, other browsers will appear that support it, but for now, Navigator 2.0 is the only game in town. Chapter 3 shows you how to track down and install your very own copy of this nifty little program.

5. You Can "Borrow" JavaScript Programs from Other People's Web Pages

Since JavaScript is embedded within HTML documents, you can surf the Web and actually see the code that other scripters have created. You'll do some poking around the Internet in Chapter 5, checking out the hottest spots for nifty scripts.

6. JavaScript Is a Language That Extends HTML; You Stick It into Your Pages Using the <SCRIPT> Tag

JavaScript has a lot packed into it (objects, functions, events, and such), but everything is designed to be easy to use and understand. As a "little sister" to Java, the new full-blown Web programming language, JavaScript gives you most of Java's power without you having to grease your hair back, switch to a plaid shirt and high-water pants, and buy a gross of pocket protectors. Chapter 4 covers how JavaScript works in conjunction with HTML.

7. With JavaScript, You Can Bypass Mastering CGI

JavaScript makes it possible to do things you couldn't do before without learning CGI (the esoteric UNIX-based programming interface to the World Wide Web). Some things will still require CGI access (you'll look at them more closely in later chapters), but for the most part, you won't need it.

8. JavaScript Is Built Around the Concept of "Objects"

JavaScript requires you to think *objectively*. By that, I mean that the language is built around the concept of *objects* or "things that represent other things." The nuts and bolts of what makes up JavaScript are covered in Chapters 6 through 14.

9. Learning JavaScript by Example Is the Easiest Approach

Learning a new language is tough. Take it slow, go easy, take small bites, and above all, *try things*. In this book, you'll find several examples of JavaScript, complete with full HTML documents that you can type in and run "right out of the box." If you want to jump right to the examples, you'll find them in Chapters 15 through 18.

10. If You Can Imagine It, JavaScript Can Help You Create It

Covering *everything* that makes up JavaScript would take a much larger (and more boring) book than the one you're holding. The intention here is to give you a taste of the power of this new language. By the time you're done with the coming chapters, you'll be able to craft some pretty impressive pages, and you'll have enough ideas to keep yourself scripting for some time to come. If you still need some help with ideas, Chapter 19 has a *bunch*.

TSSSSSS

Coffee? In My Computer? I Prefer Decaf...

Extending the Web

In the "old days" of the World Wide Web (two whole years ago), there were two ways to get information (also called *content*) to the user. The primary one was through HTML or *HyperText Markup Language*, the language used to write Web pages. HTML allows for presenting text and displaying certain types of graphics, as well as *links* to connect one page to another page—either on the same computer or somewhere else in the world. As HTML has evolved (the current standard being worked on is version 3.0), other features have been added such as forms, frames, tables, and so on. However, even with all the new features, HTML basically deals with Web content by

➤ Formatting and displaying the content of a page.

➤ Waiting for the user to click on something in the page.

➤ Depending on what the user clicked on, fetching something else (a new page) and repeating the process.

Although this provides a wealth of possibilities for content manipulation (just spend a little time on the Web to see for yourself), it doesn't allow for more advanced things like accessing a database, ordering catalog items online, or making animated graphics within a Web page. For this, you need to understand the *Common Gateway Interface,* or *CGI*.

CGI provides a means of extending the capabilities of HTML by allowing the Web designer to write custom programs that interact with Web pages to do more complex things. A CGI program is a file that resides on the Web server that the server runs in response to something inside the Web page. With it, you can...

➤ Create *image maps*, which are graphics that you can click on; different areas of the graphic behave like unique HTML links.

An image on the image map

An image map; clicking on different parts of this image determines what happens next. You used to have to know CGI programming to create one of these.

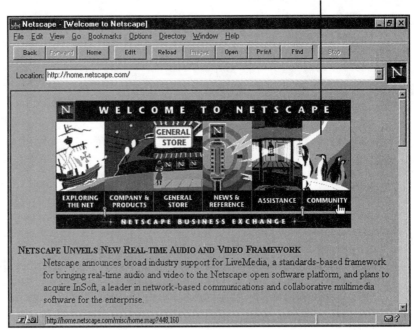

➤ Dynamically (on demand) create custom HTML pages and graphics. A common use is the "You are the 34251th visitor" line you find on many pages.

➤ Create simple animations by having CGI send a sequence of graphics to the browser. This produces the Web equivalent of a "flip-book," where one graphic replaces the previous one.

➤ Interface with a database on the server, to retrieve or add information. Online catalog ordering uses CGI, as well as the search engines (such as Yahoo, Lycos, and WebCrawler) that keep track of everything there is to find on the Web.

The downside of CGI is you *must* be a programmer to use it. Secondly, CGI requires that the user's actions be reported back to the server for interpretation and processing. The results of this processing then must be sent back to the user from this server. These extra transfers take time and reduce the "immediacy" of certain Web page interactions. Furthermore, you are limited to the CGI capabilities of your server—your provider might not offer a Web server with complete CGI tools, or any at all. Also, *multimedia* (sound, graphics, animation) has become all the rage, and everything in computers today has to have or support multimedia. CGI doesn't do this well.

Finally, to use CGI, you must have access to the CGI interface of the Web server that's serving up your pages. As mentioned, some providers might not support CGI access, or it might be offered for an extra (in many cases, costly) fee.

In other words, CGI is more complex than most Web authors are interested in, and it doesn't support all of the visually fancy things authors want to include in their pages. Something else is necessary, and that something is *Java*.

Most CGI Programs Are Written in Perl Because the Internet originated within the UNIX world (before Windows computers or Macintoshes were hooked up to it), much of what drives the Internet (and the Web) is based in UNIX. CGI stems from this same basis, and the *Perl* language is a UNIX-based language. But, a CGI program can be written in any language that the Web server supports.

Java: Web Programming for the Common Man

You can't surf the Web today without hearing about *Java*. Java, a programming language developed by Sun Microsystems, is designed to bring more power and flexibility to the presentation of material through the Web. With Java, you can...

➤ Create animations that sing and dance.

➤ Pop up prompts and dialog boxes while a user is filling out a form.

➤ Develop games and programs that actually run—right on the Web page.

➤ Calculate a loan in real-time based on user input.

➤ Display an accurate on-screen invoice reflecting a user's current purchases.

➤ Access databases and other information sources.

➤ Let your imagination wander.

Java works the floor in 3D rotating glory.

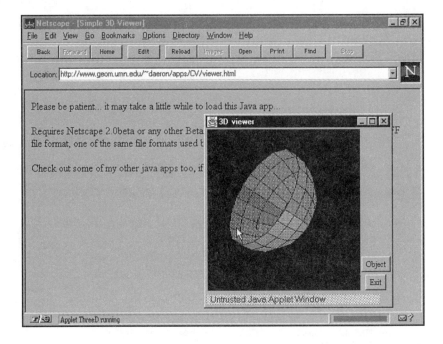

Before Java, if you wanted to view a graphic, play a movie, or listen to a sound file on the Web, you needed a *helper application* installed on your computer and connected to your browser (an independent program unrelated to the browser). Whenever a particular file (movie, sound, or whatever) was retrieved from the Web, the helper would be run to display or play back the file. If you didn't have the necessary helper, you had to find it, download it, and install it.

Java handles these things internally. No helper applications. No CGI programming. All you need is a Java-enabled browser and the Java Developers Kit (freely available from Sun's Java Home Site, http://java.sun.com). And, as an added bonus, the Java programs you create (called *applets* or *mini-applications*) will run on *any* Java-enabled browser on *any* platform: Macintosh, Windows, or UNIX. You don't need to create a program for each machine type. One size fits all.

However, Java is not without its problems. It *is* a programming language and, as with all programming languages, you must learn it relatively well in order to use it. The applets you create must be *compiled* before you can use them. A compiler is a special program that reads your own program and crunches it into machine-readable binary code. Compilers can be a hassle, because you have to use them every time you make a change to your program, and they can take a long time to compile a program. Currently, there aren't any nice programming editor/compiler packages available that allow you to easily build Java applets, although several are being developed.

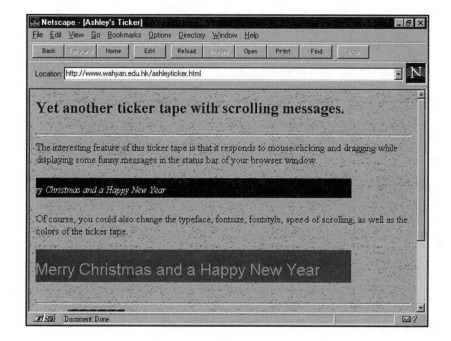

Scrolling ticker tapes—trust us; they scroll.

So, what you need is a way of getting the capability of Java without the added baggage of a full-blown programming language. Once again, Sun comes to the rescue (with help from Netscape) with *JavaScript*.

Enter JavaScript

JavaScript is a scripting language specifically designed to work with the World Wide Web. With JavaScript, you can take the power of HTML and the World Wide Web and extend it in a variety of ways.

Once upon a time (not too long ago), Sun Microsystems conjured up the complex and powerful programming language now known as Java. Although Java is highly capable, it's best suited for more complex tasks, and to be programmed by experienced users. Netscape Communications saw the need for an in-between language—one that would allow individuals to design Web pages that could interact with the user, or with Java applets, with a minimum of programming experience. Always one to be first on the block, Netscape whipped up LiveScript.

LiveScript was more of a proposal than an actual language, but it convinced people that this "bridge-the-gap" idea was attractive. LiveScript was designed in the spirit of many simple scripting languages, but tailored with capabilities specifically designed for Web pages (HTML and form interaction, for example). Sun Microsystems decided to get in on the act, and Sun and Netscape held hands and announced the newly named JavaScript.

JavaScript is freely available for licensing, so that anyone who designs a Web browser may implement it. The idea behind this is to make JavaScript a programming standard. Although Netscape Navigator is the first (and the only, at this writing) browser that supports JavaScript, the above licensing means that there will likely be others.

What's a Scripting Language?

It's impossible for a computer program to be all things to all people. Software publishers try their best to make sure their programs can handle most of what users want, but they can never anticipate everything. To make their programs more flexible, many provide the ability to extend or change how their program behaves through a *script*.

Scripts are nothing more than a sequence of program instructions (called *statements*). The program steps through the statements one at a time and performs whatever the script tells it. This is exactly the same as "programming," except that scripts tend to have simpler rules and require less learning time. Some examples of programs that provide scripting are dBASE, Paradox, and Microsoft Access (although there are many more). Some examples of stand-alone scripting languages are Perl and REXX.

Script languages make extending these packages easy. You don't have to be a programmer, purchase an expensive compiler, learn some strange, pseudo-English language, and start wearing plaid shirts with pocket protectors.

Based on Java, JavaScript supports most of Java's expression constructs (another word for *statements*). However, JavaScript doesn't require a compiler or a knowledge of programming to get up and running. All you really need is an understanding of HTML and a little logic.

Like Java, JavaScript is built on the concept of *objects*. Unlike Java, JavaScript provides a basic collection of *objects* for you to work with. You can't create new objects or object types, but the ones provided give you a great deal of power.

What's an Object?

Like the word implies, an *object* is a thing—*any* thing. The term object is used to generically group a collection of different things together. In the world of computers, *objects* are different pieces (or building blocks) that make up a computer system or program. Using objects shields a programmer (or a JavaScript writer) from having to understand how the operating system works.

You can think of objects as little black boxes. You poke things into it (called *setting properties*) and in response, the black box does something. Actually how it works isn't important, just that it works. This is the basis for the concept of *object-oriented programming*, where the programmer is more concerned with what an object is doing than how it gets the job done.

For example, if you had a "screen object," you could change the color of the computer screen by telling the screen object to set its color property to, say, green. Whether the computer is a Macintosh or an IBM PC, the object would do the same thing (although in different ways).

In Chapter 6, you begin an up-close and personal look at objects in their natural habitat.

The Least You Need To Know

In this chapter, you took a quick look at the origin of JavaScript. You learned how the World Wide Web got its start through HTML, and how HTML was extended and enhanced through CGI programming. You discovered that Java came into being to satisfy the need to do more through the Web than either HTML or CGI could provide. Finally, you learned that JavaScript took Java one step further by making the same power of Java available to Web authors who don't want to learn how to program.

Now, it's time to start jivin' with JavaScript. But first, you need a browser that supports (can understand the commands of) JavaScript. Currently, the only browser that provides JavaScript power is Netscape Navigator 2.0. In the next chapter, you take a tour through the latest version of the most popular browser on the Web.

Part 2
Let's Get Jivin'!

Alright, now you're hooked. You've gotten a "taste of the bean" and you want to put a little sugar (or whatever sweetener you prefer) on your Web site. You want to get rolling. To do that, you need a few things, not the least of which is a browser that can handle JavaScript.

At the present time, only Netscape Navigator 2.0 supports JavaScript (other companies have licensed JavaScript technology for inclusion in future versions of their browsers...but they haven't released them yet). So, set up Navigator 2.0, kick the tires, and check out what's really brewing on the Web.

Chapter 3

Netscape Navigator 2.0: The World Wide Web on a Caffeine High

In This Chapter

➤ Setting up Netscape Navigator 2.0

➤ Browsin' and jivin'

➤ Documentation: It's all in there!

➤ Canned applets (delicious!)

Let's Brew Up a Browser

Whereas JavaScript is the language, Netscape Navigator 2.0 is the browser that understands the language (making all those nifty, little scripts sing and dance on your Web page). In the future—perhaps by the time you read this—other browsers may also support JavaScript, such as Microsoft's Internet Explorer. At this writing, though, Netscape Navigator 2.0 is the only game in town. Before you dive headlong into the world of creating JavaScript pages, you need to get comfortable with the browser that plays it all back for you (or whoever else accesses your pages).

Where Can I Get a Cup?

But I Already Have Netscape 1.2! If you're already using Netscape Navigator (perhaps you purchased it or downloaded version 1.2 some time ago), you still need to upgrade to version 2.0. Netscape Navigator 2.0 is the version that supports JavaScript. If you stay with version 1.2, you won't be able to see the "special effects" that JavaScript produces.

To dig that Java jive, you need to get Navigator 2.0 up and running. To get your copy from the Internet, grab your current browser (any browser will do) and point it at:

http://www.netscape.com/

Follow the links to the "Downloading" section (or you can click one of the **Netscape NOW 2.0** buttons you'll find liberally sprinkled throughout the pages). Follow the instructions to pick the correct version (Netscape Navigator has versions available for Macintosh, Windows 3.x, Windows 95, Windows NT, and several flavors of UNIX) and begin the download process. This file is over 3 megabytes in size, so once you start the download, you might want to go get a cup of *real* coffee!

All Right...Now What?

Once you download the file, simply run it—either by double-clicking on it or specifying its name in the Windows Run dialog box, which you access by selecting **File**, **Run** in Windows 3.1's Program Manager or **Run** from the Start Menu in Windows 95. In a perfect universe, the rest of the process should be automatic, and Netscape will walk you through the installation.

After Netscape is installed and working, you may delete the installation file you originally downloaded. However, it might be wise to keep it around until you're confident that Netscape is working, just in case reinstallation is necessary. Wouldn't want to have to download that 3-megabyte file all over again.

Running the .exe file that contains Netscape.

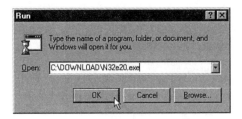

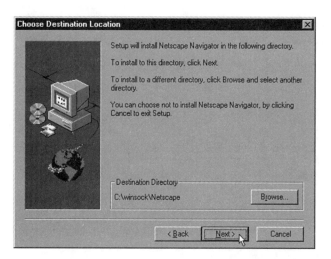

The installation program steps you through the whole process.

An .EXE File That Unpacks Itself?

This is a *self-extracting archive*, and it's nothing but a fancy way to easily get a compressed file decompressed on your computer without having to figure out how to run (or find) a decompression program (such as WinZip or PKUNZIP). Compressed files are actually collections of files or entire directories packed into one physical file (it's easier to download one large file than 500 small ones). Many of the files you'll find online in and around Web sites are in this format. However, it doesn't hurt to keep a copy of the most popular decompression programs within reach, because you might run into some compressed files that won't extract themselves.

When Netscape completes installation, it will create a Program Group with appropriate icons. In Windows 95, it will plop a shortcut to the Navigator on the desktop, all ready for launching.

That's it; you're set. Double-click the **Netscape Navigator 2.0** icon and you're off and perking!

Macintosh and Power PC

Macintosh and Power PC (running the Mac OS) users have it a little easier when it comes to installing Navigator. The file you download is not only *self-extracting*, it's also *self-installing*. Once the download is completed, you'll have an icon that, when double-clicked, will do all the unpacking, installation, and icon creation for you.

Make Sure You're Connected

Netscape Navigator must assume that you already have a properly configured Internet connection. It has no way of knowing this for itself, so if your Internet connection is not working, Netscape will launch but not be able to connect anywhere. You don't need to make any special Internet configurations for Netscape to work—you simply must have a "regular" working Net connection. Most users of Windows 95 use Dial-Up Networking to create this connection; if you're not sure how to set this up, check out one of the several online tutorials at http://www.windows95.com. (Of course, you may have to use someone else's machine to use this tutorial in the first place.)

Just Browsing

With Navigator 2.0 installed, you're ready to take off on a totally new Web adventure; launch Netscape, and you're poised to take on the world. Or at least the World Wide Web.

The first thing you see is the Netscape home page:

Netscape Navigator 2.0, up and running.

The toolbar—

The Location window—

Directory buttons—

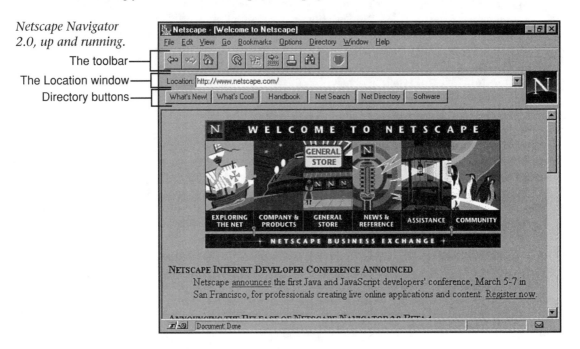

The top portion of the browser window is chock-full of buttons that allow you to "drive" the Navigator around the Web.

The Navigator toolbar.

The *toolbar* consists of the topmost series of icons in the Navigator window. These are the most commonly used buttons for accessing the major features of the Navigator. From left to right, briefly consider each:

Back   Brings you to the previous Web page visited.

Forward   Assumes that you have already gone Back from a page; brings you to the page visited subsequent to the current one.

Home   Brings you to the defined starting page; by default this is Netscape's home page, although you can set it anywhere you like by selecting **Options**, **General Preferences**, **Appearance** from the Netscape menu bar.

Edit   The Edit button exists only in the Netscape Navigator Gold edition and is used for editing a Web page.

Reload   Re-retrieves the current URL in question from the server. Sometimes, a page does not load properly; other times, you need to use this button to refresh information that may have changed on the page.

Images   If you have not configured for automatic image loading (**Options**, **Auto Load Images**), then this button will load all of the images for the current page.

Open   Allows you to enter a new URL to connect to; for connecting to a new Web page.

Print   Just what you'd think: prints the current page to your printer.

Find   Allows you to search for text in the current page.

Stop   While a page is loading into your browser, you can click this button to abort the retrieval—perhaps it is taking too long, for instance. Netscape will try to display whatever amount of the page that it has retrieved, if possible. (Often, this is the text without the images.)

The Location window resides below the toolbar. Here, you see the official URL for the current Web page loaded into Navigator. In short, it shows you the address of where you are. Another way to connect to a new page, in addition to the **Open** button on the toolbar, is to simply click within the **Location** window and enter a new URL; then press the **Enter** key. There is a little selection doohickey at the far right of the Location window (a down-pointing arrow symbol), which allows you to select a URL from a list of recently visited sites.

Finally, a row of directory buttons hangs just under the Location window. These buttons automatically bring you to Netscape pages concerning their respective topic. Thus, the **What's New!** button springs you to Netscape's page of new sites. **What's Cool!** avails you of Netscape's subjective picks of "cool" sites. The **Handbook** button leads to online documentation for using the Navigator. Net **Search** offers you a page of resources that allow for searching the World Wide Web. You can find a breakdown of Web sites by topic via the **Net Directory** button. Lastly, you can shop for Netscape software through the **Software** button.

Take note of the Netscape "N" logo on the right side of the window. This logo serves two purposes, other than being a constant source of self-promotion. First, it indicates whether Netscape is currently retrieving data. If so, you will see the "N" slightly animated, with little comets or shooting stars flying behind the "N." When no data is being retrieved, the icon sits still. Second, if you click on the "N" logo, you'll be taken directly to Netscape's home page.

If you've used the previous version of Netscape (version 1.2), you might note that this much-touted version 2.0 doesn't look much different. Don't worry; the fun stuff is under the hood: in the pages, not (visually) in the browser.

Check This Out...

Choose Your Own Adventure: Pages

The World Wide Web (and browsers that use it) handles information using the concept of pages. A page is one window-full of information, although some windows may allow you to scroll up and down them if the page is longer than your screen. As you move from page to page, you create a history of the places you've been. The Forward and Back buttons allow you to move throughout this history list (which you can see by clicking the **Go** menu). It's an easy way to explore down one path and then "back up" to some point and go in a different direction.

Configuration Bonanza

Much of the Netscape Navigator's behavior is dependent on its many configuration settings. You can truly customize this baby, short of pinstriping (well, you could do that, too, but I doubt your monitor manufacturer will take it back). The Options menu is your starting point, where you'll look mostly at those options that might have some relevance to Web pages with JavaScript.

The General Preferences Command

This is where the majority of effective settings lie. The General Preferences window (which appears when you select **Options, General Preferences**) contains seven tabs, labeled "Appearance" through "Language."

➤ **Appearance**   First, you can select what style toolbar you prefer. If you can live without the iconic pictures, a text-only toolbar saves screen space, allowing more content to fit in the browser window.

On startup (launching the browser), you can select whether to have the Web, News, or Mail be your first window. You can also select whether to have an initial Web page upon startup, and if so, which one.

Lastly, you can configure link characteristics. Links are highlighted in the Web page, and can also be underlined for easier recognition if you enable the Underlined option. Netscape will keep track of which links you have followed and will highlight those in a different color upon future visits to a given Web page. You can determine how long Netscape should remember followed links by configuring the Expire option either to **Never Expire** (Netscape Navigator will always remember them), or to some number of days (it will remember them only for that long, and then treat them as unfollowed).

➤ **Fonts**   These are cosmetic options, and you might want to experiment here. Look for fonts that meet your preferred balance between the amount of content on-screen and readability. The Proportional font refers to the font that most Web page text will be rendered in. The Fixed font is used for unformatted text, which arises less frequently in Web pages. Encoding should be set to Latin1 for English language usage.

➤ **Colors**   Here, Netscape allows you to configure your preferred Web page colors. You can select colors for various states of a link, as well as for the background of the page. You can even set a graphic texture for the background via the **Image File** selection. However, as the settings window explains, some Web pages define their own colors and backgrounds. With the check box provided, you can select whether to always use your preferred colors, or to allow pages to define their own. In most cases, it's best to allow pages to define their own—since that's part of the author's design—so not checking this option is the best option.

➤ **Images**   Many Web pages contain images (also known as *inline images* or *inline graphics*). These settings allow you first to determine how Netscape will choose image colors. **Automatic** is probably the best option; for users with lower color displays, **Dither** might produce better-quality images but will take somewhat longer to process. Lastly, you can tell Netscape whether to show images in-progress as they download, or wait until they're finished downloading before popping them onto the page. This is largely a matter of personal preference.

➤ **Apps** Netscape needs to know the locations of a few external programs that may be called from a Web page. Some pages have links that lead to Telnet addresses—Telnet requires a separate program. Thus, you must tell Netscape where your Telnet program is. Users of Windows 95's built-in networking already have a Telnet program in C:\Windows\telnet.exe. TN3270 is a specific Telnet protocol that sometimes requires a separate program—not all Telnet programs support TN3270. If you have a TN3270 program, enter it here, but if you don't really know, just leave it blank. Not many Web pages are going to require this.

The View Source option lets you choose a text viewer. This will be launched if you select **View**, **Document Source** from the Navigator menu bar. It is used to display the page in its native HTML, should you be so interested. Leaving this setting blank will use Netscape's built-in viewer, so you needn't configure this unless you have a preferred text viewer.

Finally, Netscape needs a **Temporary Directory** for any "scratch pad" space it needs. Usually a directory such as C:\WINDOWS\TEMP or C:\TEMP is a good choice.

➤ **Helpers** The Helpers settings allow Netscape to use external programs for a variety of needs. Many times, Web pages contain links to files of types that the browser itself is not equipped to view—these might include sound/audio files, certain image files, any special file types such as RealAudio files, 3D VRML files, and so on. The helper definitions tell Netscape which programs to launch when it encounters one of these file types. Although it appears confusing at first, the helper settings screen is decipherable.

The top window contains a list of "known" file types. They are written in a strange way, but usually you can tell by reading their names what sort of files they refer to (for example, "application/zip" refers to a .ZIP file). Beside each file type listing is a column that indicates what the current configuration is: what to do with that file type (ask the user, let the browser handle it, save it, or run a specific program). To the left of that are the file name extensions that relate to that file type (thus, zip would be a file name extension for a zip file type). Netscape Navigator comes with a large list of file types pre-installed. Many of these are also already preconfigured. If you highlight a file type, you can then reconfigure what to do with it in the entries below the file type window.

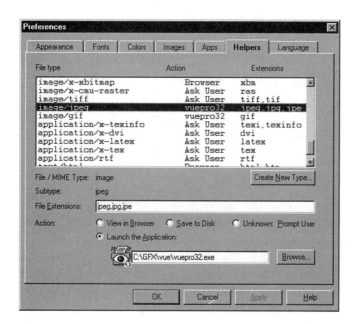

The Helpers applications settings.

This includes listing the file name extensions, and whether to save the file, ask the user, or launch a specific application. You don't often need to work with these helper settings, but it's useful to understand what they mean. If you find that a certain type of file is not being viewed/played/launched properly, the first course of action is to run to the helper settings and check the configuration for that file type. Is the file type listed? Is it configured to launch a program? Do you actually have the program it is configured to launch?

➤ **Language** The language setting isn't used terribly often. It allows you to select a "preferred" language. Some servers offer a document in several languages—if you have selected a preferred language that the server can offer, it will. Most people, most of the time, leave this setting blank, since English is obviously assumed by default.

The Mail and News Preferences Command

Netscape Navigator also includes a built-in e-mail facility and Usenet newsreader. These settings affect the operation of both. By and large, e-mail and newsreading are not Web functions, and thus have little relation to JavaScript.

When you select **Mail** and **News Preferences** from the Options menu, you see another Preferences dialog box, which contains five tabs filled with more settings. In brief, the

25

most important of these settings involves entering server names; your Internet service provider should have supplied you with names for POP, STMP (both for e-mail), and NNTP (for news) servers. Fill these in the appropriate places where the Mail and News preferences ask for them.

Also, be sure to fill in at least a name and an e-mail address in the Identity tab of this Preferences dialog box. This way, if you do send e-mail to someone else via a Web page, it will have the proper return address.

The Security Preferences Command

In the Preferences dialog box that appears when you select **Options**, **Security Preferences**, consider one option: the one labeled **Disable Java**. If you check this option, Java applets will not be run. However, this does not affect JavaScript programs. At least, as of the version of Netscape Navigator 2.0 at this writing, JavaScript programs are always executed, without relation to enabling or disabling Java support itself (remember that Java and JavaScript are virtually two different creatures).

Where Are the Manuals?

There aren't any. At least, at this point in time, there are no existing, "print" manuals that cover JavaScript or its use with the Netscape Navigator. That situation may or may not change by the time this book hits the shelves.

Netscape does, however, provide relatively thorough JavaScript documentation on its Web site, including tutorials, examples, and reference material. You can find this at

```
http://home.netscape.com/comprod/products/navigator/version_2.0/script/
```

In addition, check out the JavaScript Support Page maintained by the authors of this book:

```
http://www.winternet.com/~SJWalter/JavaScript/
```

Either place provides you with a wealth of additional knowledge (possibly more than most mortals would care to know). For the bulk of this book, however, you'll be looking at the author's JavaScript Support Page (add it to your bookmark list; then tell your friends!).

Applets and Oranges

Netscape Navigator 2.0 not only supports JavaScript but also its big sibling, Java. Java is a full-blown programming language, allowing you to do some absolutely phenomenal things through the Web (JavaScript is no slouch, and you'll be pleasantly surprised by how powerful it really is).

Although this book is not about Java itself, it would serve you well to understand the differences between the two. They are, after all, easy to confuse given that they both share at least part of the name Java.

Java is a high-level programming language—those readers familiar with C or especially C++ will understand what that means. Java is, in fact, a close relative of C++. This makes it very powerful—a creative programmer will have a lot of latitude. A Java program is known as an "applet" (small application), and these applets can be included at various points in Web pages.

Java applets can perform virtually anything the programmer can figure out how to program, from user interaction to calculations to graphical events such as animated pictures or text. The sky's the limit with Java, but there is a price to pay: it has a high learning curve and isn't necessarily the ideal programming language for a novice user.

Enter JavaScript. JavaScript was inspired by Java; in other words, the two are based around many shared concepts. However, it is far simpler to program. There are fewer rules and fewer concepts that require a computer science degree for you to program in JavaScript. In theory, this does limit the "sky" as far as JavaScript vs. Java goes. However, most novice users with limited or no programming experience should find JavaScript quite accessible and capable of many Web page needs. The language is small and compact, making learning and programming JavaScript quite manageable and, dare I say, even fun. Readers with experience programming in Pascal or scripting in PERL will find JavaScript a breeze.

If you are curious or adventurous, and want to learn more about Java itself, you might start with Java's official home page at

```
http://java.sun.com
```

In addition, while you're here, don't forget to check out Chapter 22 of this very book. It's way near the back.

The Least You Need To Know

This chapter showed you how to start with the Netscape Navigator 2.0 browser. You grabbed a copy from the Internet, installed it, and fired it up. You tried the few buttons that run the browser and spent some quality time configuring. You now understand the difference between Java and JavaScript, and why this book is about the latter.

However, the real fun begins when you start creating your own JavaScript pages, complete with animation, sound, and other nifty things. In order to start with that, you need to see how to plug scripts into your Web pages—and that's what you'll look at next.

Tag...You're It!

Giving HTML a Caffeine Boost

If you're interested in learning JavaScript programming—and I assume you are; this is the wrong book to be reading just for fun—then you must be at least somewhat familiar with HTML by now. To briefly recall, HTML is a markup language used to "describe" how a Web page should look. Web browsers such as Netscape then interpret these markup *tags* and render the page to the screen. HTML is expressed through tags, which are written in the form `<TAG>`. Most tags must surround the text on which they operate, and, therefore, have to be paired in the manner `<TAG>` `text to affect` `</TAG>`. This is basic HTML and should not be coming as new information right now; if so, I strongly recommend that you read a primer on HTML, such as Que's *The Complete Idiot's Guide to Creating an HTML Web Page*, by Paul McFedries.

Tag Attributes

Because this chapter refers to *attributes* of an HTML tag several times, you need to know what they are. As stated, a typical HTML tag looks like <TAG>. However, many tags accept further specifications that determine their final effect, such as <TAG attribute1=x attribute2=y>. That's all there is to it—when you use a tag that requires or may include attributes, it will be pointed out within the chapter.

The <SCRIPT> Tag

The tag to know for JavaScript programming is the <SCRIPT> tag. In short, it looks like this:

```
<SCRIPT attributes> JavaScript program code</SCRIPT>
```

The opening <SCRIPT> tag has two attributes that it may include:

```
<SCRIPT language="JavaScript">
```

This is the standard opening <SCRIPT> tag. It simply defines the start of JavaScript program code, and the language the code is written in (which, obviously, is JavaScript). Note that the JavaScript official documentation claims that the language attribute is mandatory; that is, you cannot simply begin a section of code with <SCRIPT> alone. However, at the time of this writing, <SCRIPT> alone does, in fact, work normally—but one cannot guarantee that will be the case when you read this. You mark the end of a JavaScript code section with <SCRIPT>.

The URL (Earl) of Web?

URL stands for **Uniform Resource Locator**. It's a fancy way of identifying anything on the Internet (a file, a document, a graphic, a web site) anywhere in the world with a unique *address*. Think of it as a global CyberZipCode: No two web pages, FTP files, UseNet newsgroups, Gopher menus, or whatever can have the same URL.

As an alternative to writing the JavaScript code within the Web page source itself, you can refer to JavaScript code that is saved in its own text file elsewhere. This will behave just as if the code were typed directly into the Web page source (as it is in all of these examples). The following is the general format:

```
<SCRIPT src="URL to your script file"></SCRIPT>
```

This would be an efficient way of reusing the same JavaScript code in several Web pages, without having to explicitly enter it into each one. You'd merely insert the call to the file. The text file of the JavaScript program must have a file name ending in `.js`, as in the following example:

```
<SCRIPT src="http://myscript.js"></SCRIPT>
```

You place JavaScript code between <SCRIPT> tags wherever you want the code executed within a page. A tiny example of the HTML code of a Web page, with embedded JavaScript code, might look like this:

```
<HTML><HEAD>
<TITLE>My Nifty Web Page</TITLE>
</HEAD><BODY>
<H1>Welcome to my Exciting Home Page, Where I talk about ME</H1>
<SCRIPT language="JavaScript">
JavaScript program code goes here
</SCRIPT>
</BODY></HTML>
```

Note that you needn't put all of the JavaScript code within one set of <SCRIPT> tags. You can use numerous <SCRIPT> </SCRIPT> pairs wherever in the page you want to include JavaScript code. Having said that, there are three caveats to note:

➤ Place all JavaScript function definitions between the <HEAD> </HEAD> tags at the top of the HTML page. That is:

```
<HEAD><SCRIPT language="JavaScript">
function func1 (x, y, z)
 { statements }
function func2 (x, y, z)
 { statements }
etc.
</SCRIPT>
any other HTML commands that should go in the HEAD section
</HEAD>
```

Functions must be defined before they can be called—you may not understand what that means just yet, but after Chapter 9, the skies will clear. To briefly summarize, a *function* is a section of code that performs a specific task. It is like a self-contained miniprogram. For many reasons, in other areas of JavaScript code, you will find the need to *call* these functions—that is, refer to them by name and have them executed. You'll learn about functions in gruesome detail throughout Chapter 9. In the meantime, simply remember that the above will ensure that all functions have been defined before they are called in any JavaScript code further down in the page.

➤ Any and all JavaScript code applies only to the page it resides on, including function definitions. Therefore, if you have a set of function definitions that you intend to use on several pages, a time-saver would be the following: compose the function definitions and save them as an individual text file, with a name ending in `.js`, such as `myfuncs.js`. Then, in the `<HEAD>` section of each page, include those function definitions with the `<SCRIPT src="http://myfuncs.js"></SCRIPT>` tags, rather than writing them out by hand all over again.

➤ Lastly, you should consider enclosing all JavaScript code within HTML comment tags. An HTML comment tag looks like:

```
<!-- comments -->
```

Anything within HTML comment tags is ignored by most browsers—except Netscape 2.0, which will recognize the presence of the JavaScript code and not ignore it. The rationale behind this is that other browsers that know nothing of JavaScript might display the code in the Web page itself, which would not be desirable at all. Therefore, in the end, the recommended manner of including JavaScript code into a page is as follows:

```
<SCRIPT language="JavaScript">
<!--
 JavaScript program code goes here
-->
</SCRIPT>
```

It doesn't matter where your JavaScript statements go in your page; they are always evaluated (a fancy term for "made ready to run") *after* the page has finished loading into the browser.

Rules of the Web

You need to keep some fundamental rules in mind when you're building your JavaScript pages:

➤ JavaScript scripts (enclosed within a `<SCRIPT>` tag) are not evaluated until *after* the page loads.

➤ Scripts stored as separate files (read in with the SRC attribute) are evaluated *before* any in-page script commands.

What about Browsers That Don't Read JavaScript?

If someone comes across your Web page with an old browser that doesn't understand JavaScript and the `<SCRIPT>` tag, what happens? Nothing drastic, but the results aren't necessarily pretty. What the user will see (in addition to the other things on your page) is your script statements, as though they were a paragraph you typed in for display.

This is a problem. A creative HTML writer can design pages that will work without JavaScript (having, for example, less user-interactivity) but, unless the script statements are in an external file, they will be displayed along with everything else...unless you use this little trick: Hide the script statements inside an HTML comment tag.

Hide them inside a comment? And they still work? YES! Comment tags identify parts of an HTML document that you want the non-JavaScript browser to ignore and not try to format or display. Using comments inside the <SCRIPT> tag gives you the added benefit of not having your JavaScript statements displayed by browsers that can't handle JavaScript. So, if the following page was loaded by a JavaScript-less browser:

```
<HTML>
<HEAD>
<SCRIPT LANGUAGE="JavaScript">
<!-- Hide the script statements from browsers that can't handle them
function dosomething()
{
    alert("JavaScript...in hiding.")
}
-->
</SCRIPT>
</HEAD>
<BODY>
<BR>
If you can't handle JavaScript...you won't see anything above this line.
</BODY>
</HTML>
```

In this example, if met by a non-JavaScript browser, only the text "If you can't handle JavaScript..." will appear on the screen. The JavaScript code between the <SCRIPT> tags will be completely ignored because it resides between comment tags <!-- -->. The magic is that a browser that *can* understand JavaScript will not ignore the code between the comment tags, because it is aware of this little trick.

Just a reminder: Although using the comment tag is a good idea when scripting (there still are many browsers out there that don't support JavaScript); all that happens is that the script statements won't be displayed when the page is formatted. The user can still view your script by using the **View Source** option on the **View** menu.

This brings up a good question: Is it possible to "protect" a JavaScript from prying eyes? Read on and see.

Shhhhh...Can You Keep a Secret?

With all the concern about security in cyberspace these days, you're probably wondering about the "secrecy" of JavaScript. After all, if your prized script is written in the middle of an HTML file, all someone has to do is select the **View Source** option on the **View** menu and your hard work is displayed plain as day...right?

Unfortunately, that is right. If you want to keep your script from being seen, place it in an external file and include it using the SRC= attribute of the <SCRIPT> tag. Just make sure that the file ends in ".js".

The Least You Need To Know

This chapter introduced you to the new <SCRIPT> tag that extends HTML to allow you to plug JavaScript commands into your Web pages. You also learned the following rules about scripts:

➤ Scripts are evaluated *after* a page has finished loading.

➤ Any functions defined in scripts are not automatically executed when the page loads. They are stored until called by something else in the page.

➤ Scripts loaded through the SRC attribute (in other words, scripts that are kept in separate files) are evaluated *before* any inline (or "in-page") scripts.

➤ Scripts can be placed inside comment tags, to keep browsers that can't handle JavaScript from displaying them on the page.

Now, it's time to take a spin out on the Web. In the next chapter, we take a break from learning the ins and outs of JavaScript, and check out what other Java-ers are brewing up.

Chapter 5

Off and Running...with Someone Else's Help

The Best Way To Learn

Starting up the learning curve with anything can be a major task, and computer-related things always seem to be the worst. After gathering up your courage to actually begin, you have a pile of books, the computer screen blinking "unknown command" at you, and a growing frustration with the inhabitants of Silicon Valley. Computer languages can be *very* frustrating.

To try to take the edge off the process and "ease" your way into the world of JavaScript, take a page from some of the computer gurus that wander the Web:

➤ *Observe* what other people are doing with what you want to learn.

➤ *Analyze* how they did it.

➤ *Adapt* it to your own needs.

In other words, *borrow from those who've already gotten the bugs out.* No, this is not plagiarism, since I'm not suggesting that you simply take someone else's hard work and put your name on it. Rather, look at the script code that they wrote and use what they did to help you better understand how JavaScript interacts with the Web. If you want to try to play with the script (make your own changes), all you have to do is save the HTML document as a file on your computer.

But, before you can learn from the experts, you have to find them.

Where Are They?

With the explosion of JavaScript on the Web today, several sites have sprung up (literally overnight) that make excellent starting points for you to explore further. In this chapter, you'll take a quick tour through several of the newest, neatest, and best places to learn more about JavaScript…and you'll pick up a little more info on Java, JavaScript's big brother.

So…do you have Netscape Navigator 2.0 installed? Good. Log into your Internet provider, fire up Netscape, and start surfin'. The tour is ready to depart—JavaScript style!

Netscape: The "Good" Got "Better"

Point your browser at:

```
http://home.netscape.com/comprod/products/navigator/version_2.0/index.html
```

You'll be whisked into the world of Netscape and Netscape Navigator 2.0, the company that developed JavaScript. Netscape Navigator has been the most popular World Wide Web browser on the Internet to date, and with JavaScript, it's going to be in the forefront for some time to come.

Netscape's pages change regularly, so you'll want to stop back from time to time to catch the latest information and updates to Navigator and the other products Netscape sells.

Finding your way from the Netscape Navigator 2.0 page to JavaScript information takes a few clicks. From the opening page, you have two equal paths. In the upper (larger) window, you can scroll down through the list of Navigator features until you see the link to JavaScript. Alternatively, the small frame at the bottom of the window contains a series of icons. Scroll to the right until you reach the Scripting icon (a typewriter).

From there, you will land smack-dab on the JavaScript page, wherein lie several examples of code, and a link leading to the "official" JavaScript documentation.

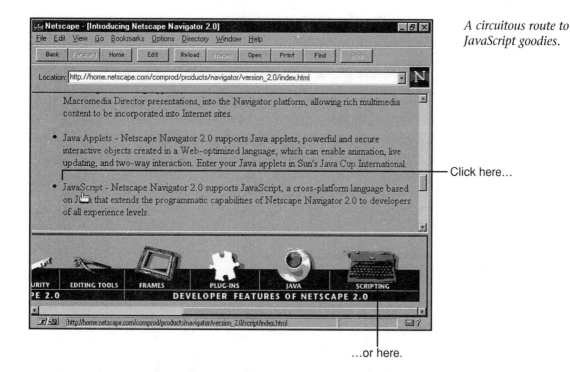

A circuitous route to JavaScript goodies.

Eyeing Some Code

Earlier I suggested that you take a long, hard look at other authors' JavaScript programs. Doing so requires that you first store a copy of the program itself, so let's see how you do that—it's relatively painless.

Several example JavaScript programs are on the Netscape JavaScript page. One of them is an "Interest Calculator," which calculates interest on a loan based on data the user inputs into the table.

Because JavaScript code is embedded within the HTML, merely save the HTML code for this page, and you will find the JavaScript program within it. You can easily see the HTML code by choosing the Navigator menu option: **View, Document Source**. Depending on what source viewer you've configured, you may or may not be able to save the file right from there. If you can't, you can simply select the Navigator option: **File, Save As**. This pops up a Save File dialog box, in which you can select where to save the file. Be sure you selected **HTML file** in the Save as Type selection of the dialog box, as pictured on the next page.

That's gonna cost ya. Calculating loan payments—oh, the fun!

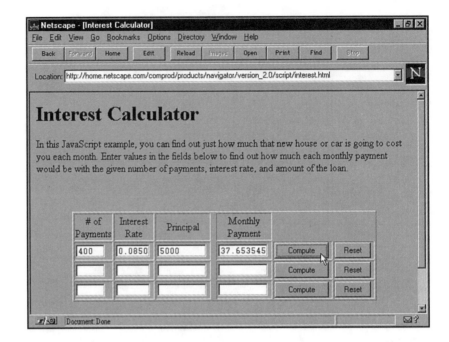

Viewing the HTML source for inspection and perusal.

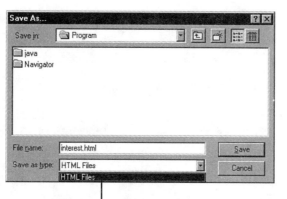

Saving the HTML source code; be sure to save it as an HTML file.

Select a file type.

The resulting file, with the name "somefile.htm" or "somefile.html" (depending on your system), is viewable by any text editor. It is simply a plain text file, and within it, you will find all the HTML tags that defined the page, including any JavaScript programs.

Gamelan

Before Gamelan, there wasn't a central clearinghouse for Java and JavaScript material. Now, if you set your browser to

```
http://www.gamelan.com/
```

Caveat Capture
There is one exception to everything we've said about capturing the JavaScript code from a page. It all assumes that the code was embedded directly into the HTML. Some authors may keep the code in a separate file, using the SRC= attribute of the <SCRIPT> tag. In these cases, you can't retrieve the JavaScript program code.

you'll find an excellent collection of JavaScript pages, Java applets, and other Java-related nifties. The folks at EarthWeb (who maintain Gamelan) are updating the site *daily,* so there is always something new to check out. Gamelan breaks Java applets down into categories, and the areas covered are rather diverse: animation, communications, finance, games, special effects, networking, and so on. There's also an impressive list of links to other Java and JavaScript sites around the Net. At last glance, there were over 180+ sites in Gamelan's listing alone!

While you're poking around Gamelan, you might want to check out the *Java Message Exchange* (you'll find it listed in the *sites* category). The Message Exchange is a message board for the purpose of exchanging information on Java, JavaScript, and new Java/Script sites.

Gamelan: Learn to pronounce it right, and you're on your way to geekdom!

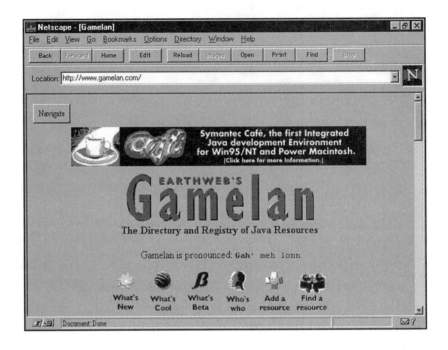

JavaScript Index

While Gamelan is Java-generic (it covers both Java and JavaScript), the *JavaScript Index* is devoted to JavaScript and its uses. Check out

```
http://www.c2.org/~andreww/javascript/
```

and you'll find a comprehensive categorical breakdown of JavaScript pages and implementations. Some are pure JavaScript; others merge JavaScript with Java and other HTML techniques.

One of the nice sections found on the JavaScript Index is its *Widgets* section. *Widgets* are little gadgets that do various things. From the standpoint of JavaScript, a *widget* is a little script that does something nifty: a scroll bar, a background changer, a pop-up help display. Widgets make great little scripts that you can borrow and put together with other scripts to create truly unique Web pages.

To borrow a widget, simply follow the same procedures outlined earlier with the Netscape example: go to the page with the JavaScript program, and then save the HTML source—either by viewing the source and saving it from there, or by using the **File**, **Save As** option from the Navigator menu.

Dimension X

No discussion of Java and JavaScript would be complete without mentioning the innovative crew of Dimension X. You can check them out at

```
http://www.dimensionx.com/dnx/java.html
```

Primarily focusing on Java rather than JavaScript, Dimension X is worth a peek, if for no other reason than to see what they've done with Java's graphics power. They're also in the process of developing several packages designed to make creating three-dimensional graphics in Java a snap. So if you're into cool graphics, these guys are worth keeping an eye on.

This is just the tip of the iceberg. More and more sites are appearing every day. So many, in fact, that it's becoming harder and harder to keep up with them. But, if you want to do a little one-stop shopping, you can check out

```
http://www.winternet.com/~sjwalter/javascript/
```

You'll find links to other sites, new and cool scripts, nifty tidbits and tutorials on Java and JavaScript—and a chance to give me a piece of your mind.

41

Sample Platter: What You're Likely To Find

Now that you know where to look for lists of JavaScript-powered pages, here's a sampling of the many diverse things those pages can do.

JavaScript 1040EZ   Just in time for April 15, here's a site that uses JavaScript to fill out the 1040EZ (known by some wags as "1040 STU-PID") form.

```
http://www.homepages.com/fun/1040EZ.html
```

You have a company known as Home Pages to thank for this little marvel.

Unit Conversion Calculator   These few nifties can convert from various units of measurement to others, all with the magic of JavaScript, authored by Jonathan Weesner.

```
http://www.cyberstation.net/%7Ejweesner/conv.html
```

Mastermind   If you have any idea how to play the game Mastermind, JavaScripted by Ian Cameron, then this page might appeal to you.

```
http://dingo.uq.edu.au/~zzdcamer/master.htm
```

The Game of Nim   A battle of wits; take on the Towers of Hanoi puzzle, you vs. JavaScript, as coded by Raul Garcia.

```
http://www.primenet.com/~raul/nim/nim2.htm
```

ColorCenter   This nifty JavaScript incarnation allows you to test various Web page color combinations—a quick way to decide what colors will work in your own design. By Bill Dortch of hIdaho Design.

```
http://www.hidaho.com/colorcenter/
```

Scrolling Text and Banners   Some textual animation for those with a sweet tooth for eye candy; this script is the spawn of Craig Slagel.

```
http://www.boots.com/~craigel/java2.htm
```

SuperSearch   A JavaScript tool that allows the user to simultaneously submit search data to several Web search engines.

```
http://www.wineasy.se/robban/seek1.htm
```

The Least You Need To Know

You've taken a whirlwind tour around the globe and through the Internet, and have found that Java and JavaScript are expanding at an explosive rate. You've seen that there are *hundreds* of sites (more and more springing up each day) with scripts and applets that you can download and use or adapt to your own needs. You also learned that using someone else's scripting ideas as a basis for your own is as simple as saving the script document and editing it.

Now that you have a few scripts from other JavaScripters, you're probably wondering what the devil those new lines in the script actually mean. That's what the next chapters cover: the inner workings of JavaScript.

Part 3
JavaScript: Espresso for the Masses

No matter how you cut it, JavaScript is a programming language…of sorts. It has rules, commands, special words that do special things, and a way of putting things together that you must be familiar with if you want to become a power JavaScripter.

The good news is that what makes up JavaScript is fairly close to English and (with a little logic thrown in) is very easy to use. Also, because it's a scripting language, you don't need a fancy compiler or another program to turn your script into something your browser can deal with. In fact, all you really need to create your own scripts is a browser, a simple word processor, and this book.

In this section, you step through the parts that make up the JavaScript language and see how they work together and what they do.

Chapter 6

Objects, Names, and Literals

In This Chapter

➤ Variables, such as the weather

➤ Value Village—the variable's better half

➤ Literal(ly)

➤ Objects: variables with an attitude

Welcome to JavaScript. What *is* a JavaScript? Quasi-technically speaking, it is a programming language that enables you to expand the functionality of your Web pages. JavaScript programs reside within the HTML code of a page and allow you to perform a variety of tasks that interact with the user or the user's input. JavaScript is relatively easy to program, even for those unfamiliar with computer programming, and is not generally intended for creating extremely large or complex programs. Any readers who have had experience with any other programming languages will find JavaScript extremely accessible. New users might want to read the following chapters a few times, to grasp the concepts involved.

Debate: Script or Program?

What is the difference between a programming language and a scripting language? Technically, JavaScript is scripting, not programming. Thus, its code is a script rather than a program. Generally, programming languages are more complex, require more specific instructions and definitions from the programmer, and are suitable for creating large, efficient applications. Scripting languages are "looser"—they require less discipline and complexity on the author's part, and are more suited to small tasks here and there. JavaScript borrows some from programming languages such as Pascal and C, and some from scripting languages such as Perl and REXX. Among the variety of programming and scripting languages around, JavaScript is one of the easier and less complex of them.

What's in a Name? (A Variable Name, That Is)

One of the basic fundamentals of a programming language is the *variable*. A variable is essentially a label to which you assign a "value" (what this value may be, you'll learn about shortly). Variables are also commonly used in mathematics, so anyone who recalls having stayed awake during those classes may still be scarred by such statements as "x=5." Good, this trauma will help you when it comes to JavaScript (and students always want to know of what use algebra will be!).

JavaScript will have variables all over the place, many of them created by you, the programmer. So, first spend some quality time understanding the ubiquitous variable.

Because it is a label, the variable is used to refer to a given "value" in a program. The value that the label refers to may change, although the label will stay the same. For example, at one point in our program, the variable "x" might refer to the value "5," but at a later point in the program, "x" might refer to 10. This is not arbitrary—perhaps we have used "x" to track the number of items a user has chosen to purchase, and one user ordered 5 while another bought 10. The variable (also known as a *name* or *variable name*) allows us to instruct the computer to perform a series of tasks or calculations, whatever the actual values may be. This, in a sense, is the heart—or one of the hearts (if that's possible)—of a program, and a JavaScript program in particular.

Tom, Dick42, and _Harry

Generally, it is up to you, the programmer, to decide on variable names. JavaScript does have a few rules that govern what names are allowable:

➤ The variable name must begin with a letter or an underscore character ("_").
The first character of a variable name cannot be a number or some other
nonalphabetical character.

➤ You cannot use a space within a variable name.

➤ JavaScript is *case-sensitive*. As far as JavaScript is concerned, "a" is a completely
different letter than "A." This has two major ramifications:

Watch your variable names—although "cost" and "Cost" and "COST" are all valid
variable names, they are all different variable names.

Built-in JavaScript "statements," which you'll learn about in subsequent chapters,
are all lowercase. You'll be reminded of this when the time comes.

➤ You cannot use a "reserved word" as a variable name. A *reserved word* is a word that
JavaScript already uses for some other purpose, such as a built-in command (an
expression, object, or function, covered later). Briefly now, JavaScript reserves the
word "if" for programming purposes. Therefore, you cannot create a variable named
if. For a complete list of JavaScript's reserved words, see the appendix, "JavaScript:
The Complete Overview," at the end of this book.

Other than the preceding rules, JavaScript doesn't care what you choose to name a
variable. As far as JavaScript is concerned, the same variable name will always refer to the
same value placeholder, whether that name is x or inventory. However, *you* should care.
As the programmer, you want to maximize your ability to understand and follow your
own program. This is especially true when you inevitably must *debug* it (that is, find
where problems are and attempt to fix them). So, it is in your best interest to make up
variable names that hold some human meaning in relation to the values that they will
represent.

For example, let's suppose that you have a Web page used to sell a product. You're
hawking novelty mugs with pictures of your dog wearing a bikini. The prices of these
may vary, depending on how many mugs the consumer chooses to purchase at one
time. The first variable you'll need to name is the one that refers to the number of mugs
ordered. Remember, you can name this variable anything (within the rules above), such
as x or bazoo. But, for the sake of programming clarity to the human mind, mugs is probably a good choice for a variable name. Perhaps orders would suffice, too, but you see the
concept.

There is a second variable in the preceding example, and that is the price of each mug.
The single-mug purchase price might be $9.95, but perhaps two mugs sell for $15.95, and
three for $22.95. Because the price may vary, and cannot be assumed to be constant, it
will require a variable name, as well. So, again, we could name the price variable mary, or
y, but something like price or cost seems to be the more reasonable choice.

Full of Value(s)

As you've read, variables are references to values. So, now that you understand what a variable is, look at the values a variable may hold. In JavaScript, a variable may refer to three types of values, plus a special bonus value. This doesn't make sense yet, but bear with me.

➤ **Numeric value**   This is what first comes to mind when people think of a variable. As in the previous examples, a variable name may refer to a numeric value, such as price referring to the value 9.95, or mugs referring to the value 2.

➤ **String value**   A *string*, in programming parlance, is a group of characters that are not a numeric value. For example, "bob" is a string. "]]]#!!!" is also a string. A string can be any length and can be made up of any characters, including numbers. Thus "a" is a string, and so is "400". Note, though, that the string "400" is not the numeric value 400. It is merely the characters "4," "0," and "0." It does not hold mathematical meaning to the computer. A variable may refer to a string. For example, you might create a variable surname and it may refer to the string "Caruthers". Or maybe you have a variable model, which could refer to "C3PO".

Notice how strings are always enclosed within quotation marks. Do the same in JavaScript code. The only way for JavaScript to distinguish between a variable name cost and a string value "cost" is when you enclose string values within quotation marks. You may use either double or single quotation marks to enclose a string ("cost" or 'cost'). In the case of nested strings—where you have to insert one string value within a phrase that is already within quotation marks—use double quotes to mark out the whole phrase and single quotes to mark out each value within it (for example, "callmyfunction ('bob','jane','white')"). You will see an example of this when we discuss event handlers in Chapter 10.

➤ **Boolean value**   "Boolean" is a humorous-sounding word that simply means "true or false." It comes from the lingo of logic studies. Thus, a variable may refer to a Boolean value; that is, it can be "true" or "false." In this sense, the variable is referring to a condition, rather than substantive content as in the two previous examples.

…And the special bonus value:

➤ **Null**   Lastly, a variable may refer simply to the word and concept "null." Null, in JavaScript, means "nothing." No value, nada. Note that this is *not* zero, because zero is a numeric value. Null is simply *nothing*. A little weird, I admit, but it has its uses on certain occasions. Plus, it's good talk at parties (Joe: "So, can there ever really be total 'nothingness?'"; Bill: "Yes, in JavaScript there can be.").

Handing Out Assignments

When you create a variable name and refer it to a value, that is an *assignment*, as in, "We assigned the numeric value 5 to the variable mugs." Although you'll discover more complex assignments in Chapter 8, the basics below serve as a useful grounding (you'll learn exactly how and where to place these commands as part of a JavaScript program in Chapter 8).

Your Basic Assignment

A basic assignment in JavaScript is made with the construction var *variablename* = *value* (where var is the keyword that precedes all assignments, *variablename* stands for the name of the variable, and *value* stands for the value you are assigning to the variable). For example:

```
var mugs = 2
var price = 9.95
```

Assigning a String to a Variable

When making an assignment to a string value, it is vital to place the string within quotation marks (either the double or single kind). Here are two examples:

```
var surname = "Caruthers"
var model = 'C3PO'
```

Note that if you do not include the quotation marks, JavaScript will think you are assigning the value of one variable to another variable; for example:

```
var surname = caruthers
```

JavaScript will think you want to assign the value of the variable caruthers to surname. Since caruthers is a nonexistent variable, JavaScript will display an error message alerting you to this fact. This is not what you want in this case (though at other times you *do* want to assign one variable's value to another).

Boolean Assignments

Boolean values usually represent conditions such as matters in which there can be only a true or false status. Assigning a Boolean value to a variable simply looks like this:

```
var married = true
var dead = false
```

51

And Don't Forget Null

And, for the sake of closure, an assignment of the special bonus value, null:

```
var variablename=null
```

You may or may not encounter actual application for the null value assignment in later chapters. It's not crucial, and may not come up very often. A common programming technique when wanting a variable to contain "nothing" is to assign numerical variables the value 0 (for example, `total=0`) and to string variables, the value `""` (for example, `surname=""`). Either of these practices would work just as well as the null assignment.

The Plain (Literal) Truth

A value that is not married (assigned) to a variable is known as a *literal*. This is such a simple concept that it might actually be a tad confusing at first. To wit:

➤ The numeric value `5` is a literal.

➤ The string `"mary worth"` is a literal.

What is the point of any of this? Recall that variables are most often used to track potentially changing values. In some instances, you will want to refer to a value, but it may only be one constant amount. For example, perhaps the price of your product is 9.95, and it is always 9.95 in all cases.

In these instances, you still have the option to assign a variable name to it—this often makes reading the JavaScript program easier for human debugging purposes—but you do not *need* to use a variable in these cases. You may simply want to write out 9.95 whenever it is needed in a calculation within the JavaScript program. This is a reasonable practice in some cases, and other times it would be more comprehensible to use a meaningful variable name.

The following examples use a variable assignment and the * sign, which is a multiplication symbol (we'll learn more about that in the next chapter). To illustrate a literal versus a variable name, consider the following:

Using variables:

```
var price = 9.95
var total = mugs * price
```

Techno Talk

Stay Still A *constant* is a label whose value never changes. A typical example from "the real world" is PI. We use the label "PI" or that funny symbol (π), yet it always represents the same actual number. We may choose to use a similar technique in JavaScript programming, for ease of reading and ease of future program modifications.

Using literals:

```
var total = mugs * 9.95
```

Although both sets of commands yield the same results, there are different reasons to select one approach or the other. In the first case (using variables), the calculation for the variable total is very easy for a human reading the program code to understand (for debugging purposes). In the second case, it might not be so obvious to a human reader just what the 9.95 represents. If there is a problem with the program, analyzing it may be more difficult because of this.

Secondly, imagine that there might be many instances of calculations within the program which utilize the 9.95 price. If the price were to change, it would take some time to manually edit the JavaScript program to reflect the price changes. On the other hand, in the first example, one need only change the value assigned to price one time, and because price is used to represent the value throughout the remainder of the program, all other calculations will remain accurate as-is.

Lastly, to reiterate, all of the above assumes that the price in question will remain constant. If it may change for any reason, such as to calculate discounts, it must be represented by a variable name.

Treating Values Like Objects

So far, you've learned about two important topics—variable names and their assigned values—and one minor topic—literals. Now, it is time to move up one rung in the ladder of abstraction, to a very relevant concept in JavaScript programming: the *object*.

An object, in JavaScript, is an umbrella concept under which a set of variables resides. This may be a tough concept at first, so let's explain it several different ways. Consider a sweater. A sweater, by the JavaScript definition, is an "object" that possesses several noteworthy qualities, or "properties." For example, a sweater may possess properties of material, size, color, and price.

Note how each property sounds like the variables discussed earlier. That is exactly what they are. Thus, an object is a sort of "supervariable" that contains a set of subvariables. Another example of an object would be an individual person. A person, as an object, contains a set of properties—some of which are useful for our particular application—such as first name, surname, age, gender, and marital status.

Also take notice of how objects can fit inside other, larger objects. For example, a person object could be part of a family object. A family object might have properties such as size, ethnicity, combined income, and each person (who, in turn, possess their individual person object properties previously described). Therefore, an object can also be a property of another object. Confusing? Somewhat, but useful as well, as you shall see.

In JavaScript lingo, you denote an object and its properties in the form

```
object.property
```

For example, recall the sweater object. Imagine that in JavaScript, you create an object (for now, don't worry about *how* you create an object) called `sweater`. You then create several properties for the sweater object: `material`, `size`, `color`, and `price`. In JavaScript syntax, these would be referred to in program code as

```
sweater.material
sweater.size
sweater.color
sweater.price
```

Each of the preceding is a variable, of the same sort discussed at the opening of this chapter. Therefore, you can assign appropriate values to each of them. Examples would include

```
sweater.material = "argyle"
sweater.size = "M"
sweater.color = "violet"
sweater.price = 29.95
```

Objects are common in JavaScript programs, so this is an important concept to nail down. Object properties exist in the order in which they were originally defined. You won't learn how to define objects until Chapter 9, but simply remember this point. In the spirit of that order, you can refer to the properties in an alternate way:

`sweater[0]` is equivalent to `sweater.material`

`sweater[1]` is equivalent to `sweater.size`

and so on.

Techno Talk

The New Math?

You may have noticed that you often start counting from 0 in programming. Why? The computer likes it that way. Therefore, in many computer counting scenarios, 0 represents "the first place," 1 is "the second place," and so on. It is somewhat confusing, which is why those who program frequently have the sort of hair that they do. In any case, it's just a matter of remembering that as you program.

For humans, `sweater.material` is certainly the preferable way to write code; however, there are times you may want to use the index numbers (the digits within the brackets) on occasions that you'll encounter later.

Objects à la Carte vs. Prepackaged

Keep in mind that you don't *have* to create objects. They're necessary only if they are useful to the tasks of your JavaScript program. A simple program that merely performs calculations using two variables may not need any objects. However, besides any objects that you may choose to create, JavaScript also includes a number of premade objects. These exist to help you achieve certain ends in your program.

Techno Talk

For the Programmers Out There... If you've done any programming in the past, you may notice the similarity between objects in JavaScript and "arrays" in most other languages. That's no coincidence—they are the same thing. You can even refer to object properties in JavaScript in a more traditional array—like fashion, such as

```
sweater["size"] = "M"
```

Before you take a closer look at some built-in objects, you need to learn about functions, all the fun of which takes place in Chapter 8.

So far, you've looked at variables, the values that may be assigned to them, literals, and objects, which are superset groups of variables (known as properties). Here, break for tea and crackers, which are provided in the rec room down the hall. See you in a bit.

The Least You Need To Know

➤ A variable name is a label that you use to refer to some sort of "value." You should choose meaningful variable names, so that you can tell what they stand for when you have to "debug" (look for problems in) your program.

➤ A value is the contents assigned to a variable. Values may take the form of numeric data, character strings, Boolean values, or the special null symbol (written as the word `null`).

➤ A literal is simply a value used in code without being assigned to a variable. That is, it is written out explicitly. Literals have specific uses in particular circumstances, but they generally make code more difficult to understand by human readers.

➤ An object in JavaScript is a superset variable, under which a set of subvariables (or **properties**) relate. It is easiest to understand by example: a sweater is an object, which possesses the properties of material, size, color, and price. Objects can also serve as properties for other objects.

Operators and Expressions

If this chapter were a sequel to the previous one—and it is—it would pick up where we left off. And it will. Variables, values, and objects are merely part of the JavaScript story. They all deal with ways to contain data. In this chapter, you're going to look at methods of manipulating data, to generate new and improved—or at least useful—data. I guarantee this will be fun, or else you get a free video rental from your local video store down the street. Tell them I sent you; they'll take care of you.

Let's Play Operation!

An *operator* is a command that interprets given values or variables and produces a result. Does that make any sense? Perhaps not, but that's a textbook definition. As usual, examples are the best explanation.

A common and easy-to-understand form of operators are arithmetic operators. They are used to perform calculations on given data. Here is an arithmetic operator:

```
+
```

Neat, huh? That's not nearly so confusing as the definition made it seem. Of course, + can't perform anything on its own—it needs data to work with. Here's where values come in, either in the form of variables or literals. In technotalk, the values used with an operator are called *operands*. Thus, consider the following:

```
3 + 8
```

In the above, 3 and 8 are operands, and the + is the operator. That example used literals for values; more commonly in JavaScript programs, you would see operands that are variables:

```
total = mugs * price
```

The asterisk (*) is the operator for "multiply." JavaScript offers a wide array of arithmetic operators, which you can use with your values, be they literals or variables (or variables in the form of properties of objects). The following table attractively highlights some of the common arithmetic operators available in JavaScript.

Common Arithmetic Operators for Fun and Profit

Operator	What It Does
+	addition
–	subtraction
*	multiplication
/	division
%	modulus (returns the remainder of a division)

One Lump or Two? Binary and Unary Operators

The preceding arithmetic operators are known as *binary* operators. This is because they work their magic given two values (binary meaning "two"). That is why the binary syntax, as illustrated in the examples, can generally be described as

```
operand1 operator operand2
```

A couple of notable *unary* operators exist. These only call for one operand, and it will be a variable. There are three unary operators in JavaScript to know: increment, decrement, and negation. Here's an example of each.

Unary Increment: ++

This operator will increase, by one, the value of the operand (variable) supplied to it. Thus, mugs++ will increase the value of the current value of mugs by 1. You might (as detailed further later in this chapter) use this in an assignment:

```
sales = mugs++
```

Note the position of the ++ relative to mugs. In the preceding example, sales will be assigned the current value of mugs, and *then* the value of mugs will be increased by 1. This is as opposed to

```
sales = ++mugs
```

Here, mugs will *first* be increased by 1, and *that* result will be assigned to sales. This is an important distinction, because if you use one but meant the other, your later calculations may be off by 1.

Unary Decrement: --

This operator works just as the unary increment, but in the opposite direction. It decreases the value of the specific variable operand by one. Therefore, the operator mugs-- will decrease the value of mugs by 1.

You can use the unary decrement operator in assignments just as you use the unary increment. Again, keep in mind the difference between --mugs and mugs-- when used in an assignment (as explained in the previous unary increment section).

Unary Negation: -

Finally, there is the unary negation operator. Simply, it negates the value of the operand. Thus, if the variable mugs currently holds the value 5, then

```
-mugs
```

Would return the value -5. If mugs was already -5, then the unary negation operator would return the value 5 (because the negation of -5 is 5).

No More Math—but More Operators

There are several other varieties of operators besides arithmetic. Each one works by relating two or more variables together in some way. Operators are of central importance in JavaScript programming, as they are the main way to evaluate current conditions and change future conditions. Let's take a spin through the nonarithmetic operators: assignments, comparisons, and logicals.

Assignment Operators

You've already encountered one form of assignment operator: the equal sign (=). This is the most basic and common assignment operator and, as discussed, is used to assign one value—either a literal or a variable—to a variable.

```
price = 9.95
price = cost
```

In the first case, a literal is assigned to the variable `price`. In the second case, the current value of the variable `cost` (whatever that may be) is assigned to the variable price. Simple enough.

The other assignment operators are shortcuts to arithmetic operators, which combine assignments and arithmetic in one fell swoop. Witness:

```
total += price
```

In longhand, using the aforementioned arithmetic operators, the above could also be written

```
total = total + price
```

One common application of this technique is in updating a running total. Perhaps you're keeping track of cumulative gross profit and want to keep adding any new purchase orders to that gross. If the current value of `total` was 10, and price was 5, then the above would sum those two values and assign the new result (15) back to the variable `total`. Note that both of the above methods produce exactly the same result. The += method is simply shorter to write.

Similarly, you can also use the following hybrid assignment operators:

```
total -= price SAME AS total = total - price

total *= price SAME AS total = total * price

total /= price SAME AS total = total / price

total %= price SAME AS total = total % price (see arithmetic operator table)
```

Comparison Operators

Often, you have to compare two values to make some sort of determination of what to do next. These comparisons can grow to be quite complex, but you will, of course, start with the basics. The rationale behind these operators should be fairly understandable if you can avoid getting bogged down in the symbols.

The most basic and obvious comparison operator is the equals operator (==). This operator can compare two values, and determine if they are equal. The result of any comparison, including this one, is true or false.

Here is a very simple equality comparison:

```
mugs == 10
```

If the value of the variable mugs is 10, and thus equal to the literal value 10, then the above comparison will yield a true result. If mugs refers to any value other than 10, the result will be false. This result is most commonly used to direct the flow of the program, or to generate a condition-specific action (detailed more later).

Similarly, you could use the not equals (!=) comparison operator.

```
mugs != 10
```

Now, this is where you might get confused. The above will again compare the value of mugs with the literal value 10. However, this time we asked if they were "not equal." Therefore, if mugs is 5, then the above comparison will yield a true result. If mugs *is* 10, then the above will be false.

Two other common comparison operators are greater-than (>) and less-than (<). They are used in the following manners:

```
mugs > 10
```

If mugs is a value greater than (but *not* including) 10, the above yields true; otherwise it yields false.

```
mugs < 10
```

If mugs is a value less than (but *not* including) 10, the above yields true; otherwise it yields false.

Lastly, a pair of comparison operators are inclusive of the tested value—greater than or equal to (>=) and less than or equal to (<=):

```
mugs >= 10
mugs <= 10
```

61

These work the same way as the > and < operators, except they do include the tested value (10, in our example). Note, therefore, that if the value of mugs is 10, then both comparisons above would yield true.

Not Just for Vulcans Anymore: Logical Operators

Any of the previously mentioned folks who stayed awake in algebra class may recall that horrific week spent learning "logic." The magic words of a logician are AND, OR, and NOT. This makes for less than stimulating dinner date conversation, but it has many uses in JavaScript programs.

Logical operators are quite similar in usage to comparison operators. They also sort of "compare" two values, and provide a true or false result. The major difference in practice is that the logical operators usually "compare" comparison operators. What?? Once again, some examples are in order.

&& (aka "the AND Operator")

The && operator is given two comparisons, and if *both* are true in and of themselves, then the && operator returns a true. Try it this way:

```
( mugs > 5 ) && ( price < 10 )
```

The above first evaluates the comparison mugs > 5. This will either be true or false. Then, price < 10 is evaluated. That will either be true or false. If the first comparison is true AND the second comparison is true, then the logical operation will yield true. If either or both comparisons are false, the whole result is false.

It helps a lot to think of these logical comparisons in the context of an English sentence. We use them exactly the same way in verbal language: "If your father comes home early AND my paycheck cleared, we will go out for dinner." The example sentence contained both a logical comparison and a resulting action—for now, as far as JavaScript goes, just consider the logical comparison. The resulting actions will come later.

¦¦ (aka "the OR Operator")

The OR operator is less finicky than the AND operator. It asks that only one of the two comparisons be true to return a true for the whole logical comparison. For example:

```
( mugs > 5 ) ¦¦ ( price < 10 )
```

Just as with the && operator, both comparisons above are evaluated. If either is true, then the OR operator returns a true. Of course, if both are true, then a true is still returned. Only if both comparisons yield false results will the ¦¦ operator yield a false result.

English example: "If your father comes home early OR my paycheck cleared, we'll go out for dinner." Only one condition needs to be satisfied for the family to chow down, in this case.

! (aka "the NOT Operator")

This one is twisted. The NOT operator is a unary operator, and, therefore, takes only one operand. That operand is often a comparison operator: the negation of the comparison is returned. Try selling that on a t-shirt! To explain from another angle, if the operand is true, then a ! operation on it will result in false. And vice versa.

In the following example, let's assume that mugs holds the value 5.

```
!(mugs == 5)
```

Above, mugs == 5 results in true, because it is true. However, it's included in a NOT operation, and thus the result of the whole phrase above is false. Of course, if you're clever, you might realize that the comparison (mugs != 5) would return the same result as !(mugs == 5) (that is, false). This is correct, and, therefore, in many cases, the NOT operator is unnecessary, because the same evaluation can be made with a comparison operator. However, programmers tend to like NOT operators because they often result in more compact code (although not in the previous example, where the comparison operator is, in fact, shorter).

String Operators: The Loom of JavaScript

You've reached the last of the operators. Whew. String operators are intended to work with string values, which you should recall are not numerals or arithmetic expressions. The comparison operators can be used with strings, as well. Since strings are not numerals, how these work requires a little explanation.

Checking for equality between two strings is fairly straightforward. Suppose you supply the following test (use literals for clarity, although in many cases you'd be using variable names):

```
"dogs" == "cats"
```

Clearly, the two strings are not equal—that is, the same, and so the comparison has a false result. For two strings to pass an equality test, they have to be exactly the same, character for character.

However, "dogs" cannot be greater than "cats" (depends who you ask!), so

```
"dogs" > "cats"
```

is simply nonsensical to JavaScript. The same applies to the <, >=, and <= operators. Of course, the "not equal" != operator could apply to two strings.

The exception to the above is if the strings represent possible numerals. Let's suppose the string in question is "54". In this case, JavaScript will attempt to convert the string to a numeral for comparison purposes (remember: strings cannot actually be compared to numbers, but JavaScript automatically tries to convert the string to a number). Therefore,

```
"54" > "12"
```

does make sense to JavaScript and is exactly the same as 54 > 12. But JavaScript can perform this conversion only if the string contains only numerals; "dog54" would not be converted to a numeral, and thus the above comparison would again be nonsensical and generate an error, or unpredictable results.

Lastly, strings can be *concatenated* with the + operator, or the += assignment operator. Concatenation is the process of combining multiple strings to yield one new, bigger string. You may want to construct a message for the user, tailored to be appropriate for varying conditions. For example,

```
"dogs " + "are cute"
```

would yield the string "dogs are cute" (note the space in the above, such that the words "dogs" and "are" are not directly smooshed together). Also, if you had previously assigned "dogs " to the variable named phrase, then

```
phrase += "are cute"
```

would assign the entire string "dogs are cute" to the variable named phrase.

Full of Expressions

Programming types throw around the term *expressions*. In a sense, by now, you're already familiar with what an expression is, but I haven't explicitly defined it yet. I wanted to keep some suspense in this tale, after all.

An *expression*, in programming circles, is any "phrase" of program code that represents one evaluation, result, or assignment. You've used a variety of expressions already so far:

```
mugs = 5
(price > 10)
```

There is no critical need for a specific definition of an expression; it's just a term that programmers use to refer to these little portions of code. Every little segment covered in examples thus far is an expression. There is one sort of JavaScript that's worth special note, though.

A *conditional expression* is basically a shorthand way to assign a value to a variable based on the results of a certain condition. A conditional expression looks like this:

```
(condition) ? valuetrue : valuefalse
```

If the condition is true, then the resulting value is whatever is specified in the position where *valuetrue* is above; if the condition is false, the value returned is whatever is positioned where *valuefalse* is above. A common use for this sort of conditional expression is in an assignment operation, such that a variable is assigned the result of the above expression. Clearer example: Imagine that you include a bonus gift—a pencil—with all mug orders fewer than 10, but you include a teddy bear with all orders of 10 mugs or more. You can use the conditional expression to make this determination as follows:

```
bonus = (mugs >= 10) ? "teddy" : "pencil"
```

The variable bonus will be assigned a string value of "teddy" if there are 10 or more mug orders, or "pencil" on fewer than 10 orders.

The Least You Need To Know

➤ Operators serve to bring values and/or variables together and yield new results.

➤ Arithmetic operators are used for basic math calculations, as well as incrementing and decrementing numeric variables.

➤ Comparison operators are used to evaluate specified cases, such as whether one variable has a greater value than another, or whether they are equal, and so forth.

➤ Logical operators evaluate comparisons against AND, OR, and NOT conditions to determine whether a series of conditions are true or false.

➤ String operators compare and/or concatenate strings of characters.

➤ Expressions are JavaScript "phrases," which yield assignments, evaluations, or results.

Chapter 8

Making a Statement

In This Chapter

➤ A statement about statements

➤ Conditional: `if...else`

➤ Loop de loops: `while` and `for`

➤ Dealing with objects

➤ Leftovers: the remaining statements

➤ The philosophy of the statement

In the first and second chapters of this section on JavaScript, you've explored most of the building blocks of a mature JavaScript program. There are variables that are assigned values, and objects that are made up of subvariables known as properties. Variables can be operated on for mathematical purposes, or be compared together, or in some other way evaluated, thereby making expressions. An expression is any one "clause" of JavaScript code, such as an assignment operator or a comparison operator. Finally, then, you have the *statement*. A statement brings expressions together, with certain keywords, to make the JavaScript equivalent of an English sentence; that is, using any or all of the building blocks discussed thus far to create program logic that is the whole purpose of a JavaScript in the first place. Statements define and control the flow of the program.

Think of statements as the bones of a JavaScript program. All of the statements in your code comprise the skeleton, which determines the overall shape of the program. Peek at the sidebar on "Execute and Flow" for more understanding of this skeleton. The JavaScript language provides a small but useful set of statements that you can use to direct program flow.

Execute and Flow

Two common terms of programmer jargon are necessary in this chapter. When JavaScript reads and performs the actions specified in each statement of code, it is *executing* the program. Normally, JavaScript will execute each statement in sequence, in the order in which the statements are written. This is called the *flow*. By default, execution flow follows in sequence. Many of the statements described in this chapter are used to alter program flow—that is, to move execution to a specified region of code. In this way, you build the overall logic of the program. Doing this correctly is one of the challenges of programming, and it often takes some debugging to correct errors in your original logic.

The if ... else Statement

It's no coincidence, then, that statements are bookended by keywords that strongly resemble English language statements. One very common JavaScript statement is the If...else statement. This statement functions just as it sounds in English. The following would be an English usage version of an If...else statement:

"If I earn at least $500 this week, I can pay the electric bill, or else my lights will be shut off."

You can generate the exact same sentiment in JavaScript. You will need only two variables: income and lights. Presume that the variable income has been previously assigned some numeric value representing this week's earnings. The variable lights will be assigned on the condition of the income and will receive a Boolean value (true or false), since there are only two possible outcomes for the lights: remain on or shut off. Given all this, the JavaScript version of the above statement, using the JavaScript If...else construction, would look like this:

```
if (income >= 500)
 { lights = true }
else
 { lights = false }
```

In this statement, JavaScript would first evaluate the expression (income >= 500). If this returns a true result, JavaScript executes the statements within the first set of brackets {}. If the expression is false, JavaScript skips ahead to the else clause and executes the statements within the set of brackets immediately below the else keyword. Note that you can include as many statements as you like within the brackets of a clause, but they must be separated by semicolons (;), as in:

```
{ lights = true ;
    savings = income - bills }
```

The formatting in both previous examples is purely a matter of taste. JavaScript doesn't care where you put breaks in the lines, as long as you include all of the correct syntax (the brackets, the semicolons, and so on). However, for the human reader, keeping a consistent and somewhat logical format to the code will make debugging far easier and less insanity-inducing in the future.

Now you see how a statement in JavaScript serves as the outline in which most assignments, expressions, and function calls (we haven't covered those just yet) occur. The if...else statement is merely one way to control the logic flow of a JavaScript program.

The while Statement

The while statement is another way to control program flow and execution. It functions the following way:

```
while (condition)
  { statements }
```

In this example, the series of statements within the brackets are executed for as long as the condition specified holds true. The simplest example of a while statement is a simple *loop*. A loop results when a statement or series of statements are repeated some number of times until some condition changes. Therefore, the while statement is a classic loop. In this simple example, you will keep appending the string "repeat" to a variable named phrase, until the loop has executed 10 times:

```
count = 1
phrase= ""
while ( count <= 10 )
  { phrase += "repeat " ;
      count++ }
```

Let's consider a line-by-line analysis of the above code, which pulls together several concepts from previous chapters.

In line one, you assign the value 1 to the variable count. Because you will be using this as a counter, you must assign it an initial value. In this case, you would like count to begin with the value 1, so that is your initial assignment.

In line two, you want to be sure that the string variable phrase starts out empty. To do this, you can assign an "empty string" to it, as shown in the syntax phrase="". This will prepare the string for usage in the loop that follows.

In line three, you construct a while statement. The while loop is defined as proceeding as long as the value of count is less than or equal to 10.

In line four, you begin the statements that comprise the body of the while loop, thus an opening bracket precedes the first statement. In this line, you use an assignment operator to concatenate the string value "string" to the existing value of the variable phrase.

In line five, you increment the counter variable count by 1, using the unary increment operator.

The final result of the example will be that count will hold the value 11, and phrase will hold the string "repeat repeat repeat repeat repeat repeat repeat repeat repeat repeat". Notice that when count has reached 10, it will move through the loop one last time, adding the final "repeat" to phrase, and incrementing count to 11. Then, when the while condition is tested again, it will be false, and the loop will cease. JavaScript would then drop down to the next statement following the while condition's bracketed statements.

The for Statement

The for statement is another statement that creates a loop circumstance. It is much like the while statement, and in fact, in many programming situations, either statement could serve the same role, although their particular syntaxes differ. The real difference is that for statements are more specifically tailored to handle numerical loops. The while statement, although capable of the same (as illustrated in the previous example), is somewhat more flexible in its capability to function on conditions other than numerical loops.

The for statement is followed by an initial expression (which is often a variable assignment, but may be another statement), a test condition, a loop update expression, and finally, a block of statements to execute. An example would look frighteningly similar to:

```
phrase = ""
for (count = 1; count <= 10; count++)
 { phrase += "repeat "}
```

Watch Your Syntax

In programming, syntax refers to the "rules of grammar"—in other words, what words or symbols go where. For example, most statements begin with a keyword identifying the statement (such as for). They are followed by a set of parentheses in which special conditions are specified. All of this is syntax—the order of what goes where. If you accidentally violate a syntax rule, such as leaving out a parenthesis or semicolon, you will experience a syntax error. JavaScript will alert you of this when you try to execute the program (load the Web page), and then you'll have to fix it.

Update That Loop

In any loop, it is presumed that the variable in the test condition is going to change. Otherwise, the loop will never execute if the condition is false, or will never stop executing if the condition is true (this is called an "endless loop"). In a counting loop, you change the counter variable with the "loop update expression." This expression is part of the statement definition, as in the for statement. In this example, you use the unary increment operator as your loop update expression, thus increasing the value of the loop counter count by 1 each pass through the loop.

In line one, you assign an empty string to the variable phrase, as preparation.

In line two, define the for statement. The counter variable count is set to 1 to start with. Your test condition for the loop determines whether count is less than or equal to 10. The loop update expression uses the unary increment operator to bump the value of count up by 1.

In line three, you see the statement that makes up the loop itself. It will be executed as long as the test condition remains true. In this case, you use an assignment operator to concatenate the value "repeat" to the string variable phrase.

This example would produce the same results as the while loop: the variable count would hold the value 11, and the variable phrase would hold the string "repeat" in ten consecutive repetitions.

As stated, this is quite similar in logic to the previous while statement. The major differences are that the initial variable assignment for the loop counter and the expression that increments the loop counter are both included in the for statement definition heading (the expressions within the parentheses following the keyword `for`). This is why the `for` statement is more suited for these sorts of arithmetic loops, whereas the `while` statement is flexible enough for other sorts of loops, because it has fewer restrictions on the expressions that can affect the test condition.

The break and continue Statements: Bringing It All Together

Sometimes you will want to jump out of the execution of a loop (as in the `while` and `for` statements) in mid-loop. Here is a classic scenario that might demand this sort of "eject from loop" capability. Suppose that you want a facility in your Web page that will total the gross profit of all the purchases made from your site that day. However, you are running a promotion—every 10th purchase receives the order for free! Therefore, when calculating the total gross for the day, we must make exceptions for every 10th order.

The loop will work the following way: Look at each purchase made, and then add its price to a running total until you've reached the end of the purchases. Simple loop. Now for the exception: check each purchase to see if it is a whole integer multiple of 10 (which would mean it was a 10th purchase). If it is, do not add its price to the grand running total. This example will use the `continue` statement, which is used to drop out of a series of statements within a loop, and return to the top of the loop.

The example code contains three simple variables:

- ➤ `orders`—Holds the current number of orders for the day.

- ➤ `count`—The loop counter (this begins at 0).

- ➤ `total`—Contains the gross running total (this begins at 0).

In addition, we have one object, named `price`. Price has the properties 1, 2, 3, and so on. Each property represents one item purchased and holds the value of its price. For example, `price.1` might equal 9.95, `price.2` might equal 14.95, and so on.

Also, recall that you can refer to objects and properties in the format *object*[*property*], as in `price[1]`, which is how you will describe them within the loop code itself.

Here is the code, following which you'll consider what took place.

```
total = 0
for (count = 0; count <= orders; count++)
  { if (( count % 10 ) == 0 )
      { continue } ;
    total += price[count] }
```

Notice: Count Those Parentheses

In the `continue` statement example, take note of the line containing the `if` keyword. Note how it is followed by double parentheses. This is because you have two sets of "nested" parenthetical expressions. Nesting occurs when you have one parenthetical expression within another parenthetical expression. For example: the `if` comparison must be in one set of parentheses, as in `if ( comparison )`. However, the comparison itself is enclosed in parentheses, as in `( count % 10 )`, to prevent any possible misinterpretation by JavaScript. It's very important to keep track of your open and closed parentheses, and that every pair matches up; otherwise, you're likely to get syntax errors. And going back through your program to look for missing parentheses is less than fun.

Several concepts are going on in the previous example, all of which are covered at some point in this book.

In the first line (`total = 0`), you initialize the summation variable total to zero.

Next, you declare the parameters of the `for` loop. You begin `count` at 0 on the presumption that the properties of the object `price` also began numbering from 0. Be sure to keep an eye out for such things in your own program. You set the `for` loop condition to remain true while `count` is less than or equal to the total number of orders. Finally, you set the loop updater to increment `count` by one. Note that `count` does not increment the first pass through the loop, and thus remains at 0 until the second pass.

Below the `for` declaration, you have the set of brackets within which the loop statements are enclosed. In this case, your loop statement is an `if` statement. Recall that the `if` statement is followed by its own bracketed statements, which is why there are two sets of brackets in the example. If you follow them closely, you will see that they make sense.

The `if` statement checks to see whether the current order in question was a 10th purchase. It does this by using the "modulo" arithmetic operator. Consider: you could divide the current value of `count` by 10. If the current order were a 10th purchase (an even multiple of 10), then this division should yield a remainder of 0. The modulo operator can be used to return the remainder of a division. Therefore, the expression `count%10` will return the value 0 on every 10th purchase.

The brackets immediately below the `if` clause determine what to do if the condition is true; that is, if this is a 10th purchase. Note that your if-true statement is `continue`. This will cause JavaScript to ignore the remainder of the statements in the brackets of the `for` statement, and return to the top of the `for` loop. This will not re-initialize `count` to zero; it will just continue on with the loop as normal.

Because the previous `if` statement will ignore the remainder of the loop statement on this pass when the condition is true, you do not need an `else` statement. If the condition is false—that is, `count` represents any purchase other than a 10th one—execution will necessarily drop to the final statement in the `for` loop, which adds the value of the current property of the object `price` to the running total.

The `break` statement is similar to the `continue` statement in usage, although it behaves in one notably different way. Rather than causing the loop to skip ahead to its next trip through, the `break` statement immediately drops out of the loop entirely. That is, it aborts the loop on the spot and moves on to the next statement in the JavaScript program following the loop. If you were to replace `continue` in the previous example with `break`, then once you reached the first 10th purchase in the loop—which would be purchase number 10—the whole loop would end. Clearly, that's not what you want in this example, but in other cases, it might be.

Object-Related Statements

Two statements are designed specifically for the purpose of dealing with objects. Recall once again that an object is a variable that contains a set of subvariables known as properties. Your prototypical object example was the `sweater` object, which contained the properties `material`, `color`, `size`, and `price`.

The following statements work with a given object, to help you navigate and/or manipulate its properties. As always, this will make more sense once you look at examples.

The for ... in Statement

The `for...in` statement is a specialized loop, similar to the `for` statement, but with the purpose of looping through the properties of a particular object. Imagine again your `sweater` object. Perhaps a customer has chosen to order a sweater, and in other portions of your Web page, he has selected each property that interests him—maybe cotton, black, and XL. Of course, the `price` property is determined by you, the retailer, as a result of the sort of sweater he chose.

So, now there is a sweater object with four properties, each assigned a value. Imagine now that you are outputting an invoice to the screen for the customer to verify. Now you need to state the values of each of `sweater`'s properties. Doing so requires moving through each property in `sweater` and printing its value. Sounds like a loop! It *is* a loop! And, since it is a loop within an object, you need a `for...in` statement. *Quel coincidence!*

The loop parameters in the `for...in` statement are much simpler than the `for` statement. There is no need to initialize a counter, test for a condition, or update the counter (such as by incrementing it). The `for...in` loop works only one way: from the first property to the last in the given object. Therefore, the `for...in` statement looks like this:

```
for ( counter in objectname )
  { statements }
```

The `counter` is any variable name you want to supply as a counter. *Objectname* is the name of the object whose properties you are interested in. Let's take an easy example. Loop through the properties of the object `sweater` and add the value of each to a string. Later, that string may be used for some other purpose, such as output to the screen. Your counter will be named `count`, your object is `sweater`, and your string will be named `descrip` (as in "purchase description").

```
descrip = ""
for ( count in sweater )
  { descrip += sweater[count] + " "}
```

Voilà! In this example, you first assign the variable `descrip` to an empty string. Then you define the `for...in` statement. One statement follows within the loop. It simply concatenates the value of each property of `sweater` to the current contents of the variable `descrip`. Note that you are, in fact, adding the expression `sweater[count] + " "` to the variable `descript`. This is simply to include a blank space between each value, so that the `string` value is more readable if and when it is output later.

At the conclusion of this JavaScript program, the variable `descrip` might contain a string value such as `"cotton black XL 24.95"`. The exact order of the values in the string depends on the order of the properties in the object `sweater`, when they were originally created.

The with Statement

Yet again, you are concerned with only one object. The purpose of the `with` statement is to tell JavaScript which object you are currently concerned with. Then, any references to variables in the bracketed statements that follow are assumed to be properties of the object.

The `with` statement, in practice, looks like this:

```
with ( objectname )
  { statements }
```

Again assume your `sweater` object. Now, imagine that you are going to assign values to its properties. You don't *need* to use the `with` statement; after all, you could assign values in the format `sweater.color = black`. However, you can also use the `with` statement the following way:

```
with ( sweater )
 { material = cotton ;
    color = black ;
     size = XL }
```

Granted, the with statement doesn't exactly rival sliced bread, or those nifty sandwich makers, as far as inventions of the century go, but besides saving on keystrokes, it also helps improve the formatting and readability of the JavaScript program. Those are always positive qualities when it comes to debugging.

The Comment Statement

If you found the with statement to be short on excitement, this one is even duller. The comment statement is simply a way to insert your own comments into the JavaScript program, for future reference. JavaScript itself completely ignores them. This isn't to denigrate the utility of comments. Including comments in your program is an extremely useful way to remind yourself what the heck is going on, if you must return to the code at a later date. Programming is one of those things where, when you are steeped in the development of a program, everything you do makes sense to you; however, if you return to the program two months later to make some changes or corrections, you'll have absolutely no idea what your code means anymore. This, then, requires you to carefully reread the code to understand it again.

Therefore, including much English commentary in code is a good thing; it's just not an *exciting* thing.

Check This Out...

Comments Comments Everywhere

This is the second appearance of comments, as far as this book goes. Previously, you saw comments when we were talking about HTML code. If you recall, the big pep talk was about including the entire JavaScript program within HTML comment tags. That was to prevent non-JavaScript browsers from displaying the code on-screen.

The comments you are considering now are meant to prevent the JavaScript browser from attempting to execute in-code reminders for humans. Comments are used to explain to you, the human, what is going on in the code. Therefore, you don't want JavaScript to attempt to execute them—they'll only wind up producing errors.

There are two ways to denote comments in your JavaScript program, depending on whether they fit on one line or span multiple lines. For one-liners, simply precede the commentary with a double-slash: `//` commentary here.

For multiline comments, surround the text with a `/*` and a `*/` at the beginning and end, respectively. Here are two examples of well-commented code:

```
count = 0
// this counter will be used to track the number of sweaters ordered
for ( count=1; count <= orders ; count++ )
/* the following loop will go through each order and process them accordingly.
First, we'll check to see if the size is in stock. Then, we'll check for the color
in stock.
Lastly, we'll see if the purchaser's name is on our blacklist, in which case we
will secretly jack up the price by adding unreasonable shipping and handling costs */
```

The var Statement

The var statement is more often a matter of style than necessity. In theory, you should precede variable assignments with the word var. That is,

```
counter = 0
```

should theoretically be written as

```
var counter = 0
```

As you may have noticed, you've not been doing this throughout your examples, and I keep using the words "in theory." That's because you don't actually have to use it. JavaScript knows when you are assigning a variable, but some purists consider it good form to include the var word for program readability.

Having said that, it *is* necessary in one case to write out var; however, you haven't encountered that scenario yet. You will, when functions are discussed, which just happens to be the next chapter.

The Least You Need To Know

➤ Statements serve as the connective tissue of a JavaScript program. They control a program's flow.

➤ Statements have the syntax *statement definition*, followed by *statements to execute if definition true* that are enclosed in curly brackets { }.

➤ The `if...else` statement tests a condition and executes the stuff within the first set of brackets if true, or it executes the stuff within the second set of brackets if false:

```
if (condition) {statements if true} else {statements if false}
```

➤ The `when` statement sets up a loop if the given condition is true:

```
when (condition) {statements}
```

➤ The `for` statement sets up a loop which performs the bracketed statements until a specified counter meets a condition:

```
for (initialize counter; condition; update counter) {statements}
```

➤ You can deal solely with an object using the `for...in` statement:

```
for (counter in object) {statements}
```

and the `with` statement:

```
with (object) {statements}
```

➤ Commenting your code is unexciting, but strongly recommended. Use `//` before single-line comments, and surround multiline comments with `/*` and `*/`.

Conjunction Junction, What's a Function?

If statements are the connective tissue of a JavaScript program, functions are the blood. See, that high school anatomy course has really paid off. Any JavaScript program beyond the most basic is going to include functions. Some are prebuilt into JavaScript (as described in the Appendix at the end of this book), while others you will create.

That's great, and very nice to know, but what is a function? A very *apropos* question, but could you ask it again, and this time a little louder?

What Is a Function?

Much better. A function is like a miniprogram unto itself. It can be "called" from the rest of the JavaScript program. A function is composed of JavaScript code, which, if executed, accomplishes some task. The set of code composing the function is given a name or label, of any sort you want. Therefore, this name comes to represent a particular function, or set of code. Creating a function is not the same as calling a function. In this chapter, you will see how a function is "defined" (that is, how you write out the code that belongs to the labeled function). To be executed, a function needs to be called from some other section of JavaScript code. You will see how this is done, as well.

Check This Out...

Calling All Functions! When you "call" a function, it means that you instruct JavaScript to execute that function. Remember that a function is a mini-program of JavaScript code. So, "calling" it means to execute the code which comprises a particular function.

You often use a function to define a procedure that will be called upon regularly. This way, a set routine is programmed and named, and can be called repeatedly without being redefined over and over. To make an analogy to real life, throughout the day you have many functions in your daily activities. You might consider sleep a function. Eating lunch is a function, and so forth. Between these predefined activities, you act out other tasks, which sometimes are similar to loops and conditional statements.

For example, perhaps you are watching television. While doing so, certain conditions may occur: if hungry; if sleepy; if bladder full. These are like conditional statements in a JavaScript program. Upon evaluation of these conditions, you may choose to call upon a predefined function. For example, if hungry, eat lunch; if bladder full, run to bathroom. In each case, eat lunch and run to bathroom are functions, because they refer to a defined series of actions. That series, however, needs to have been defined only once sometime in the past. For instance, the function "run to bathroom" may have been "defined" when you were toilet-trained. From then on, you could simply call that function to execute it when necessary. A vivid image, no doubt.

So far, in the statements you have used in this book, you have called upon only very simple actions. Soon you will learn how to create and define functions—whole sets of actions that can vary in size from one statement to a whole other program in and of itself—which can then be called from statements.

The Role of Parameters

Functions frequently, although not necessarily, accept parameters when they are called. A parameter is a specified value, which somehow plays a role in the doings of the function's actions. Let's recall the lunch function, from real life. Although the procedure for eating lunch is predefined, there are a few variables you do need to take note of. The most obvious being, what food will you be eating for lunch? What beverage will accompany this food?

Function Notation

You specify the variables included in a function by listing them within parentheses beside the function name. An example might be `lunch` `(food,beverage)`. It is common practice, in a book such as this, to write a function name in the format `lunch()`. This simply means that you're speaking of the function named `lunch`, although you're not considering its particular variables at this time.

In this sense, you can say that the function `lunch()` takes two parameters: `foodstuff` and `beverage`. When you feel peckish just around noon, you call your lunch function with these two parameters; you would notate it the following way:

```
lunch ("pizza","Coke")
```

In this example, you invoke your `lunch()` function with the specifics of a pizza and a Coke. Similarly, functions in JavaScript can also take parameters. When you define the function—which you will do shortly—you must decide which parameters the function will require. When you define a function, you don't know what the specific parameter values will be. That is determined when you call the function, somewhere else in the JavaScript program. When you define the function `lunch()`, you might name the parameters `foodstuff` and `beverage`, for instance. Only when you later call the function `lunch()` will you use actual values for these parameters.

As you will see in later examples, the names you choose when defining the parameters become variables within the function. Consider that you have defined a function `lunch(foodstuff, beverage)`. You may later call this function with specific values, such as `lunch("pizza","Coke")`. Within the JavaScript code that comprises the function, `foodstuff` is a variable that would now contain the value `"pizza"`, and `beverage` is a variable that will now contain the value `"Coke"`.

Returned Results

At the conclusion of a function, it is often (but not always) the case that you will want to return some sort of result to the program that called it. Again, with the lunch example, you might say that the function `lunch()` accepts two parameters, `foodstuff` and `beverage`, and returns one result: a variable called `satisfaction`, which will contain a logical value `TRUE` or `FALSE`.

By this logic, the `lunch()` function processes the specific foodstuff and beverage specified to it (`"pizza"` and `"Coke"` in this case), and then returns a true or a false value for the variable `satisfaction`. The calling program (in this example, that would be you, the person) then examines this result and decides what to do from there. It may choose to call the function again with new parameters (if, say, `satisfaction` was returned as false, you would want to run for more food), or it may choose to move on with the remainder of the program (if `satisfaction` is returned as true).

Now I'm Hungry—Defining and Calling a Function

The formal template for a function definition looks like this:

```
function functionname (parameter1 , parameter2 , etc.)
  { statements }
```

Therefore, the formal JavaScript definition for the `lunch()` function would have looked like this:

```
function lunch (foodstuff , beverage)
  { eat foodstuff  ;
    drink beverage ;
    satisfaction = (evaluation of satisfaction) ;
    return satisfaction }
```

Of course, the statements within brackets in this example are all fake, since there are no real JavaScript statements that define the eating of food. Remember that the above function is *not* executed unless it is called from somewhere else in the JavaScript program. Merely defining it does not execute it.

An important word about parameters, briefly touched upon earlier: when you name parameters in the function definition, you are essentially creating variables. Whatever values are passed to the function in the function call, will be assigned to the variables you have named in the function definition (in the order that they are listed in the function call). So, if you called the previous function with the call

```
lunch ("pizza" , "Coke")
```

then within the statements of the function `lunch()`, the variable `foodstuff` will contain the string value `"pizza"`, and the variable `beverage` will contain the string value `"Coke"`.

In this function call, you have passed literals as the parameter values. Alternatively, if you call the function with

```
lunch (choice1 , choice2)
```

then within the statements of function `lunch()`, the variable `foodstuff` will contain the value of the variable `choice1`; likewise, `beverage` will contain the value of the variable `choice2`. In this function call, you have passed the contents of variables as parameter values.

Would You Like Parameters with That Function?

A function does not *have* to accept any parameters. The one you are writing may not need any. In these cases, you simply continue to use the `()` where they are required (in the function definition and function calls), but leave nothing in between; for example:

```
function noparams () {statements}
```

or

```
noparams ()
```

More about Function Calls

You'll see several function calls in action in later examples, but for now, you should get a grasp on the two forms of function calls. Previously, you have just seen one common form—the plain function call. It exists, as written, in the following form:

```
functionname (parameter1, etc.)
```

However, recall the role of the "return" value. In the `lunch()` example, after the function completes (the meal has been consumed), the function returns the value of the variable `satisfaction`, which is a logical value of true or false. Where does this value get returned *to*? Mid-air? In the plain function calls above, the value is not returned anywhere. It has nowhere to go. To make a function call that can accept a returned value, you make the call within an assignment. For example:

```
morefood = lunch ("pizza", "Coke")
```

In this case, the function `lunch()` will be called, and the food will be processed just as in the plain function call. In addition, the logical value that is returned from the function will be assigned to the variable morefood. From there, you might use morefood in future conditional evaluations later in the program.

Therefore, for the calling program to accept a return value from a function, the call is made in the form

```
variableforreturn = functionname (parameter1, etc.)
```

Let's Make a Function!

Now you're ready to define a real JavaScript function. No more talk about lunch. You will build on an example already coded in the previous chapter. In Chapter 8, you wrote a small segment of JavaScript code that calculated the daily gross profit on product purchases via our Web page. The special exception was that every 10th purchase was free, and thus added zero to your cumulative total.

Now, turn that segment into an official function.

The task: calculate daily gross profit, leaving out every 10th purchase from the total. Return total gross.

First, define the function, which will be called promotion():

```
function promotion ( orders, price )
```

Notice that you are sending two parameters to the function: orders, which represents the total number of orders for the day; and price, which is an object, in which each property is a price of sale for a given order.

Note that price is an object, which must have been created prior to calling the function; however, you have not yet covered creating objects, because doing so is a variation on creating functions. For now, assume the object price was created elsewhere in the JavaScript program. By the end of this chapter, you'll know how to create objects for real.

Finally, write the { statements } section of the function. This is based closely on the continue statement example from Chapter 8.

```
{
var total = 0 ;
for (var count = 0; count <= orders; count++)
 { if (( count % 10 ) == 0 )
    { continue };
   total += price[count] } ;
return total
}
```

For the most part, the above is the same as the code in the continue example. There are a few differences to note:

➤ **The semicolons** Remember that each statement within a bracketed section needs to be separated by semicolons. In this case, the variable assignment to `total` is one statement, the *entire* `for` statement is one statement, as is the `if` clause within the `for` statement. The final statement—`return`—does not need a semicolon because it is the final statement before the closing bracket. If you read this paragraph while referring back to the code above, it does make sense.

➤ **The `var` statement, which is used twice** In the previous chapter, we dissed the `var` statement as being superfluous except for a special case. Welcome to the special case. The "special case" is when you're making new variables within a function. Any variables you create *solely for use within the function*, such as a loop counter, should be made with a `var` statement. When done this way, the variable will hold its value only within the function statements. For one thing, this would prevent you from overwriting the value of a variable of the same name which exists in the rest of the JavaScript program.

Motherly Advice

The var situation above is why it is "recommended" to always use a var statement when assigning values to variables. Doing so would prevent any possible mistakes caused by forgetting to use a var statement when necessary. Ultimately, the choice is yours. If you trust yourself to re-member to use var statements within functions, then you may opt to forego them elsewhere. On the other hand, if you tend to forget where you put your pen down five seconds ago, perhaps the recommended var usage is the way to go.

The Whole Burrito—A Finished Function

For the purposes of science and education, in the previous example, you sort of decapitated the function definition from the entire function body. Now, you'll re-animate the two parts and wind up with one fully mature, living, working function.

```
function promotion ( orders, price )
{
var total = 0 ;
for (var count = 0; count <= orders; count++)
  { if (( count % 10 ) == 0 )
      { continue };
```

```
            total += price[count] } ;
        return total
        }
```

Because this function's entire purpose in life is to calculate and return a value, you want to call it in an assignment. So, wherever it is in your JavaScript program that you want to execute this function and use its result, you would call it with an expression such as:

```
    total = promotion ( orders, price )
```

Although you needn't call the function with variable names that match the parameter names, in this case, you have done so, simply because the variable names are equally sensible labels in both portions of the program.

Making the Call

A function call can be made in any valid location for a statement. For example, you might include a function call in an `if...else` statement, as in

```
    if (hunger = true)
      {morefood=lunch ("pizza", "Coke")}
    else
      {watchtv ("NBC")}
```

Here, the fictitious function `lunch()` is called if the `hunger` condition is true, and the equally fictitious function `watchtv` is called if the hunger condition is false.

Also note that a function can call another function in the course of its `{ statements }`. However, there is an important rule (looked at again in a later chapter) that a function must have been defined before any calls are made to it. Therefore, if you are calling one function from another, the function being called has to have been defined previously in the JavaScript program, before the definition of the function making the call.

Top Loading

Because functions must be defined before they can be called, the best way to avoid potential problems is simply to place all function definitions at the top of your JavaScript program, above any other programming. Some people recommend placing all of the function definitions at the very top of the Web page, between the <HEAD> and </HEAD> tags, so that they will always be loaded before anything else. You'll see an example of this in a later chapter.

Even more interesting, a function can be passed as a parameter to another function. This makes sense if you think about it. Consider the `promotion()` function defined earlier. It returns a result, the gross profit for the day. Perhaps you have another function, `weekly`, which performs a weekly gross summary and takes two parameters: total sales for the week (`wkorders`) and gross daily profit for the current day (the `promotion()` function). It returns the value for current gross weekly sales. One might then call `weekly` with the statement

```
weektotal = weekly (wkorders , promotion (orders, price))
```

Method Programming

Supposedly, Marlon Brando was a classic method actor. Now, he was largely before my time (and I stress "largely"), but there are methods in JavaScript programming, as well. Follow closely: in JavaScript, a *method* is a function that is a property of an object.

Thus far, you have seen one type of object property: the common garden-variety variable. An example was

```
sweater.color
```

However, it is possible for the property, rather than a variable, to be a function. Thus, imagine you have a function that calculates the price of a sweater based on other characteristics, such as its material. The function itself doesn't matter now. You'll just assume that the function `fprice()` has been defined, and takes the parameter `material`. It is assigned to the object property `price`. Now your whole `sweater` object looks like this:

```
sweater.material
sweater.color
sweater.size
sweater.price ()
```

The first three properties are variables, and thus may be assigned values, or may be assigned to other variables; for example:

```
sweater.material = "argyle"
```

or

```
buystock = sweater.material
```

However, the fourth property is a method—that is, a function within the object, and, therefore, assigning a value to it is nonsensical. Rather, it is something that you call.

For instance, you might call the method `sweater.price()` and assign the returned result to some other variable:

```
total += sweater.price ()
```

That's really all there is to a method. It is simply a function, just like those discussed throughout this chapter; the only difference is that it exists as a property of an object, rather than "on its own." Methods are created when an object is created. You haven't yet learned how to create an object, and doing so is the only remaining building block you need to know for writing full-fledged JavaScript programs. Therefore, Que proudly presents...

Object Creationism

An object is, truth be told, a function. To use an object, such as `sweater`, in your program, you first need to define its function. This will provide the structure for the object.

The function, in this case, takes parameters that represent each property. But, as you'll repeat, the function merely defines the structure of the object; it does not create the object itself. Thus, although you are ultimately interested in creating a sweater object, its definition needn't be called `sweater`. Imagine, for example, that you sell several sorts of topwear, such as sweaters, t-shirts, and tank tops. All of these may be defined by the same object *definition*. Later, you'll create separate objects to represent each. Do this by example.

For your first example, simply define a `topwear` object that does not contain a method. Rather, it contains three regular variable properties: `material`, `color`, and `size`. Succeeding the function definition, watch the `{ statements }` section.

```
Function topwear (material , color , size);
  {
     this.material = material ;
     this.color = color ;
     this.size = size
  }
```

Again, this example merely defines the structure of the object; it does not actually create an instance of the object. You'll do that in a minute. Note, in the example, the usage of the term `this`. In a sense, think of it as JavaScript shorthand for "this object which you're considering." There is another situation in which you will use the `this` keyword, in a later chapter. For now, just note its usage in defining an object.

At this stage of the play, you have created the skeleton for any object that will be based on `topwear`. By skeleton, I mean that you have defined what sort of properties and methods this object would contain. But, you haven't yet created an actual instance of an object, such as a `sweater` object with properties containing actual values. You do that by assigning the above function to a variable, using a special function call known as the `new` function call. Example:

```
sweater = new topwear ("cotton" , "black" , "XL")
```

This example accomplished two feats. First, it created an actual object `sweater`—just like the one you've been referring to throughout these chapters (except this one doesn't have a `price` property). Second, it assigned some values to each of sweater's properties. There-fore, after executing the above expression, the following now exists in the mind of your JavaScript program:

`sweater.material`	which is currently the value `"cotton"`
`sweater.color`	which is currently the value `"black"`
`sweater.size`	which is currently the value `"XL"`

Now, this object and its properties may be used in the program, in any of the circum-stances which you've used objects in.

You can create any number of new objects based on the `topwear` object definition. Simply use the `new` function call; for example:

```
tanktop = new topwear ("nylon" , "white" , "M")
tshirt = new topwear ("twill" , "pink" , "XXL")
```

Now, you have `tanktop.material`, `tanktop.color`, `tanktop.size`, and so on and so on, for as many new objects as you choose to create. Go wild.

Method Making

Defining an object that contains method properties is basically the same procedure as above. Recall that a method is a property that is, itself, a type of function. So, re-create the `topwear` definition to include a price calculating function—the one based on material, which you used in an earlier method example, and called `fprice`.

First, you have to create the `fprice()` method definition (here, you'll use some silly formula to determine the garment price):

```
function fprice ()
// Base price is $10, add various amounts based on material
 { var startprice = 10.00 ;
    var addcost = 0 ;
    if (this.material == "cotton") { addcost = 5.50 } ;
    if (this.material == "nylon") { addcost = 2.50 } ;
```

```
if (this.material == "argyle") { addcost = 20.00 } ;
return startprice + addcost }
```

Notice the usage of `this.material`. This is a useful form of JavaScript shorthand. Because `fprice()` is not an independent function, but a method of an object, *this.property* refers to properties in the parent object (topwear). Now that this method definition is created, you will include a call to it in your `topwear` object definition.

```
function topwear (material , color , size)
   {
      this.material = material ;
      this.color = color ;
      this.size = size;
      this.price = fprice()
   }
```

Finally, create the new object `sweater` once again.

```
sweater = new topwear ("cotton" , "black" , "XL")
```

This time, the object `sweater` contains the properties

```
sweater.material
sweater.color
sweater.size
sweater.price
```

To access the price of a particular sweater, you would call the method `sweater.price` with an expression such as

```
price = sweater.price ()
```

So...quick quiz. Given all of the above, what would the value of `price` be?

Answer: `price` is assigned the value of `sweater.price`. `sweater.price`, in turn, refers to the method `fprice()`, which is part of the object `sweater`. `sweater` is an object with properties defined by the definition `topwear`. `sweater.material` holds the value "cotton". `fprice` calculates a total cost based on this `material` property, which works out to 15.50. Therefore, `sweater.price` holds the value 15.50, and finally then, `price` is assigned the value 15.50.

As is good practice when reading programming books, read the previous passage a few more times and follow its logic through the code segments illustrated in the example.

Congratulations are in order. This completes the last of the building blocks of JavaScript programming. Everything you do from here on in JavaScript is based on chapters 6 through 9, which explained variables, objects, literals, operators, statements, functions, and methods. The next few chapters will explore how these apply to specific JavaScript and Web-related applications. There will now be an intermission for rest and recovery (*for me*, that is—*you* can continue reading whenever you like).

The Least You Need To Know

This chapter strongly demands a close reading. Nonetheless, contractual obligations being what they are...

➤ A function is a self-contained program code element that is defined one time. It may be called upon by the remainder of the JavaScript program at any time to perform its actions.

➤ Functions may accept parameters—values given to them upon calling—and may return results to the calling program.

➤ Functions are defined with the statement

```
function funcname (parameter1, parameter2, etc.) { statements }
```

➤ Functions can be called with a plain call:

```
funcname (parameter1, etc.)
```

or in an assignment operator expression if returned results are desired:

```
variable = funcname (parameter1, etc.)
```

➤ Object definitions are created by defining a function that describes the properties of the object (*really, it's a good idea to read the chapter to grasp this*).

➤ Methods are functions that are properties of objects. First, their functions are defined, and then they are assigned to a property in the object definition.

➤ An actual instance of an object is created by making an assignment operator call to an object-defining function using the keyword new. Huh?

```
objectname = new objfunction (property1, property2, etc.)
```

➤ All functions should be defined in the JavaScript program prior to any other code.

Chapter 10

An Eye on Events

In This Chapter

➤ Behind the events

➤ Watching and waiting

➤ Ready, set, trigger—event handlers

➤ Homework examples

Welcome back from intermission. (I had cookies.) Some might think it odd to progress four chapters into JavaScript programming, and have yet to even mention HTML in this part of the book. After all, JavaScript is all about Web programming, and HTML is the standard fashion for Web pages. You might think to yourself at this point, "Great, now I understand the building blocks of JavaScript, can write functions and loops, and can create objects—but how do I make something useful out of all this?"

In answering this question, you'll look at the first of several Web-page specific facilities of JavaScript; in this case, event handling. In short, that is the capability for your JavaScript program to recognize and react to user actions within a web page. Let me just finish this last cookie I sneaked in from the rec hall.

The Main Event

By and large, the execution of your JavaScript programs needs to be "triggered" by something. Although you may, in some cases, want code to execute immediately upon loading the page, much of JavaScript's usefulness comes in its capability to be triggered.

Consider the mugs and sweaters you've been selling in program examples in the previous chapters. Most of those examples revolve around calculations you would make upon receiving a new purchase order from a Web user. Thus, receiving a new order would be a trigger to those JavaScript programs. Anything that might trigger execution of JavaScript code is known as an *event*.

Events are most often triggered by the user of your Web page. Common events include clicking on page elements (radio buttons, form submit buttons, URL links, and so on), entering values, and positioning the mouse pointer over certain elements. Your JavaScript program and/or programs that reside in the HTML source of the page will usually be triggered by these various events. Therefore, you need to learn what these events are, how to watch for them, and how to trigger JavaScript code in response.

Who They Are

Each event has a name by which you'll refer to it, so the logical place to begin is a name and description of each event which JavaScript is capable of recognizing. The events are as follows:

Click

The Click event occurs when a user clicks the mouse button on either a link or a form element. Form elements include buttons, check boxes, and "reset" or "submit" buttons.

Focus

The Focus event occurs when a user clicks the mouse or uses the Tab key to bring attention to a given form element. That is, when a user clicks on a form element to activate it, preparing it to accept entry, a Focus event has occurred. Note that this is different from when the user enters data into the element—focus merely occurs when the element is activated for entry. Some use the Tab key to move between form elements; this, too, triggers a Focus event as each element becomes active.

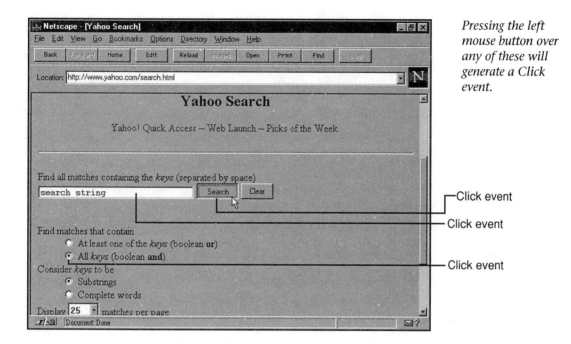

Pressing the left mouse button over any of these will generate a Click event.

─Click event

─ Click event

─ Click event

Blur

The Blur event is the opposite of the Focus event; it occurs when a user removes the focus from a currently in-focus form element, either by clicking or tabbing to another form element (thus moving the focus to a new element), or by clicking on some inactive region of the page, thus removing focus from any element.

Change

The Change event occurs after a user modifies the input into a form element, such as a text input area. It also occurs if a selection is made from a selection box (the form element that allows a user to make a selection from a scrolling list of choices). Note that the Change event occurs only after a modified entry loses focus. That is, the moment a user begins entering data into a form element, the Change event is *not* triggered. It is triggered when they're done, indicated when they remove focus from the element, such as by clicking elsewhere.

Modifying the text input area or choosing from the selection box generates a Change event once focus leaves the element.

Text input ——

Selection box ——

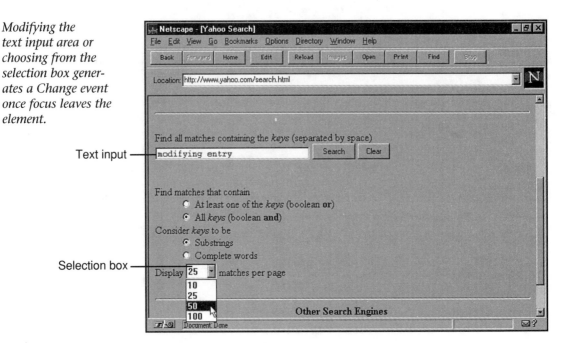

MouseOver

The MouseOver event occurs when the mouse pointer is moved over a link. You may have noticed, while using the Web, that when you move the pointer over a link within a page, the URL address of that link appears in a status line. That is an example of a MouseOver event having occurred.

Select

A Select event occurs when a user selects text (dragging the mouse across an area of text while holding down the left button, highlighting it) within a form's text entry element. A user might do this just before modifying the text in the entry.

Submit

A Submit event occurs when a user clicks the "Submit" button of a form element. Note that this event occurs *before* the form is actually submitted (as defined in the <FORM> tag). This allows you to trigger JavaScript code that might perform some analysis or evaluation, and as a result allow or prevent the form from actually being submitted.

The preceding are the basic events that may occur in a Web page as a result of user interaction. From these events, you will choose which are relevant to watch for within your particular page, and what JavaScript code to trigger as a result.

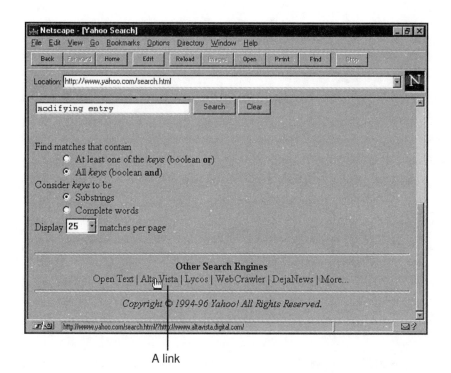

The mouse pointer is over the link, generating a MouseOver event.

A link

One Eye Open—Watching for Events

You specify events to watch for, in the case of each particular page element (link, form, and so on), in the form of an attribute of the tag that defines that element. Event attributes take the form `onEvent="JavaScript code"`. Let's consider a simple example; specifics make more sense than general definitions.

Recall the link tag in HTML. In typical HTML, you would define a link the following way:

```
<A HREF="url to link to">Text to appear highlighted in page</A>
```

The user browsing your web page sees "Text to appear highlighted in page" as a colored link. If he clicks on that link, he is taken to the new page defined by the URL specified in the HREF attribute above.

In the previous text input form, the user has selected some text just prior to modifying it, generating a Select event.

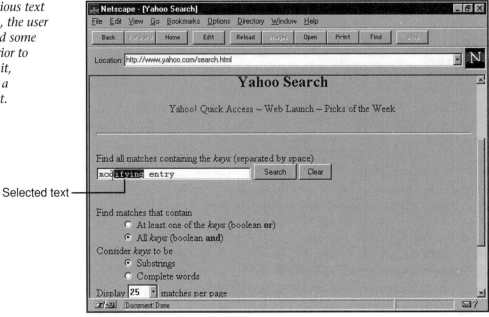

Selected text ⎯

This is typical HTML. Now, let's add event watching to it. Suppose you want to launch a certain JavaScript program if the user moves the mouse over the link. That would require a MouseOver event trigger. Recall that you watch for an event with the attribute—in this case, onMouseOver="*JavaScript code*". Thus, you add this attribute into the tag that defines the link, modifying the example as follows:

```
<A HREF="url to link to" onMouseOver="JavaScript code">Text to
  appear highlighted in page</A>
```

Keystone Caps

Remember that JavaScript is case-sensitive. It matters, within JavaScript code, whether you refer to a variable with upper- or lowercase letters. Referring to JavaScript statements with uppercase letters will result in errors. However, HTML code is not case-sensitive. Tags and their attributes can be in either upper- or lowercase, which includes onEvent attributes. However, for the purposes of book writing, onEvent is easier to read than onevent. Do remember that any JavaScript code included in the onEvent attribute between the quotation marks is subject to JavaScript's case-sensitivity.

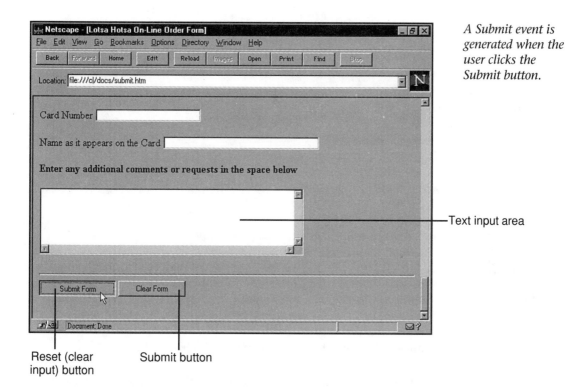

A Submit event is generated when the user clicks the Submit button.

Text input area

Reset (clear input) button

Submit button

Between the Lines—Calling an Event Handler

Let's consider the portion of the preceding that you've been labeling "*JavaScript code*", which follows the onEvent= portion of the attribute. What should go in there?

The first rule is that you must include the surrounding double-quotes as previously written. So, no matter what, the event watcher must say onEvent="*somethingsomething*". The actions specified between the double quotes are known as the *event handler*. This makes sense, because they describe how to handle the event, once triggered. The event handler *is* your JavaScript program code.

You would call basically two types of JavaScript event handlers between those double quotes: the *function call* and *explicit code*.

Function Call

The function call is the most common, and most desirable, event handler. This is why functions are so useful. In a nicely constructed web page, you define each function intended to handle a particular event at the top of the page, in the <HEAD> section. Then, in the course of the page, you call each function as required by your event watchers (the onEvent attributes).

In the case of a function call event handler, the previous link example might resemble this:

```
<A HREF="http://www.yahoo.com" onMouseOver="myfunction(parameter)">Text to appear
highlighted in page</A>
```

In this example, when a user positions the mouse pointer over the link (which would bring him to http://www.yahoo.com if he actually clicked on it), the JavaScript function myfunction(parameter) is called.

Important parameter bulletin: Note that the onEvent attribute requires double quotation marks around its definition. This means that if you want to send a string literal as a parameter in the function call, you cannot use double quotation marks to specify the literal. For example, imagine you want to call printfancy ("Nice work!") as the event handler. You have to use single quotes for the string literal; otherwise, they'll be misinterpreted as the close of the onEvent attribute. Thus, you have to write onEvent="printfancy ('Nice work!')". Something to keep in mind.

Explicit Code

Besides the elegant solution of a function call, you can write out explicit JavaScript statements within the double quotes. You can write an entire JavaScript program, of any length, although anything more than a statement or two is probably a good candidate for a function. You should remember two notable rules if you write out JavaScript code as an event handler:

➤ You cannot use any double quotation marks. You're limited to using single quotes (') anywhere a quotation mark is needed, because a double quotation mark (") would be interpreted as closing the onEvent attribute.

➤ Separate each JavaScript statement from the others with a semicolon.

Here is an example of the same link definition, but with explicit JavaScript code as the event handler:

```
<A HREF="http://www.yahoo.com" onMouseOver="total=0 ;
for (count=0;count<=10;count++) {total += 5} ;
half=total/2">Text to appear highlighted in page</A>
```

Now, I didn't say this example did anything useful—in this case, when the user moves the pointer over the link, the event handler is executed. It adds the value 5 to the variable total ten times in a loop, and then assigns half of total to the variable half. Perhaps at some later stage in the Web page, these variables will be used for some further calculations. In any case, the above is an example of explicit JavaScript code as an event handler.

You cannot specify an external file as the JavaScript event handler within the onEvent attribute. However, as previously discussed, you can include external JavaScript functions at the HEAD of the Web page with the <SCRIPT src="URL of myfuncs.js"></SCRIPT> tags, and those functions may then be called normally as event handlers in the onEvent attribute.

Examples, Exemplars, and Instantiations

At this point, you know the events, you know how to watch for them in HTML tags, and you know how to call the JavaScript event handlers. In fact, that's all you need to know. However, for the sake of clarity, we'll now run through examples of event triggers for some more types of events. Although they all follow the same rules outlined thus far, it's nice to see how a specific event is handled, to refer back to later on. Also, this chapter could use a couple more pages.

onClick

Imagine that users will click on a check box indicating their marital status. Upon clicking—whether they check it on or off—you may want to trigger a JavaScript function that uses their marital status in some other calculation. Keep in mind that forms are defined with <FORM> tags in HTML; however, the specifics of *that* are not the subject of this book. Assuming you know how to define a form element, the following is the line that defines the check box and onClick event trigger:

```
<INPUT name=married TYPE="checkbox" onClick="marstat(this.checked)">Married?
```

The preceding line first defines a check box, as per conventional HTML standards. Then you include the onClick attribute, as discussed in this chapter. Note that you make a function call as the event handler. Presumably, you defined the JavaScript function "marstat()" earlier in the page. So far, this is just like previous examples of event triggers.

What might strike you as different, upon first glance, is the fact that you pass the parameter this.checked to the function marstat(). What is this.checked? It's composed of two parts—this and checked—so let's consider each, as this concept will reappear in subsequent examples. The above is a form, and, after all, it is the data entered into this form that you want to pass to our event-handling function. A form is considered an object in JavaScript. Recall that an object possesses a set of properties. The form above happens to be a check box form, and, therefore, as far as JavaScript is concerned, a check box object. The check box object is a built-in JavaScript object, which contains four properties, one of which is named checked. The checked property is a Boolean value indicating whether the check box is checked on (true) or off (false).

Therefore, this.checked refers to the property checked, which is part of the object "this form," which happens to be a check box object. So in the previous function call, this.checked represents a Boolean value reflecting the state of the check box, and that is the parameter that the JavaScript function marstat desires.

onFocus

In this case, you will plant an event trigger that will occur if the user moves the page focus to this form. Our form will be a simple one-line entry blank, but that doesn't matter—this action is triggered by the activation of this form element, not what data is placed into it. When focus is placed on this element, an explicit JavaScript statement is executed.

```
<INPUT NAME=age TYPE="" ROWS=1 SIZE="3" onFocus="window.status='Nice
➥focus'">Your age?
```

Again, you watch for and trigger this event just as in all previous examples. Instead of calling a JavaScript function upon triggering, you execute a JavaScript statement. In this case, you assign a string value (note the single quotation marks) to an object property. We won't cover the window object until the next chapter, but for now, just note that this particular JavaScript statement will cause the specific string value to appear in the Web browser's status line.

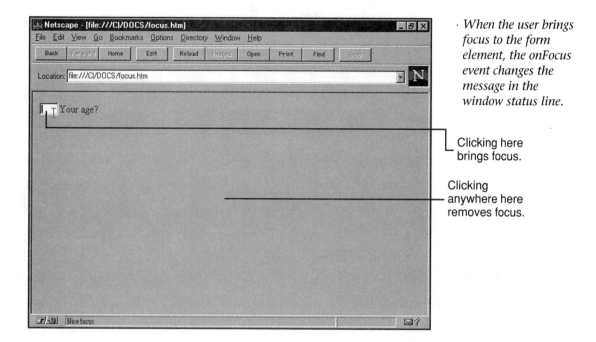

· *When the user brings focus to the form element, the onFocus event changes the message in the window status line.*

Clicking here brings focus.

Clicking anywhere here removes focus.

onSubmit

In this example, you'll watch for the user attempting to submit a form. Perhaps you offered a text box for the user to enter an e-mail address. After entering the address, the user then must hit the Submit button—typical HTML form design. Perhaps you wrote a JavaScript function that can look at the information the user entered and determine whether it is a plausible e-mail address (that is, has the proper format for an e-mail address). The following will trigger this hypothetical function, evalform (*address*), when the user attempts to submit the form.

```
<FORM onSubmit="evalform(this.email.value)">
<INPUT NAME=email TYPE="text" ROWS=1 SIZE="20">Enter your e-mail address
<INPUT NAME=submit TYPE="submit">
<INPUT NAME=reset TYPE="reset">
</FORM>
```

Once the user clicks Submit, the onSubmit event handler named evalform( ) will be called, and the entered address will be evaluated for plausibility.

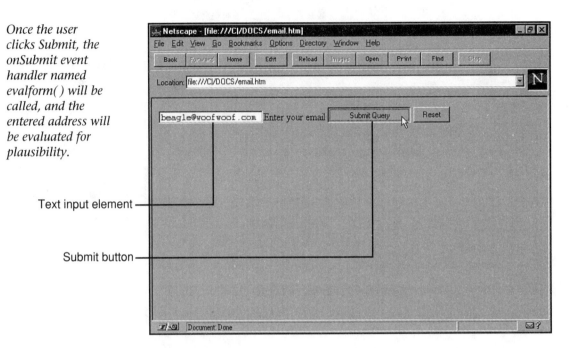

Text input element ——

Submit button ——

Alrighty then—as this is the final onEvent example, it's the most complicated. Let's tease this beast apart and see what's going on up there. For now, completely ignore the onSubmit attribute—we'll consider that last. Everything else should look like a typical HTML form. After the <FORM> tag, you define a text entry blank that is one row high and 20 spaces wide. You name this element email, as you see in the NAME= attribute. This name does not appear on the screen; it is for program reference only. The text following the <INPUT> tag will appear on the screen beside the element. Again, this is standard HTML form syntax.

Below that line, you then create another element, which is a Submit button, and below that you create a Reset button, in case the user wants to clear the text-entry element. Now, look at the event handling in this form, which is defined in the opening <FORM> tag. Because you want to call your function when the user submits the form via the Submit button, you use an onSubmit event watcher. Then, as per the previous examples, you define the event handler as a function call to the function evalform(). This should be familiar territory by now. What's worth special note is the syntax of the parameter you are sending to the evalform() function. The evalform() function—if it existed—would accept the user's input into the text-entry element of the form and determine whether it's a plausible e-mail address. You refer to this data with the name this.email.value.

104

Why? `this`, as usual, refers to the main object in question—this form. The text-entry element is a property of this form, and it is named whatever you named it with the `NAME=` attribute. (Psst—you named it `email`.) Finally, `email` itself (the text-entry element) is also an object—another built-in JavaScript object (the text-entry form element is a built-in object, which you named `email` within this particular page). One of the properties of the text element object is `value`, which contains the actual data entered into the element. So there it is: `this.email.value` refers to the data entered into the text element named `email`, which is a property of "this" form in question.

The preceding will pass the correct user input to the function `evalform(parameter)`. This function should then return a true or false value upon making its evaluation—that is, with the JavaScript statement `return true` or `return false` as the last statement in the function definition. If a value true is returned, the submission will proceed in whatever manner you intend to handle it (usually this is done with the `METHOD=` attribute of the `<FORM>` tag, but you didn't include this here because it is the stuff of HTML coding, not JavaScript). If a false value is returned, the submission will not proceed.

The Least You Need To Know

Once again, reading the full chapter is an excellent idea. The following is a fair summary, but far from detailed instruction.

➤ Anywhere you place JavaScript code within an HTML document, it must reside between `<SCRIPT>` `</SCRIPT>` tags.

➤ Include all JavaScript function definitions within `<SCRIPT>` tags, within the `<HEAD>` section of the document (that is, all the way near the top).

➤ An event is any user action such as a click, mouse movement, text selection, or form entry.

➤ Event handlers are the JavaScript programs that execute upon being triggered by a specified event.

➤ Event handlers can be triggered using the `onEvent="javascript code"` attribute within the tag defining the element being watched.

➤ Events that can be triggered include `onClick`, `onFocus`, `onBlur`, `onChange`, `onMouseOver`, `onSelect`, and `onSubmit`.

How Much Is That Object in the Window?

As you've seen, the purpose of JavaScript is to play a role in the workings of a Web page. In Chapters 6–9, you first learned the programming foundations of the JavaScript language itself. Then I ate cookies. In Chapter 10, you saw one way to integrate JavaScript programs in the functionality of a Web page—via event triggers.

Welcome, then, to Chapter 11. You now begin a journey into using JavaScript to interact with and/or control various characteristics of the Web page itself. You'll start at the top, with what is known to programming cognoscenti and exterior decorators alike as "the window."

The Looking Glass

Imagine launching your Web browser. After some hard drive activity, the browser pops onto the screen, and you are presented with an initial Web page. It is that space on your screen where the Web page appears that is the "window." In fact, your Web browser is mostly one huge window, although it has some navigational controls above the window and perhaps some status information below the window.

Your "window into the Web" is, in fact, "the window."

The window —

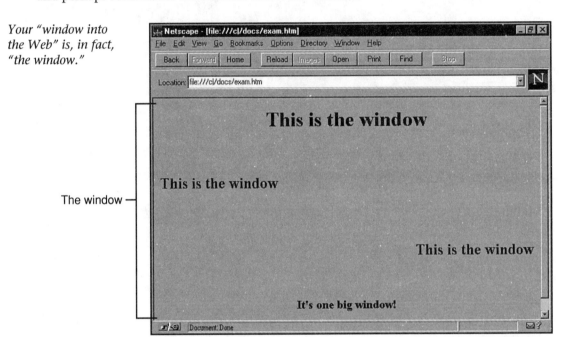

Everything that appears within a Web page, therefore, must appear within the window. For this reason, the window is called the "top-level" object. Recall the JavaScript definition of an object, such as the sweater object. Everything about the sweater—material, color, size, and price—is a property of the sweater. In this case, everything about the Web page, from its colors to background image, to form elements, and so on, is a property of the window.

In terms of JavaScript, then, the window is considered an object. When you refer to properties of the window, such as form elements in the previous chapter, you might recall that you have never explicitly written the object `window.property`. You don't usually need to, because JavaScript can assume that any other object you refer to in a program (such as a form) is necessarily a property of the window object, which is why you haven't done so.

Until now. Some goals you want to accomplish do require you to specify the window object in some way. That's the thrust of this chapter: looking at the window, rather than merely through it.

Properties

The window object contains several properties that you might need to reference, along with some nifty examples as your bonus gift. Keep reading.

The status Property

Look at the bottom of the window pictured here. The small area in the bottom frame of the window currently reads "Document: Done."

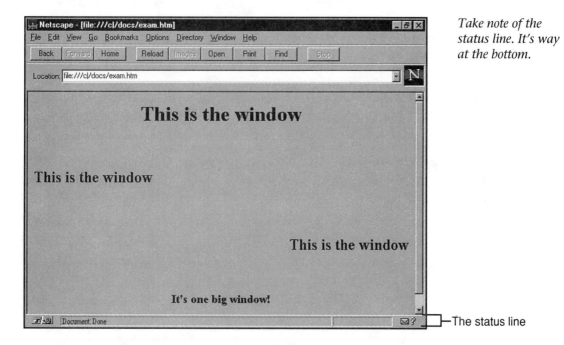

Take note of the status line. It's way at the bottom.

—The status line

This is the *status line*, and the Web browser uses it to report, well, status messages to the person using the browser. In this case, the status message tells you the document has finished loading. You, as a proprietor of JavaScript and knower of the window object can conjure up your own messages to appear on the status line.

The basic template for setting the status message text is

```
window.status = "messagetext"
```

The most likely places you would use the status property are in an onEvent trigger or the function that acts as an event handler. To create an example of the latter, you can create a Web page with two buttons on it. Label one "Try me!" and the other "Over here!". When the user clicks on either, the status line will be set to an appropriate message. You'll define a function msg(msgtext) to act as the event handler.

```
<html><body><head>
<script language="JavaScript">
function msg(msgtext)
 {window.status=msgtext}
</script></head>
<form><input type=button value="Try me!" onClick="msg('That was nice')"></form>
<form><input type=button value="Over here!" onClick="msg('Hey there')"></form>
</body></html>
```

The function accepts a parameter from the onEvent call and assigns that value to window.status. That's the relevant heart of this example. Down below, where you define the form element buttons, you use the traditional onEvent call as discussed in Chapter 10. Note that you pass string literals to the function, and, therefore, enclose them in single quotes.

If you load the above file into your Web browser, you'll see a window with two buttons. Clicking on them brings up their associated status line messages, as depicted here.

Fun with button clicking and setting the window's status message.

When the user clicks this button...

...a status message appears.

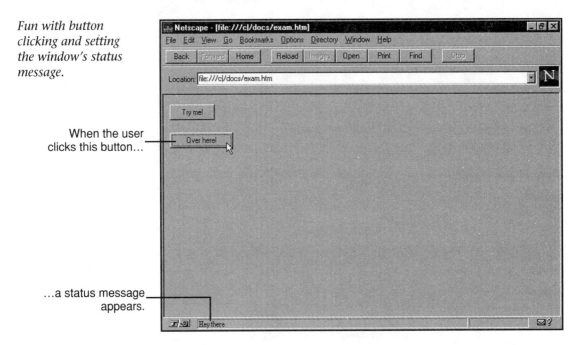

The self Object

Some claim it pretentious to refer to yourself, but in JavaScript you won't be ostracized for doing so. In fact, sometimes, you have good reason to. Technically, self is a synonym for window. Therefore

```
self.status = "Wake up!"
```

is the same as

```
window.status = "Wake up!"
```

However, the JavaScript creators realized a possible conflict. Let's say you created a form element in your page that has the internal name "status" (as defined by the NAME= attribute of the form element tag). In this case, if you ever need to refer to it in a window property construction, it's unclear whether you meant the window status line property or the form named status.

Therefore, you have the option of using self.*property* in cases where there may be ambiguity. Of course, you needn't program in any ambiguity in the first place when naming your form elements, but just in case, self is there for you.

Frames

Frames aren't discussed much in this book, as they are a Netscape HTML invention. In general, we've been avoiding overly complex HTML codes, since this is a book about JavaScript and not HTML. Nonetheless, the two are bedfellows, since they both contribute to a Web page's design and functionality.

If you don't already know how to code frames into HTML, this book isn't the place to learn—but as a reminder, frames are subwindows within the main window of a Web page. Thus, the top-level window of the Web page pictured here contains three frames:

It's quite logical, then, that each frame is a property of the window object. In turn, each frame has its own properties, because each is its own minidocument, and thus possesses the properties that any document would have (Chapter 13 covers all this).

Each frame is referred to as window.frame[0], window.frame[1], and so on. Therefore, as you'll see when we talk about document properties in Chapter 13, the properties within a frame can be described as window.frame[0].*property*. For now, this is all you need to know, that each frame is a property of the window object.

This window object contains three frames.

One frame —

A second frame —

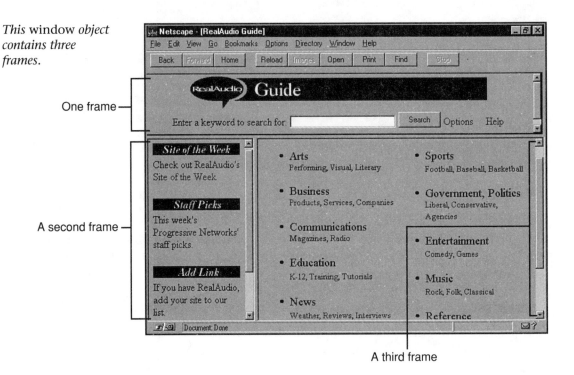

A third frame

Methods

In the spirit of "many different names for the same thing," you might remember that a method is a function that is part of an object. You coded a method called sweater.price() back in Chapter 9. Thus, the object window also has a set of methods associated with it. You can (and will) use these for a variety of useful purposes; therefore, you will now embark on a guided tour of window object methods.

alert()

What better way to let the user know something than by shoving it in his face? Enter the alert. An alert, in general-speak, is one of those message windows that pops up on the screen to tell you something. Usually, it has an "OK" button you click to signal that you've read this urgent message and would like to continue. Below is a typical alert:

Code red! Alert! Abandon ship! This is a common alert window.

Consider the hypothetical example where you requested that the user enter his e-mail address into a form text-entry element. You previously saw how you can use an onSubmit event trigger to check the user's entry for validity before allowing the submission to proceed (in Chapter 10). Let's build on that example. Suppose the submitted address is deemed nonplausible, and you want to pop up an alert telling the user that he is an abject liar.

The format for the alert method is: window.alert ("*message*")

After the user acknowledges the alert by clicking the "OK" button, JavaScript will move on to the next statement in your code or function. To reprise, your function evalform() was triggered by the following:

```
<FORM onSubmit="evalform(this.email.value)">
<INPUT NAME=email TYPE="text" ROWS=1 SIZE="20">Enter your e-mail address
<INPUT NAME=submit TYPE="submit">
<INPUT NAME=reset TYPE="reset">
</FORM>
```

Presumably, then, you have defined the function evalform() earlier in our document, and it might go a little something like this:

```
function evalform (address)
{ crucial = address.indexOf ("@") ;
    //the above uses a method of the string object to locate an at-sign in
    //the submitted form
    if (crucial == -1)
      { window.alert ("Your e-mail address is invalid! You are an abject liar!") ;
        return false }
    else
      { return true } ;
  }
```

The preceding function accepts a parameter, which is the submitted e-mail address to validate. The address.indexOf property is a method of the string object (covered in the appendix at the end of this book), which returns the position of the specified character within the string. In this case, you're searching for an @ symbol, because all valid e-mail addresses have this symbol. The position of that symbol is assigned to the variable crucial and will be a value of –1 if the symbol is not found in the string. This will be your only test, because this is simply an example.

Following that, you use a standard if...else clause, wherein if the @ symbol is not located, the window.alert method is called with an appropriate scolding to the user. Also note that the Boolean false is returned, to prevent submission of the form. Lastly, the else clause takes care of the condition where the @ was located, and simply returns a logical true, which allows the submission to proceed.

113

confirm()

The `confirm()` method is another type of message box. If you've ever used a computer—and at this stage of the book, I deeply hope you have—you've seen confirm messages. They typically pose a question or proposition, and you are asked to choose between "OK" or "Cancel."

You would use the `confirm()` method of the `window` object thusly:

```
window.confirm ("message")
```

This method returns a true value if the user opts for the "OK" option, or a false if "Cancel" is selected. In some cases, then, because a result is returned, you might want to call this method as `somevariable = window.confirm ("message")`. Next, you add a `confirm()` method to the e-mail validation function. In this case, if you determine that the address is valid, you repeat it to the user in a confirm message so that he can verify its accuracy.

Simply add the following highlighted code to your `evalform()` function:

```
function evalform (address)
{ crucial = address.indexOf ("@") ;
    if (crucial == -1)
      { window.alert ("Your e-mail address is invalid! You are an abject liar!") ;
        return false }
    else
      { message = "You entered " + address + " -- is this correct?";
        return window.confirm (message) } ;
  }
```

You've added only two lines to the previous version of this function: both occur in the true (address is valid) condition. First, you create the message to use in the `confirm()` method. You do this by making a variable `message` to which you assign three concatenated strings using the string concatenate operator (+). Below that, you call the `window.confirm()` method with the previously made `message`, which is what the user will see. Note that you make the method call as part of a return statement—the `confirm()` method will return a true or false, and you want to pass that result back to the calling form, which will then proceed with or cease the submission.

Assuming you executed your little e-mail entry JavaScript program and entered an e-mail address that passed validation, the above would generate something looking like this:

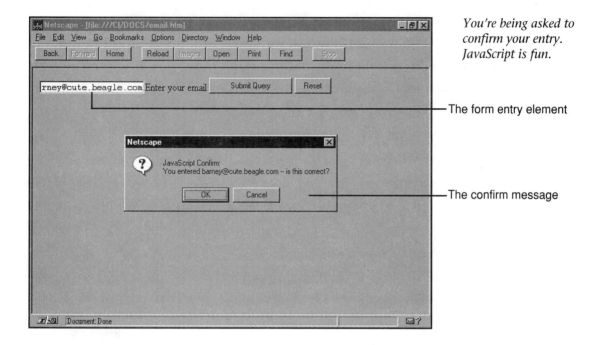

You're being asked to confirm your entry. JavaScript is fun.

The form entry element

The confirm message

prompt()

The prompt() method pops up a nifty message box, into which you may ask the user to input some sort of information. That information is then assigned to the variable to which this method is assigned, to be used as you may want for any other purpose. For this example, consider this scenario: You present a series of form buttons, each one representing an astrological sign. Somewhere in the Web page, the user is told to click whichever sign belongs to him. Upon doing so, you then prompt the user to enter his age.

The prompt() method works as follows:

```
somevariable = window.prompt ("prompt message" , defaultvalue)
```

The *prompt message* represents the proposition you want to put to the user. The *defaultvalue* represents some data that you'd like to appear in the prompt by default. If you have no preferred default value, just enter two double-quotes in that spot (like this: " ").

In this example, you'll validate the age the user enters to be somewhere within the known human lifespan. If it fails this test, a scolding alert will pop up, and then he will be asked to enter his age again. If the entered age passes, the user will be thanked. Note

115

that you don't do anything else with his age in this particular example, but, of course, you may choose to use it for any other programming purpose you like.

Here is the full code of your little programming feat:

```
<script language="JavaScript">
function getage ()
{ age=window.prompt ("How old are you?","") ;
   if ((age<1) || (age>120))
    { window.alert ("Why must you turn this page into a house of lies?") ;
      getage () }
   else
    { window.alert ("Thank you.") }
}
</script>
<FORM>
<INPUT NAME=gemini TYPE=button value="Gemini" onClick="getage()">
Click your sign</FORM>
```

Several examples are worth noting in this program. Jump to the final line first, the `<FORM>` definition. Here, as usual, you define a form element (a button) and include the `onClick` event trigger. To handle the event, you call the function `getage()`, which takes no parameters. Standard stuff.

Now up to the function definition itself, at the top of the program. The first statement in the function definition is your `prompt()` method. It will ask the user "How old are you?" and present her with an entry blank with no default value. Whatever the user enters is assigned to the variable age. You then test age for validity, using an `if...else` statement. Note the nifty conditional in the `if` clause, which uses a logical operator (OR) on two comparison operators.

Should the age be deemed invalid (outside the range 1–120), an alert pops up accusing the user of duplicity. Note that after the accusatory alert, the function `getage()` is then called again. Yes, it calls itself. That will essentially restart the function, thus letting the user start all over with the age prompt.

If age falls within the acceptable range, an alert pops up merely thanking the user for his input, and thus ends the function.

The following is a picture of the prompt method in action:

Not poking or prodding, just prompting.

open() and close()

Finally, at the sunset of your journey into the window object, consider methods that give rise and fall to windows themselves.

You can use the open() method to create an entirely new browser window. That is, the current window remains in place, but a new window is opened on the desktop. The new window is essentially another Web browser, and you define its characteristics—including size, title, document to open, navigation buttons to make available, and so forth—with the open() method.

Why would you use this method? Perhaps in your Web page, you want to show the user an example of something on another web page. Rather than load that example page within your current window—thus eliminating your explanation from the screen—you might open a new adjacent window that contains the example. At the end of the example, the user could then either manually close the new window himself, or choose some "I'm done" button, which would trigger the close() method, thereby closing the new window.

The formats for these methods are

```
window.open ("UrlToOpen","windowname","feature1,feature2,feature3,etc.")

window.close ()
```

The window.close() method must be contained in JavaScript code within the window to be closed. One window can't close another window; a window can only close itself (window suicide). Therefore, using the window.close() method is simple; just include a call to it as the event handler for some element that indicates to the user that he is done with the window, such as a form button.

The window.open() method has a few more parameters, as you can see. The first two parameters are straightforward:

➤ *UrlToOpen* is the address of the document you'd like to be opened in that window (for example, http://mydoc.html).

➤ *windowname* gives the window an internal name, which may be used for other references. Note, this name doesn't seem to appear anywhere visible on the window itself.

Finally, you may provide any, all, or none of the list of possible feature characteristics of the new window. Separate each feature by a comma but not a space, just as presented in the template example for the previous method. The possible features are

toolbar=*yes* or *no*	Determines whether to include the standard Back, Forward, Home toolbar.
location= *yes* or *no*	Determines whether to show the current URL location.
directories=*yes* or *no*	Determines whether to show "What's New" "What's Cool," or other buttons.
status=*yes* or *no*	Determines whether to have a status bar at the bottom of the window.
menubar=*yes* or *no*	Determines whether to include a menu bar at the top of the window.
scrollbars=*yes* or *no*	Determines whether to create scroll bars if the document exceeds the window size.
resizable=*yes* or *no*	Determines whether the user may resize the window.
copyhistory=*yes* or *no*	Determines whether this new window should inherit the current window's session history.
width=# *pixels*	Defines how wide the window should be, measured in pixels.
height=# *pixels*	Defines how tall the window should be, measured in pixels.

How Many Pixels in an Inch?

Noncomputer nerds might not be used to measuring sizes in pixels. But that is the standard measurement tool for the images on a computer screen. For the purposes of creating your window sizes, use the following guidelines: a standard VGA screen on a 13–14 inch monitor—which is the most common screen size in use—is 640 pixels wide by 480 pixels high. Therefore, determine what percentage of the screen you want your new window to eat up, and use the 640 × 480 scale accordingly. Furthermore, many users use screen sizes of 800 × 600 on 14–15 inch monitors, while those with 17-inch monitors more commonly use 1,024 × 768 pixels. At this point, 640 × 480 is still considered the most common standard size against which to measure your windows.

Given all of the features previously described, let's create an onEvent trigger, which will create a new window using some of the above features.

```
<INPUT NAME=newwin TYPE=button value="Click me for a new window"
➥onClick="window.open ('http://
mydoc.html','newwin','toolbar=no,status=yes,scrollbars=no,
➥resizable=no,width=320,height=240')">
```

I know that looks messy, but it's really just a long list of parameters. Note the use of single quotes within the open method call, because of the double quotes that must surround the onClick definition.

As a certain animated pig who shall remain nameless used to say, "As far as window objects go, that's all folks!" (Well, he said something like that. It was a long time ago.)

The Least You Need To Know

> ➤ The entire window through which a Web page is viewed is a JavaScript object, known as window.*property*.

> ➤ All elements and characteristics of a Web page are properties of the window object.

> ➤ window.status="*message*" defines the status bar message.

> ➤ window.frame[x].*property* refers to *property* of frame number *x*.

> ➤ window.alert ("*message*") is a method that pops up an alert box.

> ➤ window.confirm ("*message*") is a method that pops up a confirmation box; it returns true if user selects OK, and false if the user clicks CANCEL.

> ➤ *somevariable*=window.prompt ("*message*","*defaultvalue*") is a method that pops up a prompt box and assigns the user's input to *somevariable*.

> ➤ window.open ("*UrlToOpen*","*windowname*","*feature1,feature2,etc*") launches a new window with *feature* characteristics.

> ➤ window.close() kills the window that uses this method call (window suicide).

Check This Out...

Assume True
If you don't specify a window feature in the open() method call, it will default to yes. Therefore, if you want a feature false, be sure to list it and assign it "no" in the open() method call.

Chapter 12

Mapping and Tracking: Locations and Histories

In This Chapter

In This Chapter

➤ Picking apart a meaty URL

➤ URLs back in time

➤ Guiding visitors by the wallet

The location object refers to the current URL—that is, the address of the page currently loaded. This object provides several properties with which you can play with various characteristics of the URL. The history object contains the current list of other URLs that have been visited in the present session. It, too, can be sliced, diced, and analyzed.

Wherefore Art Thou, URL?

The location object contains the current URL. Thus, imagine that the address of your Web page is http://my.isp.com/~me/mypage.html. In that case, the location object refers to that address. The object's properties will seek out various portions of the URL. The location object is rather straightforward and nonconfusing—which is a Good Thing. The location object contains eight properties, and they behave in the following manners:

href

`location.href` contains the string value of the entire URL. Thus, given the previous sample URL, the value of `location.href` would be `"http://my.isp.com/~me/mypage.html"`.

One possible use of this property is to pass it as a parameter to the `window.open` call. Perhaps you want to open a new window, which connects to the same URL as the current window (so you can look at another portion of the same page at the same time you're looking at the current portion of the page). Simply use the call

```
window.open (location.href,"windowname","feature1,feature2,etc")
```

Now, you can also launch a new page without opening a new window. If you simply assign a new URL to `location.href`, the browser will attempt to connect to a new page. For example,

```
location.href = "http://www.yahoo.com"
```

Of course, if you do this, you'll effectively be leaving your current page, including any other JavaScript programs that are in it.

host

The `location.host` property holds only the hostname and port of the current page's URL. Looking at our previous example URL...

```
http://my.isp.com/~me/mypage.html
```

...the "hostname" would be `my.isp.com`. That's the Internet name of the computer on which the page resides. In the previous example, no port is specified in the URL, and, therefore, `location.host` will only contain the value "my.isp.com". If a port were specified in the URL, it might look like this:

```
http://my.isp.com:80/~me/mypage.html
```

"80" is the port in this example. If this were your URL, `location.host` would contain the string value `"my.isp.com:80"`. (Because the default port for a Web page is 80, it is usually not specified, but some URLs use a different port, in which case, it will be specified.) One possible use for this property is to construct a string for a user message or HTML link. That is, suppose you want to write a JavaScript function that you might use in numerous Web pages. The purpose of the function is to provide an HTML link on-screen for the user to jump to another document in a set of pages. Since your function doesn't know which machine it will be on, it could use the `location.host` property to concatenate an appropriate string, for later output in the window as a link.

Assigning a value to location.host will generate an error, because it is nonsensical. Whereas you can assign an entire URL to location.href, which would then connect to that URL, you cannot connect to just a host. Thus, assigning a value to location.host is of no use.

hostname

At the risk of sounding redundant, the property location.hostname will return just the hostname portion of the URL. Recall in the case above that host refers to *hostname:port*. hostname, then, refers only to the name. Yes, it is true: given a URL with no port specified, location.host and location.hostname contain the same value.

port

The property location.port simply contains the value of the port number in the URL, if specified, as explained previously. Note that if a port was not specified in the URL, location.port contains no value. It does not contain the default 80 port, unless the 80 was specified in the URL.

pathname

Once again, let's look at your example URL:

```
http://my.isp.com/~me/mypage.html
```

The pathname is the portion of the URL that describes the location of the Web document on the host computer. The pathname begins with and includes the slash (/) immediately preceding the hostname (or the port, if it were specified). In the above,

```
/~me/mypage.html
```

is the pathname. Therefore, this is the value that location.pathname would contain.

Assigning a value to this property, as in

```
location.pathname = "~me/otherdocs/newdoc.html"
```

will cause the Web browser to load that document into the current window. This is similar to when you assigned a value to location.href.

protocol

The protocol property contains the leftmost portion of the URL, which contains the name of the protocol to use in retrieving the specified file (Web document). The example

URL used the HTTP protocol, as is most common on the Web. However, some URLs may contain different protocols, such as

```
file://hostname/pathname
gopher://hostname/pathname
```

FTP, for instance, is the File Transfer Protocol and is another common way in which files can be delivered across the Internet. Gopher is yet another information-retrieval protocol, which had its heydey before the explosion of the Web (http—the hypertext transport protocol). Many sites still offer information via the Gopher protocol.

In your `http://my.isp.com/~me/mypage.html` example, `location.protocol` would contain the value `"http:"`. In the previous examples, `location.protocol` would contain `"file:"` and `"gopher:"`, respectively.

hash

Some URLs contain special *hash mark* values following the pathname. For example:

```
http://my.isp.com/~me/mypage.html#tuesday
```

The hash mark (#) specifies the name of an *anchor* to jump to in the Web page. An anchor is a place on a page that has been marked (via the HTML tags that make up the page) as a jump-to point. This allows users to be directed to specific spots within a page, rather than always at the very top. The above URL attempts to bring the user to the anchor known as "tuesday" in the page `mypage.html`.

Thus, the `location.hash` property would contain the value following the hash mark—in the preceding case, it would be `tuesday`.

Assigning a value to `location.hash` will cause the Web page to jump to that anchor. Note that of the properties you've seen so far, this may be one of the most useful. Because it jumps to new locations within the same page, it's more desirable than throwing out your current page, such as when you assign new values to `location.href` or `location.pathname`. You can use the `location.hash` property in event handlers, for example, to bring the user to specific locations within the current page.

search

Yet another variation on the URL is a search parameter following the pathname, denoted with a question mark (?). A form entry is probably the most common use for a search parameter. When a user enters form data into a form element and then clicks the "submit" button, the following URL is called:

```
http://some.isp.com/~someone/someprogram?formdata
```

The property `location.search` would contain the value following the question mark. The most sensible usage of this parameter would be in the page that receives the submitted form data.

For example, suppose you have two pages. One of them accepts user input in a form entry. It then sends that input to another page. This other page contains a JavaScript function that evaluates the submitted form data. Therefore, you can make a call to this function with `evalform(location.search)`, which would pass the submitted form as a parameter.

Re-Form School

As per my usual disclaimer, this book isn't an HTML guide. However, just to refresh your memory, I'll briefly mention how a form is submitted. You define a form element with the `<FORM>` tag. This tag may take several attributes, one of which is the `METHOD=` attribute. `METHOD=` may be assigned either `GET` or `POST`. This defines how the form data will be submitted to the server. The details are technical, but GET is the most popular method. It is also the method that generates the `?formdata` syntax in a URL.

The `ACTION=` attribute specifies which URL to send the submitted data to. This URL will presumably be designed to process the form data in some way.

Thus, a `<FORM>` definition might look like

```
<FORM METHOD=GET ACTION="http://some.isp.com/~someone/someprogram"
```

The preceding set of properties for the `location` object gives you all you need to pluck the current URL for any relevant information. Next, you look at the `history` object, which keeps track of previously visited URLs.

Let's Do the Time Warp Again—The history Object

The `history` object is an interesting beast. You're probably familiar with the standard browser history list. It's usually available via a menu—in Netscape Navigator, it's on the Go menu. Upon accessing the history list, you're presented with a list of the pages you accessed in this browsing session. You may then choose to quickly jump to one of those previously visited URLs.

The `history` object lets you send the user to somewhere in the history list from within a JavaScript program. The object contains two properties and three methods, so let's take a drive past each, shall we?

Historic Properties

First, here's a look at the properties: `current` and `length`.

current

The property `history.current` contains the value of the current URL. Yes, that would make it equivalent to `location.href`. Note that, as you'll see momentarily, the history list is referenced in a relative manner. That is, however many items are in the list, position 0 is the current item. This will become relevant in a few short paragraphs.

length

Depending on how many pages the user has visited during this session, the history list will be of varying lengths. The property `history.length` contains the current length of the history list.

It's worth noting that the `history` object does not contain any values that reflect the actual URLs in the history list. Therefore, you cannot, for example, perform some action that reads the value of "URL number 3 in the history list." The `history` object is designed for navigating the history list. That's where its methods come into the picture.

Ways of Old—Historic Methods

Now, here is a discussion of the `history` object's three methods: `back()`, `forward()`, and `go()`.

back()

This method has a very logical behavior: `history.back()` simply moves the user to the URL one place previous in the history list—that is, previous to the current position. It is the same as if the user clicked the "back" or left-pointing arrow in the Web browser's navigation toolbar.

Note that just as with any instance where you bring the user to a new page, you give up control from your JavaScript program. The user may never return. Or he may go anywhere else that the new page links to. Therefore, it usually makes the most sense to utilize these JavaScript methods—which call up new pages—between sets of pages you have designed. In this way, your pages can all contain appropriate JavaScript programs within each to move the user along to where you want them to go.

forward()

Can you guess what this method does? I bet you can. `history.forward()` moves the user one URL forward, relative to current position, in the history list.

go(offset) or go("substring")

Lastly, you can use the `go()` method to jump to a particular position in the history list, rather than merely one hop backward or forward. You can use this method to refer to the desired position in the history list in two different ways:

`go(offset)` accepts an integer parameter, positive or negative, as *offset*. If the parameter is a positive integer, the program will move the user that many places forward in the history list. If the parameter is negative, it'll move the user that many places backward (that is, previous to the current position) in the history list. Your current position is always place zero.

Examples:

```
history.go(2)

history.go(-3)
```

Alternatively, you can send `go()` a string rather than an integer value.

Example:

```
history.go("mugs.html")
```

In this case, JavaScript will search for the *newest* history list URL that contains the specified string somewhere within its URL string. Therefore, if the history list contains the URL `http://some.isp.com/~someone/mugs.html`, that's where the user will be sent by the above example—unless, of course, there is another URL that also contains "mugs.html" and has been added to the list more recently.

Remember that URLs are added to the history list when the user visits a page. Therefore, the URLs closest to the end of the history list are the newest; those closest to the beginning are the oldest.

In Closing...

Now, you have an eyeful of the JavaScript objects that allow you to play around with URL references. Their most applicable use is probably in guiding users around your pages, within functions that determine where to guide them based on certain conditions. For example, let's say you offer a special offer to customers who order 10 or more mugs from your page. You might want to take them to another page, on which they can select a gift of their choice. Thus, you can create a JavaScript function based on an `if...else` statement, which sends them to the gift-choosing page on the true condition (perhaps by assigning the gift page's URL to `location.href`), or doesn't send them on to the gift page in the false condition. (Or perhaps, sends them on to some other page that advertises the "buy 10, get a free gift" deal.)

Briefly:

```
function giftdeal(mugs)
{
 if (mugs>=10)
 { location.href="http://mysite.com/~me/giftpage.html" }
 else
 { location.href="http://mysite.com/~me/giftad.html" }
 }
```

The Least You Need To Know

➤ The `location` object possesses several properties that relate to portions of the current URL.

➤ `location.href` contains the value of the entire URL.

➤ Properties `host`, `hostname`, `port`, `pathname`, and `protocol` each contain the value of their respective portions of the URL.

➤ `location.hash` and `location.search` contain the values of the strings following an anchor specification and form data, respectively.

➤ The `history` object allows for navigation through the current session's URL history list.

➤ `history.back()` and `history.forward()` move the user to one URL previous or forward in the history list.

➤ `history.go(integer)` moves to the URL that is *integer* places away from the current URL; negative integers move backward (earlier) in the list from the current URL; positive integers move forward (later in the list).

➤ `history.go("substring")` moves to the newest URL in the history list that contains "*substring*" somewhere within it.

Chapter 13

The Document Shuffle

In This Chapter

➤ This is a document

➤ Colorful changes

➤ Objects of objects—links and anchors

➤ Output is good

➤ Hello, good-bye—interactive events

At various times throughout these chapters, the terms "Web page" and "document" are used somewhat interchangeably. At least, I've never made clear if there is any distinction between the two. In this spin 'round the chapter-o-wheel, you're going to look at documents. More specifically, how you can fiddle with documents using JavaScript.

This, then, is the second chapter in which you examine JavaScript practices that interact with the Web page. Previously, you saw how to affect window elements, such as by opening new windows and creating message boxes. Now, you'll define what a document is and learn how to manipulate it; if there's time, I'll also explain how to make no-fail chicken soup from scratch.

Document Defined

In Web parlance, a *document* is the file of HTML codes that describe a given page. A *page* is what appears within the browser window. A typical HTML document contains a variety of characteristics, other than the content of the page itself.

These include a background image (often called a background "texture"), background color, foreground color, and the colors of hypertext links. In traditional HTML, these traits are all defined as attributes of the <BODY> tag.

As in the case of the Web browser's window, the document object is also a built-in object of JavaScript. It has its own set of properties and methods, with which you can influence various aspects of the current document. Like your previous tours of duty, this chapter takes you through the properties and methods of the document object and shows you how to use them in everyday life.

Welcome to the Property

The document object has a whole gaggle of properties associated with it. Most of these properties mimic characteristics that may have been defined in HTML tags. But it's far from redundant mimicry; allowing you to access the properties via JavaScript opens up the possibility of changing a document's original characteristics, if you want.

The first property examples that follow illustrate this concept.

bgColor and fgColor

Two of the most basic characteristics of a document are its colors. A document has two main colors: a background color and a foreground color. The background color defines the color of the "page" itself, while the foreground color defines the color of the text that appears on the page.

In documents, colors are specified in what is known as a *hexadecimal triplet*. Each color specification actually contains three specifications: red, blue, and green. Thus, you define the background color, for instance, by specifying how much red, blue, and green to mix together to yield the final color.

Each color will have a value from 0 to 255: 0 being a complete lack of the color, and 255 being 100 percent of the color. Quick art school lesson: a background color which has 0 red, 0 blue, and 0 green would be black. A color that has 255 red, 255 blue, and 255 green (that's 100 percent of each), would be pure white.

The above explains the "triplet" part of "hexadecimal triplet." Now let's explain the "hexademical" part. See, JavaScript doesn't like "normal" numbers such as 255. It prefers a different numbering system, known as *hexadecimal*. The system we humans commonly use is known as *decimal*. Many computer programs can convert decimal numbers to hexadecimal for you, but for a brief tutorial, see the "I'm a Human Calculator" sidebar.

The value of `document.bgColor` is the hexadecimal triplet that defines the current page's background color. A possible value would be `"000000"`, or pure black. Note that the long hexadecimal number is, in fact, three 2-digit hexadecimal numbers in a row. The leftmost two digits represent the Red value, the second two represent Green, and the rightmost two represent Blue. Another possible value would be `"FFFFFF"`, or pure white. `"FF0000"` would be pure red. You can, in turn, alter the current background color by assigning a new hexadecimal triplet to `document.bgColor`. For example, regardless of what the current page's background color is, the JavaScript assignment

```
document.bgColor = "#00FF00"
```

changes the background to pure green. Note the hash mark (#) in the above assignment. It is traditional to place the hash mark in front of a hexadecimal number. If you leave it out of the assignment, it will still work, but note that if you retrieve the value of `document.bgColor`, it will contain a hash mark preceding the hexadecimal triplet regardless of whether you included it or not.

Along these same lines, `document.fgColor` will contain the hexadecimal triplet that represents the text color. And, similarly, assigning a new value to this property will change the text color.

Manipulating all of these possible combinations is a pain. Although this is the only way to fine-tune the exact color you will use, JavaScript does provide a shortcut. Instead of the hexadecimal triplet, you can assign a string literal specifying one of JavaScript's built-in color names. JavaScript has a long list of predefined colors, such as `"aliceblue"` and `"crimson"` and `"palegreen"`. Check the Appendix at the end of this book for the full list. Simply, rather than an assignment such as

```
document.bgColor="#000000"
```

you can instead write

```
document.bgColor="black"
```

131

I'm a Human Calculator

Hexadecimal is a *base-16* numbering system, which contains the base values 0–F. That is, beyond 9 comes A, B, C, D, E, and F. Your common decimal system uses *base-10* numbering, which only has the base values 0–9. Converting a decimal number, which you're used to, to a hexadecimal number, requires some addition and multiplication.

In this chapter, you're only considering 2-digit hexadecimal numbers which represent red, green, or blue values (although in decimal, these same values would be 3 digits long, since decimal has fewer possible values for one digit to hold). To convert a hexadecimal number to decimal, use the following formula:

```
(lefthand hexadecimal digit * 16) + (righthand hexadecimal digit)
Note that a hex. digit of A = 10, B = 11, etc., to F = 15
```

What?? Consider the hexadecimal value **05**

```
(0 * 16) + (5) = decimal value of 5
```

Okay, that one was easy. Consider the hexadecimal value **1A**

```
(1 * 16) + (10) = decimal value of 26
```

Another example: hexadecimal value **C5**

```
(12 * 16) + (5) = 197
```

Finally, the maximum 2-digit hex value: **FF**

```
(15 * 16) + (15) = 255
```

This should give you enough knowledge to guesstimate hex values for the color specification—from there, you can fiddle with the exact values to create the exact color you're looking for.

More Colors: alinkColor, vlinkColor, and linkColor

You can specify three other colors in a document. Each of these properties functions the same way as the previous two—they simply affect the color of different characteristics of the page.

alinkColor   Defines the color of an "activated" link. An activated link is a link that has been clicked, but the mouse button has yet to be released.

vlinkColor   Defines the color of a link that has already been visited.

linkColor   Lastly, this property defines the color of a link that has not yet been visited and is not currently being clicked.

You can use each of the above in the standard ways for object properties: you may either retrieve the value from or assign a new value to document.alinkColor, document.vlinkColor, and document.linkColor. If you've coded HTML before, you might have noticed that you can set these same colors in standard HTML tags. So why bother with JavaScript? Because by using JavaScript, you can change the colors in a given page at any time you want—on the fly—perhaps as a result of certain user events. In HTML, you can define the colors only once for the life of the page.

Again, simply because it's fun, you can define the above colors in hexadecimal triplets, or you can use any of the available predefined string literals.

The title Property

The property document.title holds the value of the title of the document as defined in the HTML tags <TITLE> </TITLE>. The title is what appears in the browser window's upper border, and in the bookmark list if the page is bookmarked by a user. The title does not actually appear within the content of the page itself.

As usual, you can retrieve the document's title from this property, or assign a new title to the document via this property.

The anchors Property

An anchor is a spot in a page that has been marked with a "name" within the HTML code. Links can then point to anchors, to send a user to specific locations within a single page. Anchors are defined in HTML with the <A NAME=> tag.

The document.anchors property is an array—that is, an object in and of itself—that contains the value of each anchor on the page, in the order in which they were defined in the HTML code. Let's imagine your page has five anchors defined within it. In that case, there are five properties in the object document.anchors:

```
document.anchors[0]
document.anchors[1]
...
document.anchors[5]
```

Each of the above contains the name of the anchor corresponding to the order in which it was defined. So, if you named and defined your anchors in the order Monday, Tuesday, Wednesday, Thursday, Friday, then each of those would be the values contained in document.anchors[0] to document.anchors[5], respectively.

You may use the property length, as in document.anchors.length to retrieve the total number of anchors defined.

133

Note that you would not use an assignment to document.anchors to bring the user to an anchor within the document. That could be done several ways in JavaScript. Remember that an anchor is specified in a URL with a hash mark following the pathname. Thus, you could assign the entire URL with a hash mark and desired anchor name to location.href. Or, if the desired anchor is within the same page as your JavaScript program, you might simply assign the anchor name to location.hash.

The links Property

In the same spirit as the anchors property, you have the links property. Most pages contain several link definitions throughout the HTML code, as created by the <A HREF=> tag.

document.links is another object array that contains each of the links specified in the current page. Similar to document.anchors, for as many links as there are in the page, there are properties of document.links, in the following manner:

```
document.links[0]
document.links[1]
...etc.
```

You can retrieve the total number of links in the document using the property document.links.length. As usual, you can change the value of a particular link by assigning a new string to one of the above properties, as in document.links[2] = "http://www.yahoo.com".

Imagine a scenario where this reassignment may be useful. Imagine that you have a link in the page that—on-screen—reads "Click here to continue". Perhaps, though, you would like that link to take some users to one URL, but other users to a different URL, depending on some other condition—perhaps depending on whether they've purchased more than a certain quantity of mugs.

Thus, you can use an if...else statement to evaluate the user's mug purchase, and on each condition assign a different URL specification to the above link. This would be transparent to the user, as he would simply click on the link labeled "Click here to continue", yet he'd be taken to an appropriate page as determined by your JavaScript program. This is exactly the same code as in the similar example from Chapter 11—except where you sent the user automatically to a new page in that example by using a location.href assignment, here you would replace that with a document.links[*n*] assignment.

Some Miscellaneous Properties

A few properties aren't of vital consequence, and don't require particularly detailed explanation. Each is relatively straightforward and may not find tremendous usage in your JavaScript programs. However, they're nice to know, especially when you get into those typical JavaScript arguments with friends and colleagues.

The lastModified Property

This property simply contains a string value reflecting the date that the document was last modified. A function might use this property, for instance, to communicate to the user how "fresh" the current page is, in case some of its information may be liable to become out of date.

The referrer Property

This property contains the URL of the page that led to the current page. That is, if the user reached the current page via a link from another page, this property contains the URL of the page that linked them here. You might consider using this property to track statistics about which previous sites users are jumping to yours from.

The location Property

Lastly, this highly redundant property contains the full URL of the current page. Yes, it's the equivalent of `location.href`.

Forms

Just as for anchors and links, the `document` object contains an array of properties for each form defined in the document. However, there's more to forms than simply a value, as was the case for anchors and links. Therefore, you will learn about forms in depth in their own chapter, 14.

Methods to This Madness

In fact, there are five methods to this madness called the `document` object. The methods of the `document` object are, fortunately, relatively straightforward *and* useful.

The clear() Method

It shouldn't take the Amazing Kreskin to deduce the function of the `document.clear()` method. Once called, it clears the contents of the current window. Note that this doesn't affect the actual contents of the document, as defined in the HTML tags. Nor does the `clear()` method clear any variable values, or anything else. It is purely cosmetic—it merely clears the display window. Of course, you may not want to clear the window unless you plan to display further text in it. Fortunately, there are two methods for doing just that.

write() and writeln()

You can use both of these methods to output HTML to the current window. As the parameter to either method, you pass on a string that contains the HTML code that contains what you want sent to the window.

For example, suppose you want the string "Thank you for ordering" written in the window in large type. The HTML <H1></H1> tag is one way to generate text in a large font size. Therefore, you could simply use the method call

```
document.write ("<H1>Thank you for ordering!</H1>")
```

Alternatively, you might have constructed a string somewhere else in your JavaScript code and assigned that to a variable, such as phrase. In this case, you can simply pass the variable phrase as the parameter to the method call:

```
document.write (phrase)
```

The difference between write() and writeln() is that the writeln() appends a *newline* character to the end of the output. A newline character is basically like a carriage return. However, keep in mind that these methods output their parameters as HTML. And, remember that HTML ignores newline characters when it comes to outputting to the screen.

What does the above mean? It means that HTML does not insert line breaks in screen output unless you specify a line break using either the <BR> or <P> tags. Any "natural" line breaks in your HTML code, such as from hitting return, are ignored. The only time this is not true (and carriage returns are honored) is for text that resides between <PRE> </PRE> tags. Those tags define a section of text that is "preformatted," and it appears on-screen in the browser's defined monospace font (often Courier). (Remember that a monospace font is one in which all characters have equal width.)

Thus, in most cases, there will be no effective difference between the write() and writeln() methods, unless your string parameter contains HTML code that places the output within <PRE> </PRE> tags.

Bonus Events

It so happens that the document object also has two relevant event triggers worth mentioning: onLoad and onUnload.

The onLoad Event

You can use this event trigger to launch a particular JavaScript program or function upon the completion of initially loading the document. Perhaps you coded a JavaScript function that displays an alert message to the user before he even begins reading the page. The onLoad event would be useful for this purpose.

You include the event as an attribute of the document's <BODY> tag, as in

```
<BODY onLoad="welcome()">
```

In this example, the onLoad event handler is set to call the function welcome(), which performs some feat of programming, such as popping up an alert window that requires the user to read an important disclaimer before he begins looking at the page. (Users will likely find this very annoying, but you could program it.)

Watch Your HEAD The <BODY> tag occurs very early on in the HTML document. This highlights the need to define your functions as early on in the document as possible—specifically, within the <HEAD> </HEAD> section, which is one of the only places you have an opportunity to do so prior to the <BODY> tag.

The onUnload Event

This event is triggered when the user "unloads" or exits the document. It, as well, would be defined as an attribute of the <BODY> tag. You might, for example, use this to show a message to the user after he chooses to leave your page, such as by calling a function that writes the text "You come back now, you hear?" into the document window.

```
<BODY onLoad="welcome()" onUnload="bye()">
```

As it stands, the only major aspect of JavaScript remaining to be covered is the forms objects. And—wouldn't you know—I have it covered. Next chapter in fact, so don't stop reading here. This is like the last 50 steps in an 8K run...just a few more properties...maybe a method or two...you're almost there.

The Least You Need To Know

➤ The document is the HTML file that loads as a Web page in the browser window.

➤ JavaScript contains a document object, which possesses a number of properties through which you can read or modify characteristics of the current document.

➤ You can use document.bgColor and document.fgColor to alter the colors of the background or foreground text, respectively. Colors are defined in hexadecimal RGB values.

➤ document.anchors and document.links are arrays that contain the values of a document's defined anchors or links, respectively. For example, document.link[2] refers to the second link defined in the document.

➤ You can use the method document.write("*string*") to output HTML tagged text to the current window.

➤ Use the event triggers onLoad and onUnload to watch for users opening or exiting your page. Both are defined as attributes in the <BODY> tag.

Chapter 14

Fiddling with Forms and Emulating Events

Welcome to the end of this semester's JavaScript course. You'll close out the day with some fun stuff—just like the last day of class in grade school, when you cracked the windows, broke out the Yahtzee, and ate pizza on the same desk you took math quizzes on. Actually, I'm just fooling. This chapter is about form objects and emulating events, neither of which hold a candle to pizza.

Behind the Form

The form is a staple of virtually any page that interacts with the user. Forms can take the "form" of several incarnations, from buttons to checkboxes to blank text-entry boxes. You will probably want to create JavaScript functions that in some way interpret the data produced by these forms.

Because of our close examination of forms in this chapter, you'll break with tradition and refresh yourself with HTML form tags.

You define a form in HTML with the tag <FORM>. This tag may contain several possible attributes:

METHOD=get or post	How to submit form data (get is the default, and it's the usual method).
ACTION=URL	Where to submit form data.
TARGET=name of window	Which window to display responses to the form in (usually this attribute is left out, unless you want responses to be generated in a new window).
onSubmit="*JavaScript code*"	The event handler for a submit event.

Forms are made up of *elements*, as they are known in HTML-speak, which the user uses to indicate responses. Form elements include generic buttons, radio buttons, checkboxes, text entries, and Submit and Reset buttons. A form can have any number of these elements in it. An element is defined with the <INPUT> tag, which also takes a series of attributes that define the form element. We can't go into detail for each element, but as a refresher, a typical definition for a button element might look like

```
<INPUT TYPE="button" name="ad" value="Click to see our Ad" onClick="showad()">
```

Any elements defined within one set of <FORM> </FORM> tags are considered to be part of one form. Just as there can be any number of elements within one form, there can be any number of forms within one page.

Within the context of JavaScript, each form element is also a JavaScript object. Therefore, each checkbox, text input area, and so forth has its own set of properties. Although referenced in more detail in the appendix at the end of this book, "JavaScript: The Complete Reference," the properties of these objects are typically parallel to the HTML attributes of the element. There are also properties that contain status information about the element; for instance, the checkbox object contains the property "checked," which contains the current logical status of the checkbox element. Having established all this, let's begin looking at how the forms object works within JavaScript.

Element and Object

To avoid confusion throughout this chapter, let's clear up the interchange between the terms "element" and "object." A form element, such as a checkbox, is an "element" when you are speaking from an HTML perspective. The same checkbox is *also* an object, when speaking from a JavaScript perspective. At times, I may seem to use these terms interchangeably—because they do refer to the same ultimate "thing"—but when I say "element," I'm looking at it from an HTML point of view, and when I say "object," I'm considering it from a JavaScript point-of-view.

Object of Form

The previous chapter briefly mentioned that forms was a property of document. This is true, but furthermore, document.forms is an object itself. Each form within the document is one property of document.forms. This is important, so let's take this concept again slowly.

Remember that a form is defined by anything between one set of <FORM> tags:

```
<FORM>
form element definitions
</FORM>
```

Thus, document.forms[0] refers to the first form defined in the document. document.forms[1] refers to the second form; that is, any form elements defined within a second set of <FORM> </FORM> tags somewhere else in the document.

Now, each form in a document is *also* an object. Therefore, document.forms[0] is an object whose properties are each an element of that form. The elements are referred to in the manner document.forms[x].elements[y]; where x is the form in question, and y is the element within that form.

Imagine that your HTML document contains the following lines:

```
<FORM>
<INPUT TYPE="button" name="ad" value="Click for Ad" onClick="showad()">
<INPUT TYPE="checkbox" name="married">Are you married?
</FORM>
```

This form contains two elements: a button and a checkbox. If this is the first form defined in your document, you can refer to its parts in the following manner:

➤ `document.forms[0].elements[0]` would contain the definition for the button element.

➤ `document.forms[0].elements[1]` would contain the definition for the checkbox element.

What does it mean when I say, "would contain the definition for the button element"? It means that the value of `document.forms[0].elements[0]` in this example would be the following string:

`"<INPUT TYPE="button" name="ad" value="Click for Ad" onClick="showad()">"`.

Shortly, you'll see how to refer to specific portions of each element, rather than simply its entire definition.

Properties of Forms

The `forms` object, like every other object, has a set of built-in properties. Basically, these simply help you to retrieve or modify the main attributes of the form, as follows.

The action Property

This property allows you to retrieve or alter the value of the action attribute of the form in question. For example, perhaps you want to submit the form data to one URL if the user has bought more than a set number of mugs, or another URL if they purchased fewer. You might use the classic `if...else` statement to change the property `documents.forms[0].action`. Perhaps, this would take place in a function called `buymugs(mugs)`, which accepts the parameter of how many mugs were bought. The function would be called as an event handler from the event trigger `onSubmit`, an attribute of `<FORM>`.

Below, let's play out the code for this scenario:

```
<SCRIPT language="JavaScript">
function buymugs (mugs)
  {
    if (mugs>=10)
      { documents.forms[0].action = "http://invoice1.htm" }
    else
      { document.forms[0].action = "http://invoice2.htm" }
}

<FORM method=get onSubmit="buymugs(this.quantity.value)">
<INPUT TYPE="text" name="quantity" ROWS=1 COLUMNS=3>Quantity of order
</FORM>
```

142

Looking first at the HTML code, you define a form that contains one element: a text entry box that is three spaces wide. This text entry box is given the reference name "quantity". The FORM definition specifies an onSubmit event handler. It calls the function buymugs() with the parameter this.quantity.value. This construction should seem slightly familiar from Chapter 10. this refers to this whole object—the form—from which you are interested in the property "quantity", which is the specific element within the form named "quantity". value is a property of the text entry object, which contains the user-inputted data.

The function itself is rather the same as previous functions you coded in these chapters. It simply uses an if...else statement to determine a condition and modify the ACTION= attribute of the first form in your document accordingly.

The method Property

Just like the action property, the method property refers to the METHOD= attribute of the FORM definition (don't confuse this property name with the JavaScript function known as a "method"; they are unrelated). You can similarly use this to change the METHOD of a particular form from GET to POST, or vice versa, should you so desire. A function exactly like the one used above would do the trick, as in

```
documents.forms[0].method = "get"
```

The target Property

This property allows you to retrieve or modify the TARGET= attribute of the FORM. You use it just like the method and action properties.

Elements, Up Close and Personal

We touched on the fact that the array (or object) elements point to each particular element within a given form. Good. Recall again the example in the form you defined earlier in this chapter: document.forms[0].elements[0] would contain the definition for the button element. Now, the button element in question here also contains several properties of its own. Consider the button element definition again:

```
<INPUT TYPE="button" name="ad" value="Click for Ad" onClick="showad()">
```

The button has a name, which in this case is "ad". Thus, you can retrieve or modify its name in JavaScript with a reference to

```
document.forms[0].elements[0].name
```

You might assign the value of the preceding line to a new variable, or assign a new string to the line. Each particular form element has its own slightly different set of built-in properties. The button object contains a `name` property, as you've just seen, as well as a `value` property. In the case of the button, the `value` property (as well as the value HTML attribute), is the text that appears on the button itself on-screen. Thus, you can also refer to the value of

```
document.forms[0].elements[0].value
```

The checkbox Element

Because each form element serves a slightly different purpose, each object has a slightly different set of built-in properties. Let's consider the checkbox element, defined in a way such as:

```
<INPUT TYPE="checkbox" name="marstat"
onClick="married(this.marstat.value)">Married?
```

Let's imagine that the preceding is the second element of the same form that contains the previous button, thus making it `documents.forms[0].elements[1]`. The `name` property of this checkbox object works the same way as the `name` property of the button object.

The checkbox object also contains two unique properties: `checked` and `defaultChecked`. These are logical values that, when assigned a true or false value, determine the starting state of the checkbox, before the user gets his hands on it. Sometimes, you might want a checkbox to begin in a checked state; you can do so either in the HTML definition of the element, or by assigning a true value, as in the following:

```
documents.forms[0].elements[1].checked = true.
```

Note that the `value` property works differently for the checkbox than for the button. In the preceding checkbox, the property `documents.forms[0].elements[1].value` is a Boolean that contains the state of the checkbox. This is what you would refer to if you were processing this form. Note, in the `onClick` call in the preceding example, how you call the hypothetical function `married(this.marstat.value)`.

In the "Built-In Objects" Appendix at the end of this book, you can find details of the properties available for each particular form element object. Here, you looked at only the button and checkbox elements.

The this Object

One of the most important constructions with which you refer to form elements is the `this` construction. By now, you've seen it pop up several times. Take an official look at it now.

Clearly, a construction such as `document.forms[0].elements[1].value` is somewhat long and unwieldy. However, when you are referring to form elements from within a particular form definition, you don't have to use such a long construction.

If you are between `<FORM>` `</FORM>` tags, the form to which you are referring is a given: *this form*. Therefore, `document.forms[x]` can be assumed.

Secondly, you can refer to individual form elements by their name, rather than `elements[y]`, which makes more sense to the human programmer. Thus, the first element—a button—in your continuing form example from above, *could* be called `elements[0]` *or* it could be called ad. Recall that you named it ad with the NAME= attribute.

Therefore, when you refer to a form from within its definition—which you do anytime you define an event handler for the form or element—you can use the simpler construction `this.elementname.property`.

You've seen this in practice a few times. Here's an example that combines a couple of your previous this uses:

```
<FORM onSubmit="evalform(this.email.value)">
<INPUT NAME=email TYPE="text" ROWS=1 SIZE="20">Enter your email
<INPUT NAME="marstat" TYPE="checkbox"
➥onClick="married(this.marstat.value)">Married?
<INPUT NAME=submit TYPE="submit">
<INPUT NAME=reset TYPE="reset">
</FORM>
```

Two event handlers are defined in the preceding form. One handles the `onSubmit` event and passes to its function the parameter `this.email.value`. That, then, would be the data entered (`value`) into the form element email (the text box defined in the second line of the example).

The second event handler occurs in the `onClick` event of the checkbox element. It passes to its function the parameter `this.marstat.value`, which would contain the Boolean state of the checkbox named `marstat`.

Keep in mind, though, that this works only from within the form definition. If you want to refer to a form other than the one currently being defined, you'll need to use the full `document.forms[x].elements[y]` construction. That's the only way to explicitly specify which form or element you are talking about to JavaScript. The this construction is basically a shortcut for those instances when it can be assumed which form you're talking about.

When in Doubt, Be Specific I have found some inconsistencies to the way JavaScript handles this in practice, versus how it claims that it should be handled. The simplest solution to any strange errors or difficulties with this is simply to replace the use of this with `document.forms[x]`.

145

The Faked Event

Remember that an "event" usually occurs when a user clicks on something. There are a variety of possible events, depending on what the user clicks on. It is possible to *emulate* a click in JavaScript.

Meaning? If you have a checkbox element, you could instigate a click on it yourself with JavaScript code, rather than waiting for the user to click on it manually. Why would you want to do this? I don't know. Just kidding—actually there are a couple of possible reasons:

➤ **Guiding the user** Perhaps on your particular page, you would like to show the user what to do—sort of like a "help" procedure. This way, you can use JavaScript to go around clicking elements as an example for the user's eyes.

➤ **Straightening up necessarily related elements** We delve into this possibility below.

Imagine that you have the following two elements in your form: a checkbox, which poses the question, "Do you like spicy foods?" and a radio button set, which asks the user to choose which spicy food is his favorite. The radio buttons offer three choices: "Mexican," "Indian," and "I said I didn't like spicy foods."

Suppose the user unchecks the checkbox, indicating a lack of enthusiasm for spicy foods. In that case, it would be nonsensical for the user to then check one of the regional food types in the radio button set. But how can you prevent the user from saying he doesn't like spicy foods but his favorite spicy food is Indian?

Using event emulation! (Boy, you knew that was coming, I hope.) This would be the programming logic:

If the user clicks the radio button, check the status of the checkbox.

If the checkbox is unchecked, then emulate a click event to select "I said I didn't like spicy foods" in the radio button.

This way, no matter what the user tries to select in the radio buttons, his selection will be overridden if it conflicts with a previous selection.

You will code the above logic shortly. First let's see how to emulate an event.

It's All in the Method

Event emulators are methods of the form element objects. Each of the form element objects has a click() method. Simply call this method for the object in question and it will be clicked. Therefore, to click a *checkbox*, you might use the call

```
document.forms[0].checkboxname.click()
```

Important note: A `click()` method *does not* initiate an event trigger. Only a "real" click on the *checkbox* would trigger the `onClick` event handler, if defined. If you want to emulate a click *and* trigger the appropriate event call, simply call the proposed event handler manually after the `click()` method. For example, let's say your `onClick` event handler is defined as `"married(this.checkbox.value)"`. If you want to emulate a click *and* call the event handler, simply use the JavaScript statements

```
document.forms[0].checkboxname.click() ;
married(this.value)
```

All you did was call the event handler explicitly following the emulated click, since it would not have been triggered by the `onClick` definition.

Before you run through example code for the "spicy food" logic, remind yourself how radio buttons work. A radio button is basically a multiple-choice question, from which the user can select only one of the proposed choices. What makes the radio button slightly different from other form elements is that it may contain several subelements—that is, the radio button named `"spicetype"` could have three subelements, each representing a choice: Mexican, Indian, or Don't like.

The following is the HTML code wherein we define the *checkbox* and radio buttons for our spicy foods example.

```
<FORM>
<INPUT NAME="spicy" TYPE="checkbox">Do you like spicy foods?<p>
Please select which spicy food is your favorite:
<INPUT NAME="spicetype" TYPE="radio" value="mexican"
onClick="checkspicy(document.forms[0].spicy.checked)">Mexican
<INPUT NAME="spicetype" TYPE="radio" value="indian"
onClick="checkspicy(document.forms[0].spicy.checked)">Indian
<INPUT NAME="spicetype" TYPE="radio" value="notype"
onClick="checkspicy(document.forms[0].spicy.checked)"> I said I don't like
➟spicy foods!
</FORM>
```

Note how each part of the radio button is defined to the same NAME= attribute. This is important. Also, see how each radio button definition contains the same `onClick` event handler. Therefore, any time a user makes a choice from the radio button, the verification function `checkspicy(document.forms[0].spicy.checked)` will be called. This is the heart of our logic.

The function's role will be to look at the Boolean (logical) state of the *checkbox* named "spicy" (`document.forms[0].spicy.value`) and either allow the user's radio button selection to remain, or force a different selection. You would force a different selection under two conditions:

➤ The user has left `spicy` unchecked, in which case he must select "I said I don't like spicy foods!" from the radio button.

➤ The user has checked `spicy`, in which case he cannot select "I said I don't like spicy foods!" from the radio button. Because one of the radio buttons must be selected, in this case, you'd have to select one of the others by default, so you'll choose Mexican simply because it's first on the list.

Here is the function code in JavaScript:

```
<SCRIPT language="JavaScript">
function checkspicy (likes)
{
  if (likes == true)
   { if (document.forms[0].spicetype[2].checked == true)
      { document.forms[0].spicetype[0].click() } }
   else
   { if (document.forms[0].spicetype[2].checked == false)
      { document.forms[0].spicetype[2].click() } }
  }
</SCRIPT>
```

Use the construction `spicetype[x]` to refer to an individual choice *x* within the radio button set. Here, first consider whether `spicy` is checked true. If so, look to see if the last radio button choice (button number 2, since they start counting from 0) is selected. If so, it should not be (because the user indicated that he does like spicy foods), and so you emulate a click event to check "Mexican" (radio button choice 0).

If the user has indicated a distaste for spicy foods, look at the `else` clause above. Here, determine if the final radio button choice has been selected. If not, you emulate a click event to select it, because it must be selected in this case.

All Together Now

The tools provided throughout these chapters should serve as a good overview of JavaScript and its applications. I've avoided delving into highly complex programming examples, in part because this is an introduction to the language, and in part because such examples are more about programming science than the JavaScript language itself.

The best way to learn a programming language is, as my irritating piano teacher used to say: Practice, practice, practice. And experimentation, although she didn't ever mention that. You'll need to read these chapters multiple times, in different manners. For the first read-through, you might look to pick up the general concepts behind JavaScript programming. On a second read-through, perhaps focus on the specific syntax of the JavaScript statements and expressions.

Then, at each example, attempt to throw together your own code that is just a slight variation on the example. See if it works, and if so, vary it further with new ideas. Eventually, you work toward combining concepts from multiple examples, and before you know it, you're constructing your own programs from scratch.

One word of advice is not to be beset by frustration when programs don't work the first time through. Errors and malfunctions are the stuff that programs and programmer's lives are made of. Sometimes, the error is caused by something silly, such as forgetting a closing bracket or parentheses. Other times, you haven't a clue why the program is not working. In those cases, it's a good idea to try other approaches to the end, and see if they work. Or just scream. There is a whole science to debugging—which is of great value to learn if you become heavily involved in programming—but when all else fails, I always recommend the "clear head" approach. That is, walk away. Come back another day. Many dastardly bugs are solved this way. The rested, clear mind can solve some problems in minutes that the haggard mind struggles with for hours. A perusal through Chapter 20 might be recommended, as well, where you'll find some further consideration given to script debugging and pest extermination.

Given that not-exactly-a-pep talk, you're off and programming!

The Least You Need To Know

➤ The elements of a form are an array of properties of the `form` object. The object `document.forms[x]` contains the properties `document.forms[x].elements[y]`, where *y* is each element defined within a single set of `<FORM>` tags.

➤ You can also refer to `elements[y]` by the name of the element as defined in the `NAME=` attribute of the HTML `<INPUT>` tag that defines that element.

➤ Each form element is an object with its own properties. The property of the *checkbox* element, for example, that contains the current Boolean state of the *checkbox* is called `checked` and would be referred to as `document.forms[x].elements[y].checked` or `document.forms[x].checkboxname.checked`.

➤ `this.`*property* can be used to refer to the current form being defined.

➤ Form elements can emulate clicking themselves, with the method `document.forms[x].elementname.click()`.

➤ Emulating an event *does not* trigger any event handler specified for that event; only "real" events can be triggers.

Part 4
Scripting the Whole Bean

If you've made it this far (and your head hasn't exploded), you've made it through the worst part: learning JavaScript. By now, you might have an idea or two brewing in the back of your brain and you can't wait to get scripting to see your idea become "CyberReality." For those of you who need a little more encouragement, you'll find a collection of examples to help you start.

The example scripts you'll find in this section showcase a variety of JavaScript behavior: controlling the page, changing page attributes, randomly selecting things, and responding to the user clicking a button. Feel free to observe, analyze, and adapt these scripts to your own needs. Toss 'em in your tool kit—you'll find a use for them somewhere down the line.

Finally, as a "bonus for the brave," the last example is a look at a full-blown application: a JavaScript-enhanced eZine! If you've ever wanted to publish your ideas in a "Web-ified" way, here's a framework you can use—right out of the box!

Chapter 15

Script Example 1: Hello World

In This Chapter

➤ A simple template for creating JavaScript scripts

➤ Positioning the <SCRIPT> tag to control output

➤ Writing HTML tags from within the <SCRIPT>

➤ Providing "controlled access" to parts of the document

Putting It All Together

If you've made it this far, you probably wonder when the background information, command lists, statement explanations, and other groundwork will stop and the real fun begin: creating your own *real* JavaScript Web pages. Wait no longer—the fun starts *now*! Since no introduction to a new computer language would be complete without the requisite "Hello World" application, that's where you'll start. Your little "Hello World" script will also give you a basic HTML framework that you'll use for the rest of the examples in this book.

Check This Out...

Hello World?
Every discipline has its traditions, and programming is no exception. One long-standing ritual found in almost every introductory book on any computer programming language is to have the first program be one that displays the phrase "Hello World" on the screen.

The Basic Template

You can use the following template as a framework for all your JavaScript files. From time to time, you may want to move things around a bit, but that's what templates are for: to give you a starting point. Don't consider them the *only* way to script—just one possibility.

```
<HTML>
<HEAD>

<TITLE>Your Title Here</TITLE>

<SCRIPT LANGUAGE="JavaScript">
<!-- Hide script from non-JavaScript browsers

// your script statements go here

//-->
</SCRIPT>

</HEAD>

<BODY>

// Your HTML display statements go here

</BODY>

</HTML>
```

As mentioned in Chapter 4, the <SCRIPT> tag serves as a wrapper around JavaScript statements, and you can place it anywhere within the HTML file. For the sake of consistency, place it in the <HEAD> tag.

Hello World 1

You want to present a simple page and, when the user clicks a button, display a JavaScript dialog with the phrase "Hello World from the Land of JavaScript!" If you remember back a bit, this is accomplished through the use of an *event handler* that runs a function. The event handler you need to use is onClick, and the function is a simple one:

```
function HelloWorld()
{
    alert("Hello World from the Land of JavaScript!")
}
```

So, putting it together, you get:

```
<HTML>
<TITLE>Hello World</TITLE>
```

```
<HEAD>
<SCRIPT LANGUAGE="JavaScript">
<!-- Hide script from non-JavaScript browsers
function HelloWorld()
{
   alert("Hello World from the Land of JavaScript!")
}
//-->
</SCRIPT>
</HEAD>
<BODY>
<FORM>
Click on the button below to receive a
➥special message:
<P>
<INPUT TYPE="submit" VALUE="Click Me!"
➥ONCLICK="HelloWorld()">
</FORM>
</BODY>
</HTML>
```

Run Script, Run
"Running" a JavaScript program is as simple as loading the HTML document into the Web browser. If you've created the script file on the same computer on which the browser is installed, you will load a "local file." Do this by choosing, under the **File** menu, an option named something such as "Open file" or "Open local file."

When you fire up Netscape Navigator and run this script, you should get something like what you see in the next figure.

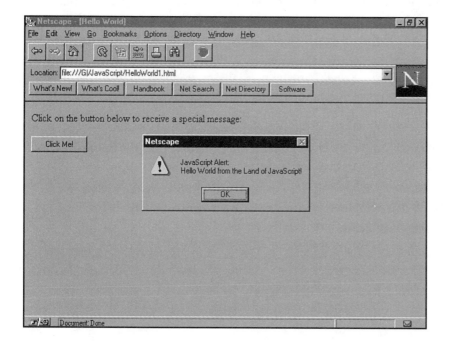

Hello World!

155

A couple of things to note. First, the JavaScript code for buttons needs to go inside a <FORM> tag; otherwise, it's simply ignored (you can test this by removing the <FORM> tag from the above script and running it again). One of the most common mistakes beginning Web writers make is to forget to use the <FORM> tag, and then they wonder why their buttons and check boxes aren't being displayed.

Note that, in the previous example, you're using a Submit button (as defined by the <INPUT> tag attribute TYPE="submit"). The Submit button also generates an onSubmit event, which you could have used to equal effectiveness as the onClick event in this case. However, the onSubmit event handler is defined in the <FORM> tag, not the <INPUT> tag. You can check this out for yourself by replacing the previous example with the following, which will yield the exact same results as the earlier example:

```
<FORM ONSUBMIT="HelloWorld()">
<INPUT TYPE="submit" VALUE="Click Me!">
</FORM>
```

Congratulations, you're now a JavaScripter!

Hello World 2

Okay, so your first little example wasn't that elaborate—you have to start somewhere! Take a little deviation from your template and look at a more significantly useful way to place text on the screen. Now, you will generate new messages directly into the on-screen document.

Remember from Chapter 13 that one of the objects JavaScript gives you is the *document* object, which provides a way to program the currently displayed document. Normally, when you load a Web page, the HTML statements within are interpreted and displayed by the browser. With JavaScript, you can write HTML statements directly into the document at any time, as generated on-the-fly by your JavaScript program. Take the following example:

```
<HTML>
<TITLE>Hello World</TITLE>
<HEAD>
<SCRIPT LANGUAGE="JavaScript">
<!-- Hide script from non-JavaScript browsers
    document.write("<H2>Hello World from the Land of JavaScript!</H2>")
//-->
</SCRIPT>
</HEAD>
<BODY>
<P>
(the previous message compliments of JavaScript)
</BODY>
</HTML>
```

Running this document produces the same output as the following non-JavaScript page:

```
<HTML>
<TITLE>Hello World</TITLE>
<HEAD>
<H2>Hello World from the Land of JavaScript!</H2>
</HEAD>
<BODY>
<P>
(the previous message compliments of JavaScript)
</BODY>
</HTML>
```

Interactive Style

Now, given the previous two examples, you might be thinking, "So what was the point of that?" Consider, though, that in the JavaScript version, you could have output that message at any time, as a result of certain conditions having been met or user interaction. In the HTML version, the message is plopped onto the screen and it's there for good. Thus, JavaScript allows you to generate on-screen messages via HTML code in reaction to conditions or user events.

Rework the first example so that you wind up with something truly JavaScripty. The following program will be a mini "tour guide" front-end to a display on the history of spices. Two buttons will appear in the window, each containing the name of a spice. When the user chooses the spice, a JavaScript function is called that generates new HTML code on-the-fly for display on the screen. This new code will display two appropriately phrased links that lead toward new (hypothetical) documents: one containing recipes that use that spice, and the other containing a history of trade for that spice. This sounds complicated, but it is, in fact, simple with JavaScript.

```
<HTML>
<TITLE>Spice Tours 96</TITLE>
<HEAD>
<SCRIPT LANGUAGE="JavaScript">
<!-- Hide script from non-JavaScript browsers
function tour(spice)
{
  recipes="<A HREF=" + spice + ".html>See recipes using " + spice + "</
  ➥A><p>";
  trading="<A HREF=" + spice + "trade.html>See history of " + spice + "
  ➥trade</A><p>" ;
  document.write("<H2>Please select one of the guided tours below<H2>") ;
  document.write(recipes) ;
  document.write(trading) }
//-->
</SCRIPT>
```

157

```
</HEAD>
<BODY>
Please click on the desired spice below:
<FORM>
<INPUT TYPE="button" VALUE="Garlic" ONCLICK="tour('garlic')">
<INPUT TYPE="button" VALUE="Cinnamon" ONCLICK="tour('cinnamon')">
</FORM>
</BODY>
</HTML>
```

The following two figures illustrate what the user would see when interacting with the this program:

Here, the salivating user can select which spice to learn more about.

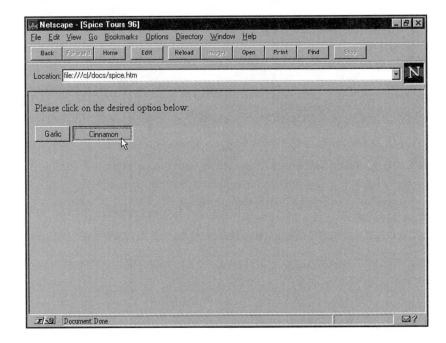

Let's consider the previous program. It basically contains two segments. The JavaScript function definition comes first, and the HTML code defining the button options comes second. First consider the HTML code. It should look familiar by now: you create a form in which there are two button elements. You labeled each button with a spice name. You could have coded as many buttons as you wanted. Both buttons contain an onClick event handler, calling the function tour(). Notice how you pass a string literal, representing the spice in question, as the parameter to tour().

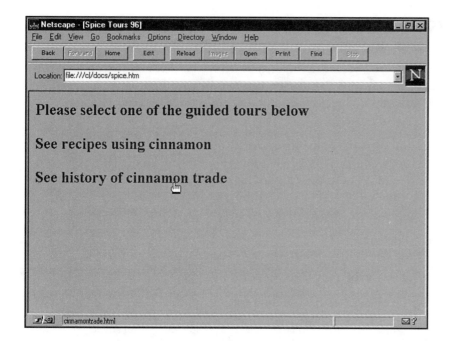

The JavaScript function then generates new HTML code to display the above spice-appropriate hyperlinks.

Now consider the `tour()` function. The first line of statements, an assignment to the variable `recipes`, looks complicated but is actually simple. The purpose of this line is to paste together a string containing the full HTML code for a hyperlink. It then assigns that whole string to the variable `recipes`. You can assume, for example purposes, that the document containing garlic recipes will be called "garlic.html," and so you use a combination of concatenations to construct this string. Recall that the variable `spice` contains either the string `"garlic"` or `"cinnamon"`, depending on which button the user clicked. Within JavaScript's mind, the following string winds up being assigned to `recipes`:

```
"<A HREF=garlic.html>See recipes using garlic</A><p>"
```

This is HTML for a hyperlink and will momentarily be output to the browser window.

The second statement line constructs a similar link, for the history of trading. This is followed by three `document.write()` statements, which simply output all this HTML to the browser window, as seen in the previous figure.

159

Web Etiquette

If you've done a bit of Web surfing, no doubt you've encountered many pages that have links "for text-based browsers" or "for non-Netscape browsers." Because there are several "standards" on the Web today, not all browsers can handle all things. Thoughtful Web authors try to accommodate this by creating different collections of pages that are tailored to different types of browsers.

Since Netscape Navigator 2.0 is the only browser that can handle JavaScript right now, it's a nice touch to make it possible for visitors who don't use this browser to still view your pages…even if it is in a reduced way. You can do this quite neatly by taking advantage of what you just learned.

Because you can generate HTML using the `document.write()` method, you can create the following JavaScript-aware page:

```
<HTML>
<TITLE>Welcome to My JavaScript</TITLE>
<BODY>
<H1>So...you're interested in JavaScript?</H1>
Hello World!  Well, you've come to the  right place for JavaScript.
But, if you don't have <A HREF="http://home.netscape.com/">Netscape
Navigator 2.0</A>, you won't be able to see any of the fun!
<SCRIPT LANGUAGE="JavaScript">
<!-- Hide from non-JavaScript browsers
    document.write("<HR>")
    document.write("<P>")
    document.write("To proceed to my JavaScript pages,")
    document.write('<A HREF="myjavascript.html">Click here</A>.')
//-->
</SCRIPT>
</BODY>
</HTML>
```

The following figure shows the result. With this little trick, you can keep people from trying to view your JavaScript pages if they don't have a browser that can handle it. That way, they won't be disappointed by the gibberish they'll see on-screen.

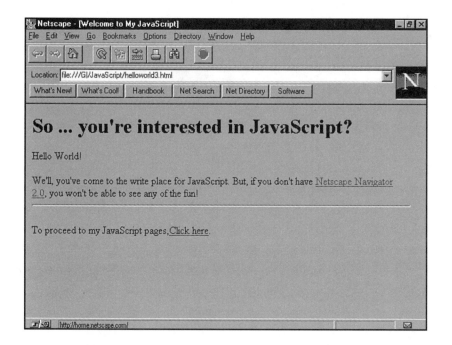

Only a JavaScript-enabled browser will display the last line.

The Least You Need To Know

Now that you've seen all that makes up JavaScript, you embarked on the adventure of creating your own pages. In your first example, you displayed a simple "Hello World" message in two ways: from within the document through the `document` object, and from the JavaScript `alert()` function. You then constructed a user-interactive program that generated context-appropriate messages on-screen. Finally, you saw that you can hide URL links inside a script to keep non-JavaScript browsers from displaying things that wouldn't work for them.

Clarify Your Marks Note that when you have to use double quotes for something else in the display line (such as a URL), you can use single quotes to bracket the entire display string. Or you can use double quotes to bracket the entire string, and single quotes within it. Either way works, as long as you are consistent; if you start the string with a double quote, be sure to bracket the end of the string with a double quote and use single quotes when necessary within. And vice versa.

Chapter 16

Script Example 2: Random Chatter

In This Chapter

➤ Generating "random" numbers with JavaScript

➤ Easily creating an array of things

➤ Making changes to the page itself (randomly)

When Is Random Not Random?

Computers are "linear" machines, very logical and precise. Humans have no problem picking a number between 1 and 10, but computers don't have the capability to randomly select things. And yet, card games, dice games—just about any game you can think of—involves some sort of random selection...and we *do* love to play games on computers. So how, then, do computers take a "shot in the dark"? By using a formula that's dependent on something that is always changing: the time of day.

Using *military time* (where hours are numbered from 0 to 23 instead of "a.m." and "p.m."), you can create a *pseudo-random number*, or a number that *seems* random because it changes every second. Simply speaking, take the hour of the day, the minute of the hour, and the second of the minute and multiply them together. Depending on the hour, minute, and second you pick, you'll have a number somewhere between 0 and 80,063 (the 59th second of the 59th minute of the 23rd hour of the day...or the second just before midnight). And, through the Date object in JavaScript, you can get the current time of day easily.

Random numbers are used commonly in computer programs, especially games. Lottery-style games, gambling games, and so forth tend to be common beginners' programs. Perhaps, if you were designing an online "store" for your wares, you might offer customers a chance at a discount via a lottery or slot-machine style game. Using the Date object, it's just a hop, skip, and a jump to implementing a random-number generator into your JavaScript programs.

Random Numbers with the Date Object

With the Date object, you can find out the current hour, minute, and second. The Date object contains a large number of methods that can be used to extract various portions of the current date and time, or set them.

First, though, you need to create a new Date object that contains the current date and time settings. This is simple:

```
now = new Date()
```

Here, now would be the name of your Date object, although you could use any legal variable name. Thus, you have an object now that contains all of the date methods. Some of the more useful ones include:

```
getDay()
getDate()
getHours()
getMinutes()
getMonth()
getSeconds()
getTime()
getYear()
```

There are also more methods for setting the various aspects of the date and other date-related tasks. For more references on these, check out the Appendix of this book, "JavaScript: The Complete Overview."

You use these methods in typical fashion; for example, let's say you'd like to know the current date. Having already created the object now, you can simply use an expression such as

```
today = now.getDate()
```

Or perhaps you might write the current day into a document message:

```
document.write ("<H2>Welcome, today is the " + now.getDate() + "th</H2>")
```

To generate a random number, you use the hour, minute, and second of the current date. All you need to do then is multiply them together and you'll have a different number for every second each day, such as with the statement

```
rannum = now.getHours() * now.getMinutes() * now.getSeconds()
```

However, under normal circumstances, this is too wide a range to deal with. Usually, when you want a random number, it needs to fall within certain bounds. For example, there are only 52 cards in a deck, unless you count the jokers, so a card game must not choose random numbers outside the range of 1 to 52. You need to be able to *limit* the range of numbers, and this is easily accomplished with a little *modulus math*.

Modulus Math?

Normally, when you divide one number by another, you get some decimal result (unless the numbers divide evenly). Modulus math is interested in the *remainder*, or what's left after you've evenly divided as much as you can. For example, dividing 10 by 3 gives you 3 with a remainder of 1 (3 times 3 is 9, plus 1 for 10). In JavaScript, modulus math is represented by the percent sign (%) and, when used in place of the division sign operator, returns the *remainder* of the division. This value will always be a number from 0 (perfectly divisible) to one less than the dividend (in our 10 % 3 example, the range of the modulus is from 0 to 2).

So, you can write a JavaScript function that returns a "random" number within a particular range as follows:

```
function random(maxValue)
{
    day = new Date();
    hour = day.getHours();
    min = day.getMinutes();
    sec = day.getSeconds();
    return (((hour + 1) * (min + 1) * sec) % maxValue) + 1;
}
```

As you can see, you get the hour, minute, and second from the Date object, then multiply them together. Finally, you modulus this number by the maxValue parameter to get a number somewhere between 1 and (maxValue - 1). Add 1 to this result (you'll see why in a moment) and return the final value. This is a handy little function to keep in your toolkit, because most uses of random-number generation will require a range limit.

165

You can then plop it into any JavaScript program where you require a random-number generator, or save it in a separate file and include it in your HTML documents with the SRC= attribute of the <SCRIPT> tag. In the case of your card game, you would pass the value 52 to random(), which would then be the maxValue.

You may be asking, "Why is 1 added to the hour and minute *before* you multiply them together?" Well, if you happen to be a late-night surfer and are trying this page out between midnight and 1:00 a.m., you'd discover that without this step you'd always get the value of 1. Remember, the hour, minute, and second are values between 0 and 59 or 23, so for the first hour of the day, the hour is 0. This would make the entire equation return a zero for one whole hour (as an experiment, try changing the function above and experimenting with the page after midnight).

Now that you can randomly generate a number within a particular range, you need to have a selection of things to randomly pick from—and that's next.

The Random Chatter Example

Create a simple example that randomly picks a phrase from an array of sentences. An "array" is simply an object, and each "array element" is one property. Every time the user clicks on the button, something new appears on the screen. Here's the JavaScript page:

```
<HTML>
<TITLE>Random Chatter</TITLE>
<HEAD>
<SCRIPT LANGUAGE="JavaScript">
<!-- Hide from non-JavaScript browsers
function random(maxValue)
{
    day = new Date();
    hour = day.getHours();
    min = day.getMinutes();
    sec = day.getSeconds();
    return (((hour + 1) * (min + 1) * sec) % maxValue) + 1;
}

function MakeArray(size)
{
    this.length = size;
    for(var i = 1; i <= size; i++)
    {
        this[i] = 0;
    }

    return this;
}

function showRandom(field)
```

```
    {
        textArray = new MakeArray(10);
        textArray[1] = "JavaScript is Fun!";
        textArray[2] = "Let's Browse the Web in Style!";
        textArray[3] = "We're now JavaScript-powered!";
        textArray[4] = "Click again, I don't like this choice.";
        textArray[5] = "And now ... something completely different.";
        textArray[6] = "So far ... so good.";
        textArray[7] = "Ok ... now what?";
        textArray[8] = "A nice choice, if I do say so myself.";
        textArray[9] = "Only one more to go ...";
        textArray[10] = "That's it!";

        field.value = textArray[random(10)];
    }

//-->
</SCRIPT>
</HEAD>
<BODY>
<H1>Random Chatter</H1>
<HR>
JavaScript can be quite a talker, and can even randomly pick things
to say.
<P>
<FORM>
<HR>
Click on the button, I'll think of something to say
<INPUT TYPE="button" VALUE="Take a chance!"
ONCLICK="showRandom(this.form.randomOut)">
<CENTER><INPUT TYPE=text NAME="randomOut" size="60"></CENTER>
</FORM>
</BODY>
</HTML>
```

There's your random-number function. In this case, it's returning a number between 1 and 10. Notice that you pass the parameter 10 (your maxValue) to random() in the function call in the final statement of showRandom(). The value it returns is used by the showRandom() function to pick a text line from textArray. The selected text is then loaded into the value property of the field that is passed to showRandom(). In the BODY of the page, you'll find the "Take a chance!" button that fires showRandom() whenever you click it, and the randomOut field that receives the text selected by showRandom().

One other thing you should see is the MakeArray() function in the <SCRIPT> tag. This is another handy little function to have around. Remember that creating an array is as simple as using new and defining the size (or number of indexes). MakeArray() provides a clean way of *initializing* any type of array to any size, setting all indexes in the array to 0 (or an empty text string). In essence, this is an automated object and property creator;

167

recall that an array is another name for a JavaScript object. `MakeArray()` simply creates an object and uses a loop to create some number of properties (array elements). This is done to create the skeleton of the array, for the same reason you created skeletons of an object back in Chapter 9.

Color Me Random

As another mini-example of random numbers, you can add another button to your page that causes the background color to change each time the button is clicked. To do this:

➤ Build an array of the color codes. As you know from your HTML experience, color codes are stored in *hexadecimal triplet* format (which specifies the amounts of red, green, and blue used in each color).

➤ Pick a color randomly from this array.

➤ Set the `bgColor` property of the JavaScript `document` object to this new value.

For a list of 138 of the most common colors, their RGB values, and their hexadecimal triplets, see "JavaScript: The Complete Reference" at the end of this book. For quick reference, here are the hexadecimal triplets for some basic colors:

Color	Hexadecimal Triplet
black	000000
blue	0000FF
brown	A52A2A
cyan	00FFFF
gold	FFD700
gray	808080
green	008000
lime	00FF00
magenta	FF00FF
maroon	800000
orange	FFA500
pink	FFC0CB
purple	800080
red	FF0000

Color	Hexadecimal Triplet
silver	C0C0C0
white	FFFFFF
yellow	FFFF00

Here's your function to pick a background color:

```
function SetBkgndColor()
{
    colorArray = new MakeArray(7);
    colorArray[1] = "#FF0000";
    colorArray[2] = "#00FF00";
    colorArray[3] = "#FFFF00";
    colorArray[4] = "#0000FF";
    colorArray[5] = "#FF00FF";
    colorArray[6] = "#00FFFF";
    colorArray[7] = "#FFFFFF";

    document.bgColor = colorArray[random(7)];
}
```

Notice that all you need to do to cause the background color to change is set
`document.bgColor`. Remember that `document` is a predefined JavaScript object that gives
you direct access to the current document and how it's being displayed (see Chapter 13
for more information on the `document` object).

Putting it all together, here's your new random chatter page:

```
<HTML>
<TITLE>Random Chatter</TITLE>
<HEAD>
<SCRIPT LANGUAGE="JavaScript">
<!-- Hide from non-JavaScript browsers
function random(maxValue)
{
    day = new Date();
    hour = day.getHours();
    min = day.getMinutes();
    sec = day.getSeconds();
    return (((hour + 1) * (min + 1) * sec) % maxValue) + 1;
}

function MakeArray(size)
{
    this.length = size;
    for(var i = 1; i <= size; i++)
    {
        this[i] = 0;
```

```
   }

   return this;
}

function showRandom(field)
{
   textArray = new MakeArray(10);
   textArray[1] = "JavaScript is Fun!";
   textArray[2] = "Let's Browse the Web in Style!";
   textArray[3] = "We're now JavaScript-powered!";
   textArray[4] = "Click again, I don't like this choice.";
   textArray[5] = "And now ... something completely different.";
   textArray[6] = "So far ... so good.";
   textArray[7] = "Ok ... now what?";
   textArray[8] = "A nice choice, if I do say so myself.";
   textArray[9] = "Only one more to go ...";
   textArray[10] = "That's it!";

   field.value = textArray[random(10)];
}

function SetBkgndColor()
{
   colorArray = new MakeArray(7);
   colorArray[1] = "#FF0000";
   colorArray[2] = "#00FF00";
   colorArray[3] = "#FFFF00";
   colorArray[4] = "#0000FF";
   colorArray[5] = "#FF00FF";
   colorArray[6] = "#00FFFF";
   colorArray[7] = "#FFFFFF";

   document.bgColor = colorArray[random(7)];
}

//-->
</SCRIPT>
</HEAD>
<BODY>
<H1>Random Chatter</H1>
<HR>
JavaScript can be quite a talker, and can even randomly pick things
to say.
<P>
<FORM>
<HR>
Click on the button, I'll think of something to say
<INPUT TYPE="button" VALUE="Take a chance!"
ONCLICK="showRandom(this.form.randomOut)">
<CENTER><INPUT TYPE=text NAME="randomOut" size="60"></CENTER>
<HR>
```

```
Or ... click here and I'll change color!
<INPUT TYPE="button" VALUE="Color Me!" ONCLICK="SetBkgndColor()">
</FORM>
</BODY>
</HTML>
```

And, here's what it looks like once it's running:

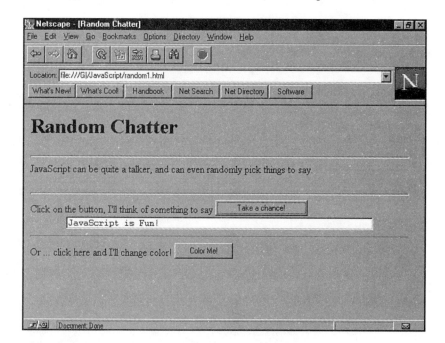

Randomly selecting text and changing document properties.

The Least You Need To Know

In this chapter's example, you learned how to:

➤ Get a JavaScript program to randomly pick from a list of selections.

➤ Create a function that you can use for a variety of things, such as the `random()` function, which can select a random number within specified bounds.

➤ Pick up a nifty little function that makes creating arrays a snap.

➤ Create a Web page that randomly displays various strings and changes color at the click of a button.

Script Example 3: Bank Loan Calculator

Math on the Web?

Web pages have been, for the most part, pretty pictures and tons of text. That's nice if all you want to do is make information available to the rest of the CyberCommunity, but for business applications, this can limit you. Previously, if you wanted to have the user interact with your pages (more than simply clicking on links and form buttons), you had to master the CGI interface (which opened a whole new world of frustrations).

With the invention of JavaScript, your pages can now do more than just display information—you can create custom information tailored to the user. You can even have your pages do mathematical calculations. The example you will look at in this chapter is a loan calculator that computes the monthly payments for a given amount of money at a particular compound interest rate, and then displays an amortization table showing what the principal and interest components are for each month's payment. This is the kind of math you'd have to deal with if you were financing a car or a home mortgage.

Why a calculator? If you were an insurance salesman (for instance), you could have your site compute the premium a person would have to pay for a particular policy. Instead of having to set up an appointment with a potential client, pitch them on the benefits of your program, and haul your laptop computer to their home to construct and print a policy; you can make your company information available on the Web. Let your users browse your policy options, make selections, and discover *right there* what they would have to pay. Then, if they're interested, they can send you e-mail to go to the next step. Makes your job easier, doesn't it (and it beats "cold calling")?

Before you dive into setting up the calculator, you need to take a look at some of the math functions that are built into JavaScript through the Math object. You can do most of what you need to with the Math object, but it does have one minor drawback: it doesn't have a method to round to the nearest penny.

Before you tackle this problem, quickly review what you can do with JavaScript math.

JavaScript Algebra 101

JavaScript's math functions provide some powerful flexibility to your scripts. Aside from the basic operations (+, −, /, and *), the Math object has additional methods that perform most of the special functions you find on today's calculators: abs(), acos(), asin(), atan(), cos(), exp(), log(), pow(), sin(), sqrt(), and tan(). Another method, random(), even generates a random number (you'll play with that in the next chapter). Additionally, parentheses allow you to group various substeps of a math equation to control what part of the equation is calculated first. Numbers in an expression are called *constants*, and *variables* are the letters (or words) that represent another value that changes depending on what's done to it.

If this looks like introductory algebra, it should; You can write JavaScript math expressions the same way you write algebra expressions. For example, adding two numbers together and assigning the result to a variable is done in algebra by:

```
a = 3 + 5
```

while in JavaScript, you would type:

```
a = 3 + 5;
```

The only real difference is the addition of the semicolon to indicate the end of the expression.

JavaScript math is *decimal math*. Any math operations performed (whether or not there are integer constants involved) are converted to decimal and the decimal is computed. So, an expression like:

```
a = 9 / 2;
```

would *evaluate* (a fancy word for "the answer is") to:

```
a = 4.5
```

This is all well and good, but what about numbers that don't produce simple decimals? If you were to type in the simple page:

```
<HTML>
<BODY>
</BODY>
<SCRIPT LANGUAGE="JavaScript">
<!--
document.write("100 divided by 3 is " + (100 / 3));
//-->
</SCRIPT>
</HTML>
```

and view it with your browser, you'd find the result displayed on the Web page.

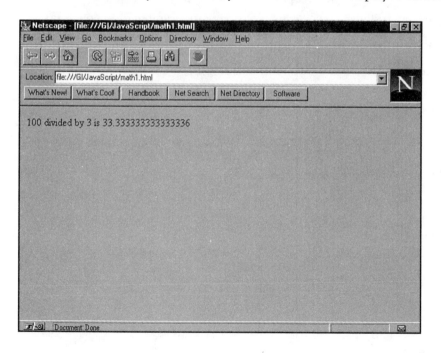

An example of JavaScript math.

That's 15 decimal places…plenty when you're doing something scientific, but *way* too many decimal places for most uses.

That Last Decimal Is Wrong!

Yep, it is. Computers aren't really good with fractions. You and I know that 1.3333333333… is the same as 1/3, but a computer needs to be *accurate*, and 1/3 as a decimal doesn't ever end. So, the computer does its best to calculate the fraction out as far as it can (called *number of digits precision*). Because a computer isn't an infinite thing (it has a fixed amount of memory, its processor chip is only so big, and so on), it has a fixed number of digits precision (in this case, 14 digits).

After the 14th digit, if the fraction is *still* going, the computer pretty much gives up. What it does next is basically anybody's guess: round up, round down, pick a number at random…anything. Because of this, the last decimal is wrong, and although there are 15 decimal places, only 14 of them are precise.

In this case (dealing with dollars and cents), you need only two decimal places. Anything after that should be dropped, not rounded (money is one area where everyone would love to round up to the nearest dollar…but it's just not done unless you're filling out a tax form). Unfortunately, there is no method in the Math object that allows you to automatically chop off those fractions of a penny. To do this, you need to "roll your own" function, using the round() method of the Math object as a basis.

Dollars and Decimals

Because JavaScript math would have you working with thousandths of a penny, you need to create a function that causes all those little copper shavings to be swept under the rug. To do that, you'll need to use the round() method of the Math object.

The round() method does just what its name implies: it rounds a decimal number to the nearest whole number. Using the earlier example, if you want to round the result of 100 divided by 3, you would type:

```
a = Math.round(100 / 3);
```

You can check this with another little short page:

```
<HTML>
<BODY>
</BODY>
<SCRIPT LANGUAGE="JavaScript">
```

```
<!--
document.write("100 divided by 3 (rounded) is " + Math.round(100 / 3));
//-->
</SCRIPT>
</HTML>
```

And you'd see:

```
100 divided by 3 (rounded) is 33
```

displayed in your browser. Using round() causes *all* the digits to the right of the decimal to be swept away and, if necessary, the number to the left is rounded up (so if you were rounding 4.6, you'd get 5). This gets half the job done (using your money example, you're rounding to the nearest *dollar*), but you want to keep two decimal places (the pennies), so you need to do a bit more math.

Since you want round() to round to the nearest penny, you need to convert the number from dollars and cents to just cents. You can do this by multiplying the dollar amount by 100 (if you have 1 dollar, you have 100 pennies), and *then* performing the round. After that, you just shift the decimal point to the left two places (divide by 100) and you have a dollar and cents amount. Simple, right?

Not quite. Remember that computers aren't very good with dividing fractions. If you were to type

```
a = 100 / 3
pennies = a * 100
document.write("100 divided by 3 is " + Math.round(pennies) / 100);
```

as a script, you'd see

```
100 divided by 3 is 33.329999999999998
```

displayed in your browser. *Still* not right, but you're getting closer. Replacing the document.write() line above with

```
document.write("100 divided by 3 (in pennies) is " + Math.round(pennies));
```

would cause

```
100 divided by 3 (in pennies) is 3333
```

to print out, so you *are* figuring the right number of pennies. The problem is the computer's inability to handle decimal division precisely.

To fix this, you need to take a different approach and just print out the number of pennies with a decimal point stuck in the middle. You can do this with JavaScript because you can take *any* number and convert it to a string:

```
strPennies = "" + pennies;
```

The `""` put in front of `pennies` causes the conversion, and `strPennies` becomes a string version of the value in `pennies`.

Now, to plug a decimal point into the middle of `strPennies`, construct another string that consists of:

➤ All the digits in `strPennies` but the last two.

➤ A decimal point.

➤ The last two digits from `strPennies`.

Remember from Chapter 6 that the `string` object in JavaScript has a `substring()` method, with which you can take a piece of a larger string. If you use a variable `len` to hold the number of digits in `strPennies`, all but the last two digits in `strPennies` would be

```
strPennies.substring(0, len - 2)
```

and the last two digits would be

```
strPennies.substring(len - 2, len)
```

Remember that the first parameter of `substring()` is the character position to *start* at and the second parameter is the position to *end before* (in the computer world, you start counting character positions at 0 instead of 1). Putting your number together:

```
strPennies.substring(0, len - 2) + "." + strPennies.substring(len - 2, len);
```

This takes 33.329999999999998 and turns it into 33.33. Putting it all together in a function:

```
function roundToPennies(n)
{
    pennies = n * 100;

    pennies = Math.round(pennies);

    strPennies = "" + pennies;
    len = strPennies.length;

    return strPennies.substring(0, len - 2) + "." + strPennies.substring(len -
    ➥2, len);
}
```

You now have a function that rounds to dollars and cents! You could extend this function to round to any number of decimal places (up to 14 decimals, at which point the computer loses accuracy), but I'll leave that as an exercise. Now, you can build the function that computes the monthly payment.

The Monthly Payment

If you've ever borrowed money (from a bank, not your uncle), you've had to pay interest, a percentage of "profit" the bank makes for letting you use its money. Being fond of math (as bank people are), the formula used to calculate the interest on a bank loan isn't a simple one, and one look at the printout that comes with loan papers (showing what your monthly payment is and what part is principal and what part is interest) proves it.

The figures in the *amortization table* show that you pay mostly *interest* (the money the bank makes) for the beginning of the loan, and then more and more *principal* (the actual money you borrowed) as you go along. This is because the interest for a given month is computed against whatever the unpaid principal is. As you make more payments, the amount of remaining principal decreases, and the amount of interest computed decreases. Since you are paying a fixed amount each month, less interest means more principal in each payment. Even banks make their money "up front."

If you look in a book on finance, you'll find that the formula for computing a monthly payment on an amortized loan is rather complex:

```
monthly = principal * rate / (1 - (1 / (1 + rate)payments ))
```

where:

Variable	Meaning
monthly	Amount of monthly payment.
principal	Total amount borrowed.
rate	Monthly rate (annual rate divided by 12 months). For example, an APR (annual percentage rate) of 12% equals a monthly interest rate of 0.01 (1%/month).
payments	Total number of monthly payments.

But, with JavaScript's Math object, this formula is easily tamed. The worst piece of it is:

```
(1 + rate)payments
```

The pow() method is designed to handle just such a problem (remember that pow() takes two parameters, and raises the value of the first parameter to the power of the second).

179

So, in JavaScript-ese, this becomes:

```
Math.pow(1 + rate, payments);
```

Putting this together with the rest of the formula, you have:

```
monthly = principal * rate / (1 - (1 / Math.pow(1 + rate, payments)));
```

And, you can now write your function:

```
function Monthly(principal, years, apr)
{
   rate = apr / 12;
   payments = years * 12;
   return principal * rate / (1 - (1 / Math.pow(1 + rate, payments)));
}
```

With this function complete, you have one last piece of your math puzzle to construct: for any given month, how much of the monthly payment is interest and how much is principal?

Amortization Tables

In an amortized loan, the interest incurred isn't computed all at once. Rather, the amount is figured out each payment period (in your example, each month) against whatever the principal is at the time, much the same way that you are charged interest on your credit card balance. Also, the amount of interest charged is the monthly interest rate (the annual rate divided by 12).

So, if you were to borrow $50,000 at 8% over 10 years (120 payments), the monthly payment would be $606.64, and the monthly interest rate would be 0.08 divided by 12, or 0.00666666666667 (remember, you can handle only 14 digits precision). At the end of the first month, the principal is still $50,000, so the interest incurred that first month would be

```
$50,000.00 * 0.00666666666667 = $333.35
```

The amount of your payment that is actually principal is what's left over after paying off the interest: $273.29. Therefore, at the end of the second month, the principal has been reduced:

```
$50,000.00 - $273.29 = $49,726.71
```

This becomes the new principal, and the process continues until all the money has been paid back.

This can be done in JavaScript using a `for` loop that runs over the total number of payments:

```
for(i = 0; i < payments; i++)
{
   interestPayment = principal * monthlyInterest;
   principalPayment = monthlyPayment - interestPayment;
   principal -= principalPayment;
}
```

Notice the use of `-=` in the loop. This is a nice shorthand for

```
principal = principal - principalPayment;
```

For each pass through the loop, `principal` is reduced by the amount of `principalPayment` (the part of the payment that is not interest). As `principal` gets smaller, so will `interestPayment`, meaning what's left over will increase...exactly what happens in an amortized loan.

Finally, you want to print out this information for each month. Using `document.write()`, you can write HTML statements right out to the current page (no need for CGI here!). Adding this to the `for` loop above gives you the monthly amortization function:

```
function MonthlyAmortization(principal, years, apr)
{
   payments = years * 12;
   monthlyInterest = apr / 12;
   monthlyPayment = Monthly(principal, years, apr);

   for(i = 1; i <= payments; i++)
   {
      document.write(i);

      interestPayment = principal * monthlyInterest;

      document.write("$" + roundtoPennies(interestPayment));

      principalPayment = monthlyPayment - interestPayment;

      document.write("$" + roundToPennies(principalPayment));

      principal -= principalPayment;

      document.write("$" + roundToPennies(principal));

      document.write("<BR>");
   }
}
```

This prints one line per payment, displaying the payment number, the amount of interest paid, and the amount of principal paid. Using `roundToPennies()`, you make sure that only dollars and cents appear. Adding a dollar sign in front of each number makes it look even better.

The `<BR>` tag at the end forces a carriage return; otherwise, the displayed data would wrap around the screen. There is, however, a better way...and you'll look at that next.

Forms in a Function

A better method of presenting a table of information like this would be to use the `<TABLE>` tag in HTML to format your information automatically (saves having to compute widths and margins and all that ugly stuff). But, can you create a table dynamically? Yes, and you won't believe how easy it is.

Remember that the basic structure for an HTML table is

```
<TABLE>
<TR>
<TD>column 1</TD>
<TD>column 2</TD>
</TR>
</TABLE>
```

This displays a table of one row and two columns. Since the `document.write()` function allows you to write out HTML statements as well as regular (display) text, you can just as easily write out table control tags.

Look back at the `MonthlyAmortization()` function. Each pass through the `for` loop generates one row of information. This means that you can rewrite this loop with `<TR>` and `<TD>` tags:

```
for(i = 1; i <= payments; i++)
{
   document.write("<TR>");

   document.write("<TD>" + i + "</TD>");

   interestPayment = principal * monthlyInterest;

   document.write("<TD>$" + roundToPennies(interestPayment) + "</TD>");

   principalPayment = monthlyPayment - interestPayment;

   document.write("<TD>$" + roundToPennies(principalPayment) + "</TD>");

   principal -= principalPayment;
```

```
document.write("<TD>$" + roundToPennies(principal) + "</TD>");

document.write("</TR>");
}
```

This generates a table exactly the right size and makes sure everything lines up the way you want it to. The only thing left is to add a table heading and put your page together.

Amortized Loans: The Whole Picture

With the individual pieces built, you can now construct the entire page:

```
<HTML>
<HEAD>
<TITLE>Loan Calculator</TITLE>
<SCRIPT LANGUAGE="LiveScript">
<!-- hide from non-JavaScript browsers

function roundToPennies(n)
{
   pennies = n * 100;

   pennies = Math.round(pennies);

   strPennies = "" + pennies;
   len = strPennies.length;

   return strPennies.substring(0, len - 2) + "." +
   ➥strPennies.substring(len - 2, len);
}

function Monthly(principal, years, apr)
{
   rate = apr / 12;
   payments = years * 12;
   return roundToPennies(principal * rate / (1 - (1 / Math.pow(1 +
   ➥rate, payments))));
}

function MonthlyAmortization(principal, years, apr)
{
   payments = years * 12;
   monthlyInterest = apr / 12;
   monthlyPayment = Monthly(principal, years, apr);

   document.write("<CENTER>");

   document.write("<H1>Amortization Table</H1>");
   document.write("<HR>");
```

```
document.write("<TABLE BORDER>");

document.write("<TR>");
document.write("<TH COLSPAN=4>");
document.write("$" + roundToPennies(principal));
document.write(" at " + roundToPennies(apr) + "%");
document.write(" over " + years + " years.<BR>");
document.write("Monthly payment: $" + Monthly(principal, years, apr));
document.write("</TH>");
document.write("</TR>");

document.write("<TR>");
document.write("<TH></TH>");
document.write("<TH COLSPAN=2>Payment</TH>");
document.write("</TR>");

document.write("<TR>");
document.write("<TH>Month</TH>");
document.write("<TH>Interest</TH>");
document.write("<TH>Principal</TH>");
document.write("<TH>Balance</TH>");
document.write("</TR>");

for(i = 1; i <= payments; i++)
{
    document.write("<TR>");
    document.write("<TD>" + i + "</TD>");

    interestPayment = principal * monthlyInterest;
    document.write("<TD>$" + roundToPennies(interestPayment) +
    ➥"</TD>");

    principalPayment = monthlyPayment - interestPayment;
    document.write("<TD>$" + roundToPennies(principalPayment) +
    ➥"</TD>");

    principal -= principalPayment;
    document.write("<TD>$" + roundToPennies(principal) + "</TD>");

    document.write("</TD>");
}

document.write("</TABLE>");

document.write("</CENTER>");
}

function compute(form)
{
    if((form.principal.value.length != 0) &&
       (form.apr.value.length != 0) &&
       (form.years.value.length != 0))
```

184

```
      {
        principal = eval(form.principal.value);
        apr = eval(form.apr.value) / 100.0;
        years = eval(form.years.value);

        if(years == 0.0)
        {
           alert(
           "You have no monthly payment, since the number of years is zero.");
        }
        else
        {
           MonthlyAmortization(principal, years, apr);
        }
      }
      else
      {
        alert("You must fill in all the fields.");
      }
}

//-->

</SCRIPT>
</HEAD>

<BODY>

<CENTER><H1>Loan Calculator</H1></CENTER>

<HR>

<CENTER>
<FORM>
<CENTER>
Fill in the fields, then click
<INPUT TYPE=BUTTON VALUE="Amortize!" onClick=compute(this.form)>
</CENTER>
<P>

<TABLE BORDER=3>
<TR>
  <TD>Amount of the loan ($)</TD>
  <TD><INPUT TYPE=TEXT NAME=principal></TD>
</TR>
<TR>
  <TD>Annual interest rate (%)</TD>
  <TD><INPUT TYPE=TEXT NAME=apr></TD>
</TR>
<TR>
  <TD>Total number of years</TD>
  <TD><INPUT TYPE=TEXT NAME=years></TD>
```

185

```
</TR>
</TABLE>
</FORM>
</CENTER>

</BODY>
</HTML>
```

As you can see, this script also demonstrates the use of HTML tables to create a page that has a pleasing layout.

A loan amortizer in JavaScript.

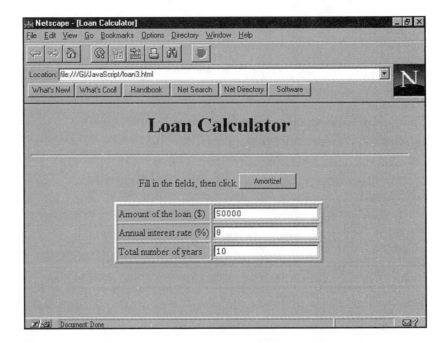

Once the user clicks **Amortize!**, the monthlyAmortization() function goes to work, producing the amortization table. Additionally, you'll notice (when you try this in your browser) that this method of writing directly to the active page causes the page to be reloaded with the new data.

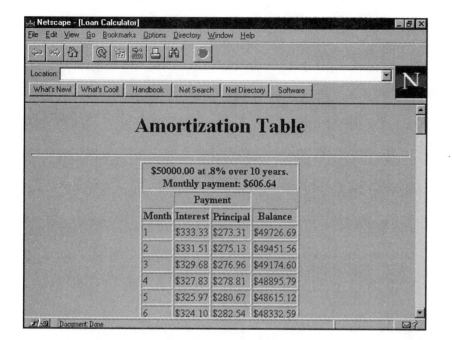

The amortization table produced by the calculator.

The Least You Need To Know

This chapter presented another math example: computing the monthly payment on a loan and producing an amortization schedule based on that information. You learned how JavaScript deals with decimal numbers and learned a way around JavaScript's lack of "number of decimal places" control. You also learned a way to format the page using HTML tables to create a pleasing layout, as well as how to get JavaScript to create a table for you dynamically...customizing your pages to the user's specific needs.

It Looks Different, But It's Still the Same Page Any HTML statements that are written with document.write() aren't written back to your page. They are created by the browser when needed but are not saved back over your page on your site. This way, you can run the program again and again with different figures.

Script Example 4: Blackjack

Game Time

In our final example, you take a break from the monotony of loans and other boring subjects. It's time to play a few hands of cards and prove that JavaScript is an effective environment for game creation. To this end, you'll cook up a little script that plays a simple game of blackjack.

First, define the ground rules for the game:

➤ For this demonstration, Aces have the value 11.

➤ All "face" cards (Jack, Queen, and King) have the value of 10.

➤ All cards will be dealt "face up." This means you'll know what the dealer (house) has from the start.

➤ The deck is "infinite," meaning you can draw more than one Ace of Spades in a row. For those of you fond of Las Vegas or Atlantic City, this is called a *multiple-deck shoe.*

➤ The user will click a Hit or Stand button, depending on whether they want another card.

➤ Once the user clicks Stand, the dealer starts drawing cards. The dealer continues to draw until either the house's hand totals more than 17 or the house busts. In other words, the house stands on 17.

➤ Once both the dealer and user stop taking cards, the winning hand is the one closest to 21 without going over (busting).

➤ If the dealer and the user have the same total at the end of a hand, they "push" (tie), and no one wins or loses.

Okay, so we cut a few corners with the rules. If you want to extend the game to handle such things as splits, doubles, betting, and Aces that are 1 *or* 11, please feel free.

Pick a Card

In Chapter 16, you saw how to create a function to generate a random number between 1 and some maximum value using the JavaScript Date object to get the current time (hours, minutes, and seconds). Since time is constantly changing, this provides a very basic, *pseudo-random* (almost random) generator. For review, here's the random() function:

```
function random(maxValue)
{
    day = new Date();
    hour = day.getHours();
    min = day.getMinutes();
    sec = day.getSeconds();
    return (((hour + 1) * (min + 1) * sec)  %  maxValue) + 1;
}
```

This works quite nicely for your purposes, because you need to randomly pick two things for each card "drawn" from the deck:

➤ The suit: Spades, Clubs, Diamonds, or Hearts.

➤ The face value of the card: Ace, 2–10, Jack, Queen, or King.

Since there are four suits, you can write a function to pick a suit by randomly generating a number between 1 and 4:

```
function pickSuit()
{
```

```
    suit = random(4);

    if(suit == 1)
        return "Spades";

    if(suit == 2)
        return "Clubs";

    if(suit == 3)
        return "Diamonds";

    return "Hearts";
}
```

You really need to check `suit` only to see if it's 1, 2, or 3. If it isn't one of those, it must be 4 and you don't have to use an `if` statement to make sure. This is an "old programmer's trick" that saves a few keystrokes and a couple of steps when the program is running (if you want to drop a buzzword at your next party, this is called *program optimization*).

The next step is to pick the card from the suit. There are 13 cards in each suit: Ace, 2 through 10, Jack, Queen, and King. You need your card picker to return two things: the value of the card (a number from 2 to 11...remember, Aces are 11) and the *name* of the card (either the card number or the word "Jack," for instance). This causes a bit of a dilemma: `"Jack"`, `"Queen"`, `"King"`, and `"Ace"` are all strings, but `"2"`, `"3"`, `"5"`, and so on are numbers. You need both.

Since you need two distinct things from your card picker, make two distinct functions: one to return the value, and one to return the name. The value function simply takes the number of your card (a number from 1 to 13) and returns a value from 2 to 11:

```
function cardValue(card)
{
    if(card == 1)
        return 11;

    if(card > 10)
        return 10;

    return card;
}
```

If the card is 1 (an Ace), you say it's worth 11. If the card is a face card, its number will be 11, 12, or 13, so you say it's worth 10. Otherwise, it's worth the number that's passed in.

Figuring out the card name is similar:

```
function cardName(card)
{
```

```
    if(card == 1)
        return "Ace";

    if(card == 11)
        return "Jack";

    if(card == 12)
        return "Queen";

    if(card == 13)
        return "King";

    return "" + card;
}
```

Since each face card has a different name, you can't just say, "If it's greater than 10 ...," so you need a separate if statement for each face card. Finally, the number (spot) cards are simply returned, but you convert the value to a string (using the " " + trick).

Now, you can construct your PickACard() function:

```
function PickACard(strWho)
{
    card = random(13);
    suit = pickSuit();

    alert(strWho + " picked the " + cardName(card) + " of " + suit);

    return cardValue(card);
}
```

Return the card's value from PickACard() so you can use this function to add to the totals in the dealer's and user's hands. Also, the parameter strWho gives you the flexibility to call PickACard("You") or PickACard("Dealer") and have the alert() dialog say "Dealer picked..." or "You picked..." without having to write two separate functions (remember Rule #3 of JavaScript programming: *Never do more typing than you have to*).

You can test your card picker with the following short page:

```
<HTML>
<TITLE>Pick a Card</TITLE>
<HEAD>
<SCRIPT LANGUAGE="JavaScript">
<!-- Hide from non-JavaScript browsers
function random(maxValue)
{
    day = new Date();
    hour = day.getHours();
    min = day.getMinutes();
    sec = day.getSeconds();
```

```
    return (((hour + 1) * (min + 1) * sec) % maxValue) + 1;
}

function pickSuit()
{
   suit = random(4);

   if(suit == 1)
      return "Spades";

   if(suit == 2)
      return "Clubs";

   if(suit == 3)
      return "Diamonds";

   return "Hearts";
}

function cardName(card)
{
   if(card == 1)
      return "Ace";

   if(card == 11)
      return "Jack";

   if(card == 12)
      return "Queen";

   if(card == 13)
      return "King";

   return "" + card;
}

function cardValue(card)
{
   if(card == 1)
      return 11;

   if(card > 10)
      return 10;

   return card;
}

function PickACard(strWho)
{
   card = random(13);
   suit = pickSuit();
```

193

```
        alert(strWho + " picked the " + cardName(card) + " of " + suit);

        return cardValue(card);
}
//-->
</SCRIPT>
</HEAD>
<BODY>
<FORM>
<INPUT TYPE=BUTTON VALUE="Pick A Card" onClick=PickACard("You")>
</FORM>
</BODY>
</HTML>
```

Clicking the Pick A Card button will generate a JavaScript alert box something like this.

Testing the card picker.

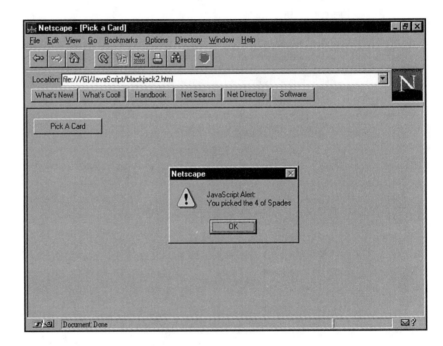

Clicking repeatedly will pop up different card selections—so your card picker works! Start putting together the game logic, beginning with the dealer (which is a little more involved than the user).

Dealer Takes a Card

The user takes a card only when he clicks the Hit me button, but the dealer must repeatedly take cards (after the user clicks Stand) until the house's hand goes over 16. This means you have to set up a function that repeats the pickacard() process until 17 is reached or exceeded. If you think this sounds like a job for a while loop, you're right.

Recall the basic form of the while loop: "While {*something*} is 'true', keep doing something else." In this case, you want to keep picking cards while the total in the dealer's hand is less than 17:

```
function Dealer()
{
   while(dealerHand < 17)
   {
      dealerHand = dealerHand + PickACard("Dealer");
   }
}
```

Simple, isn't it? The function for when the user picks a card is even easier:

```
function User()
{
   userHand = userHand + PickACard("You");
}
```

And, once everybody has taken all the cards they want, figuring out who won is a snap:

```
function LookAtHands()
{
   if(dealerHand > 21)
   {
      alert("House busts!  You win!");
   }
   else
   if(userHand > dealerHand)
   {
      alert("You win!");
   }
   else
   if(userHand == dealerHand)
   {
      alert("Push!");
   }
   else
   {
      alert("House wins!");
   }
}
```

But what are userHand and dealerHand? They could be variables, but they really are placeholders for the form fields that you need to display this information to the user on the "game board." It's time to "spread the felt" and set up the gaming table.

Deal Me In

The game page needs two fields (for the house's and user's totals), and three buttons: Hit, Stand, and New Hand. Each button will have its own onClick event handler to process taking a card (for a hit) or having the dealer take cards (if the user chooses to stand). From the functions you've compiled so far, you can see that...

> ➤ The **Hit** button should run the User() function and check to see whether the user has gone over 21.

> ➤ The **Stand** button should run the Dealer() function and then the LookAtHands() function to see who won.

> ➤ The **New Hand** button should reset the dealer's and user's hands to 0 and pick a new starting card for each.

Since you'll be dealing with an HTML <FORM>, you'll make the dealer's total field dealer, and the user's you. This means you have to replace userHand with form.you.value and dealerHand with form.dealer.value. The correct value for form can be passed into the various functions from inside the HTML form by using the this.form qualifier. For example:

```
<INPUT TYPE=BUTTON VALUE="Hit me!" onClick=User(this.form)>
```

This would pass the form into the User() function, so that you can update the user's total hand:

```
function User(form)
{
    form.you.value = eval(form.you.value) + PickACard("You");

    if(form.you.value > 21)
    {
        alert("You busted!");
    }
}
```

By replacing userHand with form.you.value, you are writing the total of the user's hand back to the form for display. Accessing the dealer's hand information is done the same way.

JavaScript Is Very Fond of Strings

In fact, JavaScript will convert any form fields that are nothing but numbers into their string equivalents. This means that, if you want to change the value of a number in a field, you should first use the `eval()` function to make sure that the field value is treated as a number, not a string.

For example, if you had a form field called `number` and it was holding the value 23, adding 5 to it by:

```
form.number.value = form.number.value + 5;
```

would result in `number` having the value `"235"`, as though you were tacking strings together. Use `eval()` to keep this from happening:

```
form.number.value = eval(form.number.value) + 5;
```

and the result will be `"28"`.

Using the `eval()` function guarantees that the information in `form.you.value` is treated as a *number,* not a *string* (JavaScript has a tendency to look at things as strings, whether they are strings or not).

With that said, here's the complete script:

```
<HTML>
<TITLE>BlackJack</TITLE>
<HEAD>
<SCRIPT LANGUAGE="JavaScript">
<!-- Hide from non-JavaScript browsers
function random(maxValue)
{
   day = new Date();
   hour = day.getHours();
   min = day.getMinutes();
   sec = day.getSeconds();
   return (((hour + 1) * (min + 1) * sec) % maxValue) + 1;
}

function pickSuit()
{
   suit = random(4);

   if(suit == 1)
      return "Spades";

   if(suit == 2)
      return "Clubs";
```

```
      if(suit == 3)
         return "Diamonds";

      return "Hearts";
   }

function cardName(card)
{
   if(card == 1)
      return "Ace";

   if(card == 11)
      return "Jack";

   if(card == 12)
      return "Queen";

   if(card == 13)
      return "King";

   return "" + card;
}

function cardValue(card)
{
   if(card == 1)
      return 11;

   if(card > 10)
      return 10;

   return card;
}

function PickACard(strWho)
{
   card = random(13);
   suit = pickSuit();

   alert(strWho + " picked the " + cardName(card) + " of " + suit);

   return cardValue(card);
}

function NewHand(form)
{
   form.dealer.value = 0;
   form.you.value = 0;

   form.dealer.value = eval(form.dealer.value) + PickACard("Dealer");
   form.you.value = eval(form.you.value) + PickACard("You");
```

```
    }

    function Dealer(form)
    {
       while(form.dealer.value < 17)
       {
          form.dealer.value = eval(form.dealer.value) + PickACard("Dealer");
       }
    }

    function User(form)
    {
       form.you.value = eval(form.you.value) + PickACard("You");

       if(form.you.value > 21)
       {
          alert("You busted!");
       }
    }

    function LookAtHands(form)
    {
       if(form.dealer.value > 21)
       {
          alert("House busts!  You win!");
       }
       else   if(form.you.value > form.dealer.value)
       {
          alert("You win!");
       }
       else
       if(form.dealer.value == form.you.value)
       {
          alert("Push!");
       }
       else
       {
          alert("House wins!");
       }
    }
    //-->
    </SCRIPT>
    </HEAD>
    <BODY>
    <CENTER><H2>BlackJack</H2></CENTER>
    <CENTER>To start a hand, click 'New Hand'.</CENTER>
    <CENTER>(Dealer stands on 17)</CENTER>
    <HR>

    <CENTER>
    <FORM>
    <TABLE BORDER=3>
```

```
<TR>
  <TD>Dealer has</TD>
  <TD><INPUT TYPE=TEXT NAME=dealer></TD>
</TR>
<TR>
  <TD>You have</TD>
  <TD><INPUT TYPE=TEXT NAME=you></TD>
</TR>
</TABLE>

<P>

<CENTER>
<INPUT TYPE=BUTTON VALUE="Hit me!" onClick=User(this.form)>
<INPUT TYPE=BUTTON VALUE="Stand"
➡onClick="Dealer(this.form);LookAtHands(this.form);">
<INPUT TYPE=BUTTON VALUE="New Hand" onClick=NewHand(this.form)>
</CENTER>

</FORM>
</CENTER>

</BODY>
</HTML>
```

From inside the browser, your blackjack game looks like this.

*Gambling with
JavaScript (it's
cheaper than Vegas).*

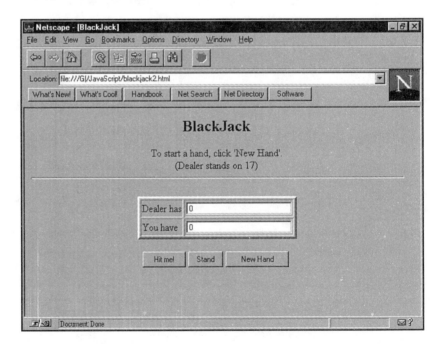

The Least You Need To Know

In this example, you looked at creating a game with JavaScript. Using the tools you've collected from previous chapters, you built a simple blackjack player. You also saw how using the `while` statement makes it possible to continue working inside a function until some condition is met. To make sure that the totals you were building in the form were correct, `eval()` makes sure that field values are treated as numbers rather than strings.

Chapter 19

Script Example 5: Creating an eZine

In This Chapter

➤ Use of <FRAME>s

➤ Multiple <SCRIPT> tags

➤ Non-Function JavaScript statements

➤ Talking between frames

Start the Web-Presses!

By now, you may be thinking to yourself, "This author stuff doesn't seem that difficult. Heck, I could write my *own* book or publish a magazine and it'd be *much* better than what this guy's written." You may be right…and through the magic of the Web, you can give it a shot. *And*, publishing on the Web doesn't require a contract with a publisher, a fleet of editors, and tons of money—just you, your browser, and an idea.

Many have already started down the path of the *eZine*, an electronic, online version of the magazines you find at your favorite bookstore. Each day, another one is "published" through the Web (I've even heard there's a 'zine about chickens). If no one reads it but you, who cares? You've made your statement, presented your case, told your story, whatever you want to do.

But *you* are a JavaScripter...you want to be different. You want to stand out in the crowd as someone who *knows* his Web. That's what this example will do for you: a Do-It-Yourself JavaScript-Enabled eZine Framework (whew!).

At the same time, you'll get a chance to see a variety of JavaScript tricks all rolled into one power-collection of pages. A few Netscape HTML enhancements are thrown in that Navigator 2.0 supports (since you need Navigator 2.0 to view JavaScript, this is a pretty safe step).

JavaScript: The eZine!

Any magazine, electronic or otherwise, consists of the following parts:

➤ A cover page

➤ A table of contents

➤ Articles, articles, articles

You can put these together using Netscape 2.0's <FRAME> tag. The <FRAME> tag allows you to break the browser's display area into subsections (each separated by a *frame*), and display a *different* HTML document in each frame. Since a picture is worth a thousand words, here's what our eZine will look like when you finish:

JavaScript:
The eZine!

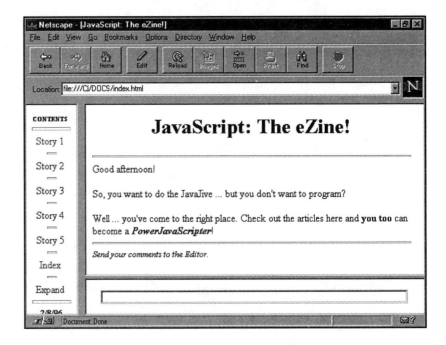

Now, let's tear this apart and look at each piece.

I've Been Framed!

The first thing you'll see is that the screen is divided into three areas. Each area is referred to as a *frame*. The *frame* that runs down the left side of the screen serves as your Table of Contents. Each link will load a particular article when clicked on. Articles that are loaded appear in the large frame on the right. When the user first loads the eZine, he is shown the cover page that you see in the figure. Finally, the third frame is a "help window," and you'll look at that more closely later.

So, the first thing you need is an HTML document that sets up your frames. This is the document that the user would load to read your eZine. By convention, the "main" or "primary" HTML document in a directory is called `index.html`, and you want to stick with convention. Here's your `index.html`:

```
<!-- index.html:  The "driver" of our eZine -->
<HTML>

<HEAD>
<TITLE>JavaScript:  The eZine!</TITLE>
</HEAD>

<FRAMESET COLS="90,*">
  <FRAME SRC="buttons.html" NORESIZE NAME="Buttons" BORDER=1 SCROLLING=NO>
  <FRAMESET ROWS="*,60">
    <FRAME SRC="coverpage.html" NORESIZE NAME="Main" SCROLLING=AUTO>
    <FRAME SRC="helpwindow.html" NORESIZE NAME="Help" SCROLLING=NO>
  </FRAMESET>
</FRAMESET>

<NOFRAMES>
<BODY BGCOLOR=#FFFFFF>

<CENTER><H1>JavaScript:  The eZine!</H1></CENTER>

<HR>

Since this is an eZine about JavaScript, you really ought to get
a browser that supports it.  Why not check out
<A HREF="http://home.netscape.com/">Netscape Navigator 2.0</A>?

<HR>

Send your comments to the <A HREF="mailto: ">Editor</A>.

</BODY>
</NOFRAMES>
</HTML>
```

The <NOFRAMES> tag is basically a wrapper for what you want to display to people who don't have a frames-enabled browser. In this case, you gently urge people to get a newer browser and, since you're also using JavaScript, I suggest Navigator 2.0.

A collection (or *set*) of frames is defined with the <FRAMESET> tag. <FRAMESET> has two attributes, ROWS and COLS, which allow us to define the width of the various frames we want. In our example:

```
<FRAMESET COLS="90,*">
  <FRAME SRC="buttons.html" NORESIZE NAME="Buttons" BORDER=1 SCROLLING=NO>
  <FRAMESET ROWS="*,60">
    <FRAME SRC="coverpage.html" NORESIZE NAME="Main" SCROLLING=AUTO>
    <FRAME SRC="helpwindow.html" NORESIZE NAME="Help" SCROLLING=NO>
  </FRAMESET>
</FRAMESET>
```

a <FRAMESET> is *nested* inside another <FRAMESET>. You can do this as deep (as many nests) as you want, but don't get carried away with it (you *can* create frames too small to display much of anything). Another way to look at your collection of frames is thusly:

> *My frames consist of two columns. The left column is 90 pixels wide, the right column is whatever's left of the screen width. The left column will be called "buttons" and will load "buttons.html". The right column is further divided into two frames, the bottom one 60 pixels tall, the top one whatever's left. Call the top frame "Main" and load "coverpage.html", while the bottom one will be "Help" and will load "helpwindow.htm".*

By using the "*" value for the frame width, you tell the browser to make that frame whatever width is left after the other fixed widths have been computed.

Also, notice the <FRAME> attributes NORESIZE and SCROLLING. NORESIZE tells the browser not to let the user grab the frame and drag (resize) it. Without this attribute, moving the mouse over the frame edge will cause the mouse cursor to change to the familiar Windows resize cursor. If the user were to grab the frame by clicking on it, the frame could be moved.

The SCROLLING attribute controls whether a scroll bar will be displayed. By default, the value of SCROLLING is AUTO, meaning that a scroll bar will appear only if the page is bigger than the frame. In this case, you don't want scrolling on the help window or the table of contents, so you set SCROLLING=NO. Setting SCROLLING=YES would make a scroll bar always appear, even if the document was smaller than the frame.

As you can see, the <FRAMES> tag doesn't really display any text. It simply defines the frames and indicates which documents should be loaded into which frames.

Now, let's move through each piece of the eZine. We'll start with the more interesting one: the help window.

Help Me!

You're probably wondering about that short frame at the bottom of the screen...the one with the words "Article #3" in it. That's the *help window*, and it is powered by JavaScript. As the user moves the mouse over the table of contents, the text in the help window will change to relate to whatever the user is pointing to. With the help window, you can display a one-line description of each link in the table of contents.

The help window is a simple FORM with one field: a text field named "helpmsg" that will receive information sent to it from the table of contents. Here's the HTML file:

```
<!-- helpwindow.html:  The eZine help window -->
<HTML>

<HEAD>
<TITLE>JavaScript:  The eZine!</TITLE>
</HEAD>

<BODY BGCOLOR=#FFFFFF>

<CENTER>
  <FORM>
    <INPUT TYPE="text" NAME="helpmsg" SIZE=60>
  </FORM>
</CENTER>


</BODY>
</HTML>
```

Nothing fancy, but with the addition of the table of contents buttons, it produces a very nice effect.

In the previous programs, all of the frames have the same "title," as defined by the <TITLE> tag. However, recall just what the purpose of the HTML "title" is. It doesn't appear anywhere within the document itself. The title pops up in two places: the upper border of the browser window, and the bookmark list. We've used the same title, "JavaScript: The eZine!" for each frame because it is appropriate for either the browser windowframe or bookmark.

You'll see the table of contents now.

The Table of Contents

The table of contents (the frame on the left) is your control center. As the user passes the mouse over one of the links, a line of text describing that link is sent to the help window frame below.

How is this done? First, remember that the helpwindow.html file contains a form with one field, helpmsg. Forms are accessible from within JavaScript, and with JavaScript, the data in form fields can be changed. Also, remember that since each frame is a document—and each document is attached to the main window—you can "reach" from one frame into another and do something to it.

First, create an array of help strings to display:

```
function MakeArray(size)
{
    this.length = size;
    for(i = 1; i <= size; i++)
    {
        this[i] = '';
    }

    return this;
}


msg = new MakeArray(7);

msg['story1'] = 'Article #1';
msg['story2'] = 'Article #2';
msg['story3'] = 'Article #3';
msg['story4'] = 'Article #4';
msg['story5'] = 'Article #5';
msg['index']  = 'Return to the cover page';
msg['expand'] = 'Remove the button bar and help window';
```

This uses your familiar MakeArray() function. It also creates your message array, msg[] *outside a JavaScript function*, making the array "visible" to any other JavaScript functions.

Now that you have the array, you need to display it. What you want to do is create a special link on the page that handles the onMouseOver event:

```
<A HREF="story1.html"
   TARGET="Main"
   ONMOUSEOVER="message('story1', this.href); return true;">
Story 1</A>
```

The onMouseOver event handler simply calls our message() function and passes an "ID tag" (the index into the msg[] array) and the HREF associated with this link. Also, notice that our TARGET is "Main". This means that the HREF that will be loaded (a story document, in this case) will be loaded *into* the frame named "Main" (the large frame on the right of the screen).

The message() function looks like this:

```
clearid = 0;

function message(button,url)
{
    if(clearid)
    {
        clearTimeout(clearid);
    }

    window.parent.frames['Help'].document.forms[0].helpmsg.value =
    ➥msg[button];
    self.status = url;
    clearid =
setTimeout("window.parent.frames['Help'].document.forms[0].helpmsg.value =
➥''", 5000);
}
```

That rather long window.parent.frames['Help']... line is what does the magic. It loads the selected msg[] text into the value property of the helpmsg field in the form of the helpwindow frame. That's a long-winded way of saying that it copies a string somewhere else on the page—but it works!

Putting this all together, here's the table of contents document, buttons.html:

```
<!-- buttons.html:  eZine table of contents -->
<HTML>

<HEAD>

<TITLE>JavaScript:  The eZine!</TITLE>

<SCRIPT LANGUAGE="LiveScript">
<!-- Hide from non-JavaScript browsers

function MakeArray(size)
{
    this.length = size;
    for(i = 1; i <= size; i++)
    {
        this[i] = '';
    }

    return this;
}


msg = new MakeArray(7);
```

```
msg['story1'] = 'Article #1';
msg['story2'] = 'Article #2';
msg['story3'] = 'Article #3';
msg['story4'] = 'Article #4';
msg['story5'] = 'Article #5';
msg['index']  = 'Return to the cover page';
msg['expand'] = 'Remove the button bar and help window';

clearid = 0;

function message(button,url)
{
   if(clearid)
   {
      clearTimeout(clearid);
   }

   window.parent.frames['Help'].document.forms[0].helpmsg.value =
   ➥msg[button];
   self.status = url;
   clearid =
setTimeout("window.parent.frames['Help'].document.forms[0].helpmsg.value =
➥''", 5000);
}

//-->
</SCRIPT>
</HEAD>

<BODY BGCOLOR=#FFFFFF>

<CENTER>

<FONT SIZE=1>
<STRONG>CONTENTS</STRONG>
<FONT SIZE=>

<HR SIZE=4 ALIGN=CENTER>

<A HREF="story1.html"
   TARGET="Main"
   ONMOUSEOVER="message('story1', this.href); return true;">
Story 1</A>

<HR SIZE=2 WIDTH=25% ALIGN=CENTER>

<A HREF="story2.html"
   TARGET="Main"
   ONMOUSEOVER="message('story2', this.href); return true;">
Story 2</A>

<HR SIZE=2 WIDTH=25% ALIGN=CENTER>
```

210

```
<A HREF="story3.html"
   TARGET="Main"
   ONMOUSEOVER="message('story3', this.href); return true;">
Story 3</A>

<HR SIZE=2 WIDTH=25% ALIGN=CENTER>

<A HREF="story4.html"
   TARGET="Main"
   ONMOUSEOVER="message('story4', this.href); return true;">
Story 4</A>

<HR SIZE=2 WIDTH=25% ALIGN=CENTER>

<A HREF="story5.html"
   TARGET="Main"
   ONMOUSEOVER="message('story5', this.href); return true;">
Story 5</A>

<HR SIZE=2 WIDTH=25% ALIGN=CENTER>

<A HREF="index.html"
   TARGET="_top"
   ONMOUSEOVER="message('index', this.href); return true;">
Index</A>

<HR SIZE=2 WIDTH=25% ALIGN=CENTER>

<A HREF=""
   TARGET="_top"
   ONMOUSEOVER="message('expand', this.href); return true;"
   ONCLICK="{
      alert('You can restore the button bar by\npressing the BACK button.');
      this.href = window.parent.frames['Main'].document.location;}">
Expand</A>

<HR SIZE=4 ALIGN=CENTER>

<SCRIPT LANGUAGE="JavaScript">
<!— Hide from non-Javascript browsers

function DisplayDate(dateString)
{
   d = new Date(dateString);

   return "" + (d.getMonth() + 1) + "/" + d.getDate() + "/" + d.getYear();
}

document.write("<FONT SIZE=2>");
document.write("<B>" + DisplayDate(document.lastModified) + "</B>");
document.write("<P><FONT SIZE=>");
```

211

```
//-->
</SCRIPT>


</CENTER>

</BODY>
</HTML>
```

Three final things to look at before moving on. First, look at the line:

```
<A HREF="index.html"
   TARGET="_top"
   ONMOUSEOVER="message('index', this.href); return true;">
Index</A>
```

Remember that assigning _top as a target effectively reloads *everything*, not just a particular frame. This is important to use, especially when you're linking to a page outside your eZine...one that doesn't support frames. Otherwise, your browser will try to load the new page into whatever frame you've specified (and if you don't specify a target, the current frame is assumed). Try to load your entire home page into a window the width of the table of contents and you'll understand why this is a problem.

Second, check out the line:

```
<A HREF=""
   TARGET="_top"
   ONMOUSEOVER="message('expand', this.href); return true;"
   ONCLICK="{
      alert('You can restore the button bar by\npressing the BACK button.');
      this.href = window.parent.frames['Main'].document.location;}">
Expand</A>
```

This does a _top load like the Index link, but it also hooks the onClick event handler to do something else very nifty. Before the URL is loaded, the HREF attribute is set to whatever the HREF is of the document currently displayed in the "Main" window. Think of it as a short way of saying, "Take whatever is currently loaded in 'Main' and reload it ... filling the full screen." Because this eliminates the frame containing the button bar, the addition of the alert() method provides an easy reminder to the user of how to get the bar back. See the figure on the next page.

Finally, the date displayed at the bottom of the table of contents has some properties of its own. It uses the lastModified property of the document object to retrieve the date that you last changed the document. With a little modification, it displays this date at the bottom of the screen. This is an easy way of showing the user *when* the eZine was created or changed. It also shows off one other important JavaScript feature: *you can use the SCRIPT tag more than once in a document.*

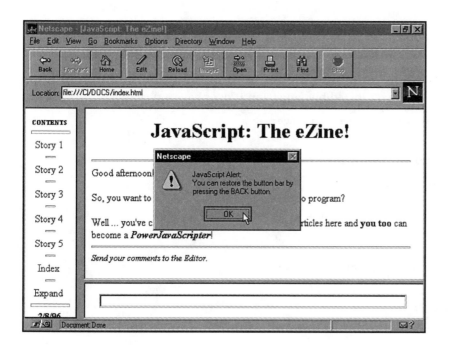

Clicking on Expand generates a reminder.

Stories

Okay, you've seen the tough stuff...you're almost done. The story1.html through story2.html files are nothing more than regular HTML files:

```
<!-- story1.html:  an example eZine story -->
<HTML>

<TITLE>JavaScript:  The eZine!</TITLE>

<BODY BGCOLOR=#FFFFFF>

<H1>Article 1</H1>

<HR>

Article 1 goes here.

</BODY>
</HTML>
```

that you can embellish to your heart's content. Just remember that if you add any links to pages *outside* your eZine, you'll want to add the TARGET="_top" attribute to the <A> tag; otherwise, things will start to look *very* strange.

213

The last part is the first part your readers will see: the cover page.

Cover (Page) Me with JavaScript

This example cover page isn't incredibly fancy, but it does have a nice touch:

```
<!-- coverpage.html:  eZine coverpage -->
<HTML>

<TITLE>JavaScript:  The eZine!</TITLE>

<BODY BGCOLOR=#FFFFFF>

<H1><CENTER>JavaScript:  The eZine!</CENTER></H1>

<HR>

<SCRIPT LANGUAGE="JavaScript">
<!-- Hide from non-Javascript browsers

d = new Date();
hour = d.getHours();

if(hour < 5)
{
    document.write("Doing a little late-night surfing, eh?");
}
else
if(hour < 6)
{
    document.write("Up early, I see!  Do you have your coffee?");
}
else
if(hour < 12)
{
    document.write("Good morning!");
}
else
if(hour < 18)
{
    document.write("Good afternoon!");
}
else
{
    document.write("Good evening!");
}

document.write("<P>");

//-->
</SCRIPT>
```

```
So, you want to do the JavaJive ... but you don't want to program?

<P>

Well ... you've come to the right place.  Check out the articles
here and <B>you too</B> can become a
<B><I>PowerJavaScripter</I></B>!

<HR>

<FONT SIZE=2>
<I>Send your comments to the <A HREF="mailto: ">Editor</A>.</I>
<FONT SIZE=>

</BODY>
</HTML>
```

Notice the JavaScript script in the <BODY>? It doesn't have any functions, just statements. This means that the statements will be executed after the page loads (and before it is displayed), even though the user hasn't clicked on anything. In this example, it uses the Date object to figure out what time of day the user is reading your eZine. Depending on the hour, it displays a different message.

There...you have all the pieces for a basic eZine. Now, get out there and publish!

The Least You Need To Know

This chapter took a final look at JavaScript by pulling different features together into a *real* application: an eZine. You learned how to:

➤ Use <FRAMES>.

➤ Catch the mouse movements and do something with them.

➤ Send information from one frame to another.

➤ Use <SCRIPT>s in both the <HEAD> and <BODY> of a page.

➤ Use more than one <SCRIPT> in a page.

➤ Use JavaScript statements outside a function, to dynamically change the document.

Chapter 20

What To Do When It Won't Work: Debugging Your Scripts

Bugs! Bugs! Bugs!

Whether it's ants at a picnic or cockroaches in the closet, bugs aren't most people's favorite critters. They get in things, spoil things, and generally cause a great deal of consternation. Their appearance usually gets a standard response: insecticide, a fly swatter, or a call to the exterminator. Bugs just aren't popular—unless you're a bug collector. (Any bug collectors out there, please accept my apology; I'll use the proper term: *entomologist*.)

Computer programs are no different from the rest of life. Programs don't always work and when they don't, it is said (in another humorous adaptation by programmers of yore), "This program has a *bug*." Whether it's termites in your walls or errors in your code, a bug is a bug, and a bug isn't good.

As you embark down the path to JavaScript enlightenment, you'll no doubt encounter a few bugs of your own. In the next few pages, you'll take a look at some of the more common causes of bugs and how to exterminate them.

The End Result

A bug can occur in two forms, one sometimes more insidious than the other. The first sort of bug makes itself quite obvious, like a cockroach in the middle of the kitchen. These bugs prevent the program from executing beyond a certain point due to some illegal statement. JavaScript can recognize these, and as we will discuss shortly, attempt to scold you.

The more insidious bugs, perhaps not unlike termites deep in the foundation, are those that are not illegal statements but are based on incorrect logic. Your program executes, because the statements are "legal," but the results are incorrect because your programming logic was flawed at some point. These can be extremely difficult to exterminate. We'll discuss such nasties second.

BZZT! The ERROR

When your bug is the result of an illegal statement, JavaScript will holler at you with a big pop-up alert box. To wit....

A JavaScript error message.

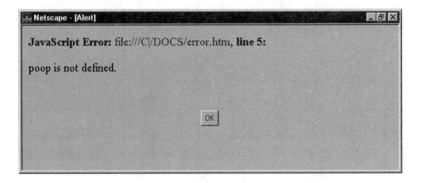

The first line of the error window identifies the file (or URL) where the bug occurred, while the second line tries to identify the bug. In this figure, the real problem was that a built-in JavaScript function was misspelled...but the error states that the function (as it was misspelled) was "not defined." This is the browser's way of saying, "I can't find a function by that name," and it makes an important point: errors that you may get in JavaScript will help tell where the bug occurred, but they may not tell you exactly what the error was. Therefore, figuring out what caused an error will sometimes require a bit of sleuthing.

Another thing you might notice is that the first line ends with the word "line," and a number. This is the line number in the HTML document where the error was found, which should at least help you find its location. Note that every line of the HTML file is counted as one line—not just those containing JavaScript code. Sometimes, unfortunately, the URL is longer than the error window, and the line number isn't displayed. You can try to grab the edge of the window with the mouse to resize it, but you won't have much luck. An unfortunate error (yep, a *bug*) in the Netscape browser is that if the URL is very long (or even moderately long), the rest of the line identifying the specific location of the bug will be cut off. Perhaps they'll fix this in a future version.

Because illegal statement errors are often the easier bugs to rid, the previous information is half the battle, if not more. JavaScript has already told you where and in which statement the problem lies. Thus, you can spelunk into the code with some accuracy to where the bug resides. From there, your final mission (which you should choose to accept) is to determine *why* the noted statement is illegal. There are several possibilities you should consider, which are detailed in the following sections.

Tpyo...er...Tipo...uh...Spelling Errors

The *biggest* sources of bugs, by far, are typographical errors. In a word: misspelling something important. Unlike humans, who can still get the general idea of what you're trying to say (whether you remember to put the "i" before the "e" or not), computers aren't so flexible. If it isn't spelled *exactly*, the computer doesn't have a clue what you mean. The problem with "typos," as they're called, is that (as you saw in the previous section) the browser isn't smart enough to say, "Ahh, you didn't spell it right." If it were, the browser would *know* what the right value was...right?

Instead, a typo can cause one of several things to happen:

➤ Nothing being displayed. This happens, for example, when you misspell an HTML tag. By definition of HTML, if a browser encounters a tag it doesn't recognize, it ignores it. This is especially a problem when you get really fancy with JavaScript, as you can use `document.write()` and string construction to dynamically build HTML statements to display (and since the HTML tags are being generated, they are harder to see).

➤ The HTML tag *being* displayed, when you want it to format text rather than show itself. Again, this is a side effect of the browser's interpretation of HTML. Sometimes, when a browser can't identify a tag, it assumes that the tag is actually text to display.

219

➤ A property value not being set or changed. The JavaScript-enabled browser will obediently set the "property" to the specific value, but since this isn't the same property that you wanted to adjust, the result will be different than you think.

➤ A "??? is undefined" message being displayed. This is most common with functions, since JavaScript *must* be able to find the function code whenever it encounters a function call.

And the list goes on…and on…and on. In a nutshell, spelling something wrong is a lot like trying to order in a French bistro when you don't speak French: depending on what word you get wrong, you could end up with anything from a scoop of sorbet to a boiled shoe. *Check your spelling!*

A Capital Idea

"Kissin' cousins" to spelling errors are errors in capitalization. The JavaScript documentation notes that JavaScript is *case-sensitive* (upper- and lowercase matter). Case *is* important, and capitalization *is* critical.

Many functions, methods, and properties in JavaScript are "compound words" made up of more than one word slapped together (for example, getDate()). In most cases, the second word is capitalized while the first word is not. If you try to type in a JavaScript component and don't capitalize the second (or third, or fourth) word, you'll probably generate an error.

The Appendix, "JavaScript: The Complete Reference," which lists all the components of JavaScript—and Chapters 6 through 14—show the proper capitalization for JavaScript functions, objects, and properties.

Matching Mates

There are many occasions in JavaScript programming when you use paired bookends, such as brackets { }, parentheses ( ), and both single- and double-quotation marks.

As with socks in the laundry, improperly matching pairs will result in a statement of problematic fashion. It is vital that every open bracket and parenthesis have an appropriate closing mate somewhere further down in the code. Where people most often lose track is when they are nesting parentheses or brackets, such as when using a loop statement within a loop statement.

It is not uncommon to find multiple closing parentheses or brackets at the end of a series of statements, which pair up with a series of opening mates earlier on. It might look strange, but an eye for an eye and a bracket for a bracket, as they say (don't they?). Something to watch for.

JavaScript Errors

If you're still stumped and you're *positive* you spelled everything correctly, then move to Phase 2: interpreting the JavaScript error message. JavaScript has a handful of errors that it kicks up for a variety of situations. Take a look at each and what to check for if you encounter one. For purposes of the "error lineup," look at the second line of text displayed in the error window. Any parts of the message that may change will be represented by a string of question marks (?????).

????? Is Not Defined

You've already met this guy. He's trying to tell you that either you misspelled something or have forgotten to include the function *body* (the guts of the function) in the script. It might also mean that the function requires an uppercase letter or two, so you might want to check the function against what you find here in the book.

????? Is Not a Function

You tried to call an object's function (for example, `document.write()`) and the function doesn't exist. Check the spelling and capitalization.

????? Is Not a Numeric Literal

You attempted to perform some sort of math operation on a string. For example, if you wanted to take the numeric value 2 and display on the screen 2nd, trying something like:

```
document.write(2 + "nd");
```

will generate this error. This is because, as JavaScript *evaluates* the expression inside the parentheses, the *type* of the expression is whatever variable type JavaScript encounters *first* when reading from left to right (or whatever way is the default for evaluation...using more than one pair of parentheses can change this order). In this example, JavaScript assumes that you want to print out a numeric value, but then you try to tack a string on the end (a no-no).

To get around this, you need to "convert" the expression to a string before you start evaluating it. You can easily do this by adding a "null" or "empty" string in front of the number:

```
document.write("" + 2 + "nd");
```

The Dreaded "Crash"

Sometimes, things get *really* hairy and you're presented with the infamous "illegal operation" dialog box.

Something's seriously wrong!

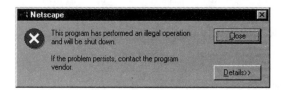

Netscape itself shuts down. First rule: *don't panic*. Chances are you've done something simple that, while the browser should have a better way of handling it, blindly charges forward until it gets hopelessly stuck.

A common way to cause this error (if you really like *creating* bugs instead of fixing them) is to try to treat a numeric value like a string and manipulate it. For example:

```
var n = 264;
document.write(n.substring(0, 1));
```

will definitely cause a crash. However, if you convert the number to a string *first*:

```
var n = 264;
var strN = "" + n;
document.write(strN.substring(0, 1));
```

then everything's fine.

Along the same lines, calling a method of a numeric variable (even if it's not a string method) will also cause Netscape to explode. There isn't any "solution" other than the punchline to that old joke: don't do it. Actually, the fault isn't yours, it is Netscape's—it should generate an error in such circumstances, not crash. Presumably, future revisions to Netscape will weed out these landmines.

Design Errors (or "Why Did My House Just Collapse?")

Often sneakier and much more difficult to track down are outcome bugs. These are not the result of an illegal statement that JavaScript cannot understand. They are the result of errors in program design, which produce the wrong results when you execute the program.

Think of an entire JavaScript program (or any computer program, for that matter) as a large exercise in logic *and* grammar. Even if your grammar is impeccable (JavaScript makes no error complaints), your logic may be flawed. It may be flawed in one tiny section of code, several tiny sections of code, or perhaps your entire design is logically flawed.

Ultimately, the only solution to these problems requires three possible steps:

1. Locate the region of code likely to contain the design flaw.

2. Follow the logic and redesign where necessary.

3. Return to step 1 if the problem persists.

Finding the Holes Where the Rain Gets In

Suppose you've written a JavaScript program that calculates a loan payment schedule. The program contains no syntax errors, but the alleged payment amount it reports is clearly incorrect. You have a design flaw (don't feel too down; virtually every program contains *some* design flaw the first time around).

To locate the region of code where the flaw is most likely, you have to consider the program itself. Presumably, you have several functions in such a program, each of which performs some calculation. Therefore, any of those would make good suspects at this point, since a wrong final tally is probably caused by an erroneous calculation.

Look at the sections of code you might suspect. Read them over carefully and follow the logic in your mind. Should no flaw be immediately apparent, then dip into the programmer's toolbox for handy debugging tool number one: the inside scooper.

One of the most revealing ways to track down design bugs is to gain some insight into what is going on "behind the scenes" while the program executes. A very common way to do this is to stick new lines of code here and there that display the current values of particular variables. This way, when you execute the program again, you have a better idea of what is going on "in there." In JavaScript, I commonly do this using the `window.alert()` method. For example, let's imagine that my suspect code looks like this:

```
function evalform (address)
{ crucial = address.indexOf("@") ;
    if (crucial == -1)
    { window.alert ("Your e-mail address is invalid! You are an abject
    ➥liar!") ;
        return false }
    else
      { message = "You entered " + address + " -- is this correct?";
        return window.confirm (message) } ;
}
```

To check behind the scenes, I might like to find out just what JavaScript thinks the values of address and crucial are. Thus, I could stick the following two lines just after the second line above:

```
window.alert ("Value of address is "+address);
window.alert ("Value of crucial is "+crucial);
```

Now, when the program is executed again, the values for those variables will be displayed, giving you some clue as to whether they are at least what you were expecting them to be or not. If they aren't, then you must begin your investigation again, but at least you've narrowed it down (do remember, though, to remove these lines of code once the program is working, since they're not intended to be part of the final program).

In addition to variable values, another common test is for program flow. Did the execution even reach your function? Perhaps your function was never even executed due to some other design flaw in your logic. You can test for this simply, just like before: stick a line somewhere within the questionable function that you're sure will generate some action if the function is, in fact, being executed. Perhaps, window.alert ("Hi function bob was just called"), for instance.

Sigh and Rebuild

Using some combination of the previous example—perhaps many times, if necessary—you will eventually track down the region of code that is logically flawed.

From there, you must determine the flaw and rebuild. The only sure way to determine the flaw, once you're certain you have the right portion of code, is to step through it mentally, bit by bit. In a Zen-like way, imagine that *you are* the computer, and attempt to interpret the code exactly as the computer would. Perhaps grab a pencil and paper and write down the values of variables as you progress through your mental exercise. This can be very tough work. Sometimes, the logic flaw will pop out to you quickly. In a most difficult case, you might be stumped. This is the "art" of programming.

Clear heads help, so time away from the screen can be of use. Equally useful are smart people, or at least experienced ones, and so there are many places on the Internet where people exchange programming hints and pose questions to others. Check out the Usenet newsgroup comp.lang.javascript for just such chatter—and support.

The Least You Need To Know

Bugs are a common problem when you're creating programs, and working with JavaScript is no exception. JavaScript tries to provide information on where the bug is and what it is, but it isn't the most accurate analysis of the problem. Furthermore, a particular bug can generate an error that makes no sense whatsoever...unless you understand a few tricks.

For the most part, mistakes in spelling or capitalization are the worst culprits when it comes to bugs. The three questions you, as a JavaScripter, should ask are:

➤ Is everything spelled correctly?

➤ Is everything capitalized correctly?

➤ Do all my open parentheses and brackets have an accompanying closed bracket or parenthesis?

If your code is free from grammatical errors, it might be suffering from design flaw. You need to examine the logic of your code.

➤ Insert `window.alert()` methods at various places that reveal the value of a variable. This gives you behind-the-scenes insight.

➤ Use `window.alert()` methods to indicate that a function is even being called at all.

225

Chapter 21

Ideas

Document Madness

Take the first example (your "Hello World" script in Chapter 15) and extend it to do other things to the page. Remember that you can access the document object from inside a JavaScript function or outside. Experiment with:

➤ Writing HTML tags inside the <SCRIPT> tag.

➤ Changing other attributes of the document (text color, link color, and so on).

➤ Placing the <SCRIPT> tag in the BODY of the document instead of the HEAD, so that any JavaScript statements that aren't part of a function are executed whenever the script loads.

➤ Use script hiding to create parts of the document that are visible only to people running JavaScript-enabled browsers.

To take one example, imagine that you'd like to present the user with an opening greeting and important message. You can ensure that the user reads this message before proceeding with the page by inserting a `window.alert()` method immediately after the `<BODY>` tag.

This will ensure its execution every time the page is loaded. Regardless of what else is in this page, you might write code such as:

```
<BODY>
<SCRIPT language="JavaScript">
window.alert("Thank you for visiting the Spice Tours 96. Before you
read on, you must be 21 to continue.");
</SCRIPT>
...rest of page HTML code and possibly more JavaScript...
</BODY>
```

Now, whenever a user accesses this page, the first encounter he'll have will look like this.

Disclaimers—the wave of the future.

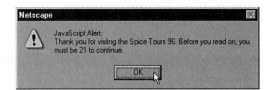

Custom Pages

Using the `random()` function you cooked up in Chapter 16, create a page that changes its appearance based on:

➤ The time of day

➤ The day of the week

➤ The month

➤ Whether it's a holiday

Or just cook up something that's different every time a user loads it. Try changing the color, the text that's displayed, or both. Many users create pages that never change again, resulting in a certain staleness. You can program in the preceding techniques to spice up a page without a lot of owner maintenance. Consider this function, which is called when the page is opened in a browser:

```
function colorday();
{
    dateobj = new Date();
```

```
    today = dateobj.getDay();
    if (today==1) { document.bgColor="blue" } ;
    if (today==2) { document.bgColor="teal" } ;
    if (today>3) || (today==0) { document.bgColor="salmon" }
}
```

Using this function, the current day would be determined and assigned to today (in JavaScript, 0 is Sunday, 1 is Monday, and so forth). From there, you simply use a series of if...then statements to assign various colors to the background depending on which day it is. Mondays are blue—clever!

Web Roulette

The window object has a method that allows you to load another URL. Write a script that randomly picks a URL from a list and takes the user there at the click of a button. For this, you'd rely on the method window.open(), which would spawn a new browser window and connect to a URL you specify. Recall that this method is described in detail in Chapter 11, and it is also referenced in the appendix reference of objects and functions ("JavaScript: The Complete Reference").

The design behind this should be comprehensible by now. This program would require three key components:

➤ An array of URLs to choose from. You'd construct this array just as you did in Chapter 16, with the MakeArray() function.

➤ The random() function, which will choose one of the URLs from the array.

➤ The window.open() method.

Given that you covered each of these components in detail previously in the book, a simple Web Roulette script should be quick work—allowing you that much more time to design the nifty roulette wheel graphics!

Tour Guide

Using the window object's URL loading method, create a sequence of pages that automatically take the user from one page to the next. You could do this as a "slide show" of your favorite work or for an automated "kiosk" that displays your company's products.

Games, Games, Games

Extend the blackjack example to handle

➤ Betting.

➤ Aces that can be 1 or 11.

➤ The house hitting on "soft 17".

➤ Splits, double-downs, insurance, and so on.

Or try your hand at writing a different game. Perhaps Poker, roulette, craps, or Hearts. You can include graphics of the cards and actually display the hands.

Would you like to play a game? By Stephen Wassell.

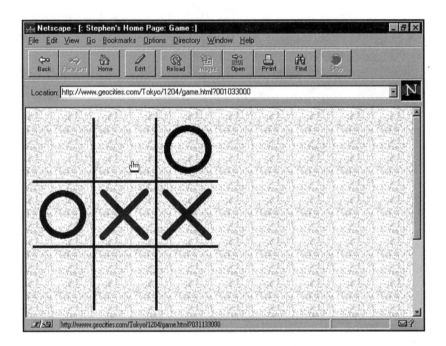

Sell T-Shirts

A basic catalog implementation might revolve around T-shirt sales. You might, for instance, include a series of images or text descriptions representing the clever witticism on each shirt.

These images or text may either be designed as HTML links, or standard HTML text accompanied by an "Add this item to shopping cart" button. Use an onClick event to catch the order, and then add the price of the shirt to a cumulative total, just as you did in Chapter 9 with your mug-selling venture.

Once the visitor clicks on some appropriate "Go to Cashier" link, you can construct an invoice and output it to the Web browser using string concatenations and the `document.write()` method. From here, you can even program in the option to remove items from the cart, in case the user has a last minute change of heart.

A Script That Writes Scripts

JavaScript's text handling allows you to build text strings out of parts of strings. Create a script that allows a user to pick options from a table and then generates an HTML document that incorporates those selections. For example, you can create a "build your own home page" or a "list of favorite links" script.

Spreadsheet

A spreadsheet is nothing more than a table that performs operations on the data in its cells. Write a script that makes a table act like a spreadsheet. With the substring parsing capabilities of JavaScript, you can even build "formulas" that are analyzed when the user clicks Compute.

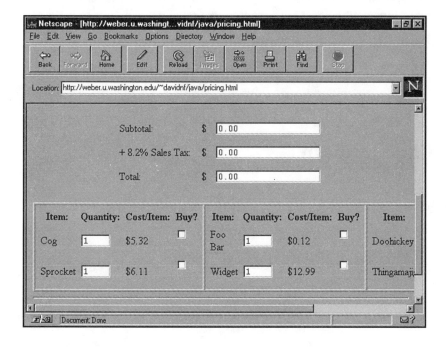

One form of a spreadsheet: a running purchase total, by David Nagy-Farkas.

Database Query Front-End

Given a table of options, the user can select various components and have the script build a query (using SQL, for example) that can be submitted to a database. To actually utilize this, you would need access to the Web server's CGI interface since JavaScript can't read information outside its document.

Loan Amortization

Take the loan calculator from Chapter 17 and extend it to compute *any* data field, based on the information provided in the other fields. You can also extend the script to compute and display the principal and interest amounts of each payment for the life of the loan.

Tutoring

You can design a JavaScript-based Website that offers tutoring services in a variety of subjects. Programming the informational text itself would be simple enough, and even customizing it to an individual user could rely on string concatenations and `document.write()` methods.

Testing skills in either flashcard or multiple-choice format could rely on regular buttons and radio buttons. Questions could either be presented in a relevant sequence or using the `random()` function. Use event handling to interpret the student's answers and provide context-sensitive responses—perhaps correct answers, explanation, or repeated attempts at the question.

Keep track of cumulative right/wrong totals and output a customized "report card" at the end of each lesson.

And the Scripting Goes On

Here are some other scripting ideas:

➤ A "quote of the day" script

➤ A full-blown calculator (simple, financial, or scientific)

➤ A board game, like Monopoly, Mastermind, or Yahtzee

➤ Whatever else you can think of!

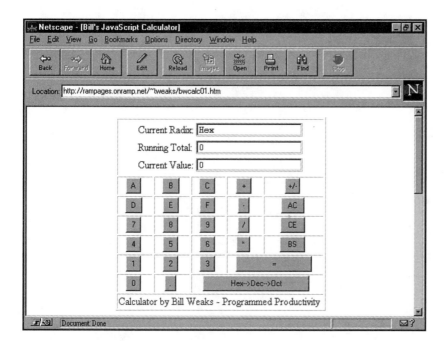

*An inspired
JavaScript calculator,
by Bill Weaks.*

The Least You Need To Know

You've only brushed the surface of what you can do with JavaScript. As a powerful extension to HTML and the Web, you can do *almost* anything with JavaScript that you can do with Java, but without having to write full-blown programs and compile them. Just about anything you can think of can be scripted, and, in this chapter, you looked at some possibilities for future exploration.

The list of ideas here is by no means exhaustive. What you can do with JavaScript is limited only by your imagination. Take a little time to explore on the Web. Check out some of the sites covered in Chapter 5. See what other JavaScripters are up to. Maybe something someone else has cooked up will fire off another idea for you to try.

When you've created your script and it is working "perfectly," load it onto your Web site and invite the world to stop by. JavaScript: better than cappuccino and twice as fun!

Chapter 22

Stepping Up to Straight Java

In This Chapter

➤ What *is* Java?

➤ The Java Developer's Kit

➤ Integrating Java into HTML

➤ How to get up and writing your own applets

JavaScript's Big Brother

If you've made it this far in the book...good for you! As you've seen, JavaScript is a *very* powerful language for extending the capabilities of your World Wide Web pages. No doubt, as you've surfed around checking out other authors' uses of JavaScript (okay, and peeked at their source code to get more ideas), you've encountered talk about a thing called *Java*. If you're the curious sort, you're probably wondering just what *Java* is...and whether it's worth looking into.

Java is a full-blown programming language, designed for the purpose of providing "truly interactive" content through the World Wide Web; Java is the language on which *JavaScript* is based. Developed by Sun Microsystems, Java attempts to bridge the "multiple platform" stew that exists on the Internet by creating applications (called *applets*) that will run on *any* computer of *any* type…as long as you have a Java-enabled browser handy. The same Java applet will run on Windows 95, Windows NT, UNIX, and Macintosh, with no need for customizing the applet to the particular computer.

Java Relies on a "Virtual Computer"

In order to pull off the trick of being able to work on a variety of platforms, Java applets actually run on what's called the *Java Virtual Machine*. Look at it this way: There are programs available today that allow you to run Windows software on a Macintosh, or UNIX software on a Windows computer, and so on. They do this by *emulating* the behavior of a particular computer type (they "pretend" to be a Mac or Windows or UNIX machine so that the software thinks it's running on the correct computer).

The Java Virtual Machine is another type of emulator, but it doesn't emulate Mac, Windows, or UNIX. Rather, it pretends to be a totally different type of system; and by defining *what* the Java computer can and cannot do, Sun was able to create a program that, no matter what physical hardware it's run on, will always look like a Java computer to the applets.

Because Java is a programming language (like Pascal, BASIC, C, or C++), to work with it, you have to write a *program*. Java programs are similar to JavaScript scripts, except that they are much more extensive and include a lot of additional material necessary to successfully complete the next phase of Java development: *compiling*. Compiling an applet means to take the program that you've written and run a special program on it that converts it from "near-human-readable" format to "Java-machine-readable" format (this is called *bytecode*)—so that a Java browser can then run the applet.

Java is an "object-oriented" programming language most closely related to C++. "Object-oriented" is a difficult concept to explain clearly, but in essence, it means that the language revolves around manipulating end-results rather than designing the tools for manipulation. An object-oriented sculptor, for instance, would be more concerned with melding together various blocks of clay than the tools that carve the clay initially. The popular construction game Lego is a nice example of an object-oriented activity.

In this chapter, you're not going to dig deep into the bowels of Java. Like JavaScript, Java is still evolving, and by the time you're holding this book in your hands, there will no doubt be newer tools for creating Java applets. Instead, you'll take a quick glance at what it takes to get an applet put together and how to link applets into your HTML pages.

To start, you'll need to do a little surfing and pick up a copy of the collection of utilities Sun puts out to aid Java programmers: the *Java Developer's Kit.*

Java Browsing

As with JavaScript, you need to use a Java-capable browser to run Java applets. At the time of this writing, there are two Java-capable browsers: HotJava from Sun and Netscape Navigator 2.0 (32-bit, although the 16-bit version is rumored to have Java support by the time you read this). It is likely that the other major browsers, such as Microsoft's Internet Explorer, will gain Java capabilities in the near future. In all cases, browsers for 16-bit platforms such as Windows 3.1 are less likely to see Java.

HotJava from Sun is the other current Java-capable browser, so let's take a quick peek at it. At this time, HotJava can only view "alpha" stage applets, and Navigator 2.0 can only view "beta" stage applets. In time, these two distinctions should erode.

The HotJava browser is available from Sun's Web site, at

    http://java.sun.com

Once you download the Windows 95 version, simply run the .exe file and it will self-extract. From there, launch HotJava by running the file hotjava.exe, which is in the newly created hotjava\bin directory.

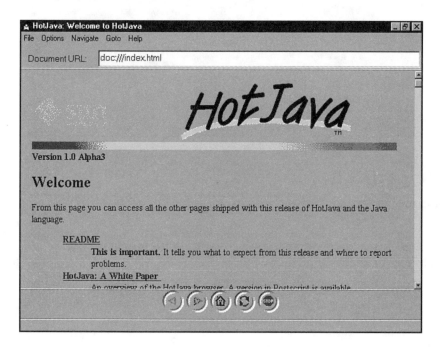

The HotJava Web browser.

HotJava is not as feature-laden a browser as Netscape Navigator, but it is simple to use. To connect to a new URL, either enter it into the URL Location box at the top of the window, or choose the menu commands **File, Open**.

At the bottom of the HotJava browser window are the five navigation buttons: Back, Forward, Home, Reload Current, and Stop.

You don't need to do anything specific to enable Java; merely opening a Web page that contains a compatible (alpha) Java applet will cause it to be loaded and run. A good place to begin is the Java Demos page, available among several other preset pages in the HotJava Help menu.

The HotJava Help menu.

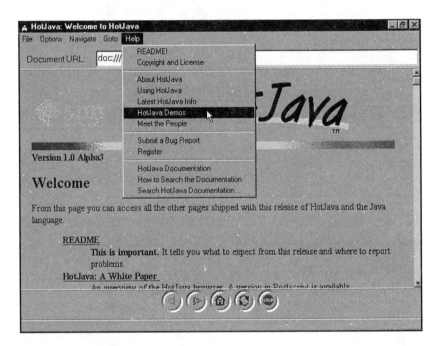

The Java Developer's Kit

Before you dive into Java programming, you need to pick up a copy of the *Java Developer's Kit* (*JDK* for short). The JDK includes:

➤ A *compiler* to turn your applet program code into *bytecode*, the language the *interpreter* understands.

➤ An *interpreter* that runs your applets, one line at a time.

➤ An *applet viewer* for testing and running applets.

238

➤ A *debugger* to help track down problems in your applet code.

➤ A collection of example applets to play with.

➤ A huge collection of documentation files, in browser (HTML) format.

➤ An *upgrade utility* to convert old applets to the new standard.

In a nutshell, the JDK has *everything* the budding Java programmer needs to start.

Why Include an "Upgrade Utility"?

There are actually two different versions of Java floating about in CyberSpace: the one that came with the HotJava browser and the one in the JDK. At the time the JDK was released, the Java language was "frozen" (no more major changes). However, there were some significant changes in Java between the release of HotJava and the introduction of the JDK.

To make the transition from 1.0 Alpha 3 (the HotJava version) to 1.0 beta (the JDK version), the JDK includes a utility to help convert old applets.

What? How much does it cost? Put your checkbook away; the JDK is available *free* off the Internet. Simply fire up your browser (any browser will do) and point it at the Sun Java Homesite at:

```
http://java.sun.com/
```

Browser your way into the Developers section and you'll find the links for downloading the JDK for your machine. The file you'll be downloading is rather large (4M or more), so once you start the download process, go get a cup of coffee.

Once the file has been downloaded,

1. Move it to the root of the drive where you want to install the JDK (c:\ for example). Make sure that you have *at least 5 Megabytes* of free space on the disk before going to the next step (that's 5 Megabytes *after* you copy the file to it).

2. Run the file (either from a DOS window, **File**, **Run** from Windows NT, or the **Run** option after pressing Windows 95's Start button).

239

*Links to download
the Java Developer's
Kit.*

The file will automatically unpack itself, create a \java directory and a bunch of subdirectories, and copy a ton of files into these new directories. When all this is done, you can delete the original file (or store it in a safe place, if you like to keep a copy around…just in case).

An .EXE File That Unpacks Itself?

This is called a *self-extracting archive* and needs only to be "run" by you. In Windows, you can choose **File**, **Run** from the Program Manager, or in Windows 95 choose **Run** from the Start Menu on the taskbar. From there, the file will decompress and install itself.

Where Are the Manuals?

One of the nice things about the JDK is the existence of very thorough documentation. What documentation, you ask? Well, if you fire up your browser and open the **\java\progguide\index.html** file, you'll be introduced to one of the nicest documentation collections on Java (and the JDK) available:

JDK online documentation.

Now, scroll down a bit. Below the **Getting Started** heading, you'll find Duke, the Java mascot (a cute little guy who looks amazingly like the Starfleet insignia)...and he's *waving* at you! You guessed it. Duke's a Java applet!

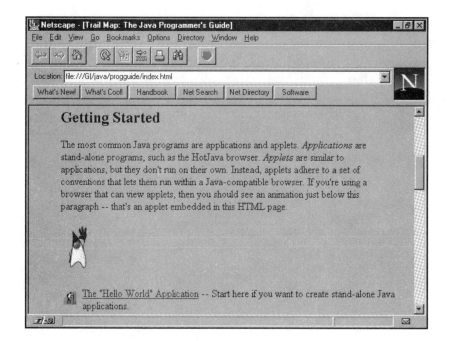

Duke waves a friendly greeting. Resist the temptation to wave back!

All of the documentation that comes with the JDK is available in HTML format, so you might want to browse around a bit right now before going further in the book. One point, though: not all the HTML files in the JDK are linked to the other files. The JDK contains a collection of document sets. You can simply list all of the JDK help files with the File Manager or the Windows Explorer, and double-click on any of the HTML files you like. They'll then be opened into your browser.

Back from your local surfing? Good! Take a quick detour into HTML and see how Java applets connect to Web pages: the <APPLET> tag.

Introducing the <APPLET> Tag

Just as JavaScript scripts are identified by their own custom HTML tag (the <SCRIPT> tag you met back in Chapter 4), Java applets are included in Web pages through their own custom tag: the <APPLET> tag. As with other HTML tags, browsers that don't support Java will simply ignore the tag, so you can safely create Java-enabled pages that don't limit their viewing to Java-enabled users (however, you *will* need to do a little more HTML to provide those who haven't caught up with the times something to look at).

The <APPLET> tag's structure is relatively simple. Actually, there are two tags that work together: APPLET and PARAMS. The <APPLET> tag looks like this:

```
<APPLET CODE="appletFile" WIDTH=pixels HEIGHT=pixels>
<!-- Alternate HTML code goes here -->
</APPLET>
```

Check This Out...

The CODE Attribute Must Be Relative
Unlike most other HTML tags and attributes that use URLs, the CODE attribute cannot be an absolute URL; it must point to something *relative* to the current directory the HTML files are in.

The CODE attribute identifies the applet program and is a file with a ".class" extension located in the same directory as the HTML document. To make your page do something for those poor souls who don't have a Java-enabled browser, you can place additional HTML statements inside the <APPLET> tag. Java browsers will ignore these statements; non-Java browsers will ignore the <APPLET> tag (which works out quite well, don't you think?).

The WIDTH and HEIGHT attributes define the size of the applet on the page. An applet's size is specified in pixels.

Additionally, there are several other optional attributes that you can add to the <APPLET> tag to modify the behavior of the tag.

CODEBASE

The CODEBASE attribute lets you specify a URL (directory path) where your applet .class files are located (if they're in a different place from your HTML documents). As previously mentioned, if you don't specify CODEBASE, the applets are assumed to be in the same directory as the HTML files.

ALT

If, for some reason, a browser understands the <APPLET> tag but can't run applets (for example, a browser that's being upgraded to handle Java but isn't quite there yet), you can specify some text to display with the ALT attribute. This is similar to the ALT attribute of the <IMG> tag, which displays the specified text string on browsers that can't show graphics (text-based browsers).

NAME

The NAME attribute does the same thing for <APPLET> that it does for other HTML tags: it gives the applet a name, allowing other applets on the same page to locate and talk with each other (much the same way JavaScript uses NAME to find and talk to different frames or fields in forms).

ALIGN

Just like the <IMG> tag attribute of the same name, ALIGN controls how the applet is lined up. Acceptable values of the attribute are LEFT, RIGHT, TOP, TEXTTOP, MIDDLE, ABSMIDDLE, BASELINE, BOTTOM, and ABSBOTTOM.

VSPACE and HSPACE

These attributes also behave the same way their <IMG> tag counterparts do: they specify the amount of space (in pixels) to leave above and below (VSPACE) and on each side (HSPACE) of the applet.

Passing Applet Parameters

Those of you who remember the days of DOS (those glory days before Windows, X-Windows, and the Macintosh made pictures out of everything) might recall that you could run some programs by typing the name of the program and adding additional information on the command line before pressing the Enter key. These additional pieces of information were called *parameters*.

You Can Spot Old (pre-JDK) Applets Easily
If, as you surf the Web, you come across an applet that's implemented in HTML using an <APP> tag instead of the JDK <APPLET> tag, you've found an old applet.

It's possible to create applets that can take *parameters* (in the case of applets, parameters are additional options that are unique to the applet and aren't covered by other <APPLET> attributes). Passing parameter values to an applet is done with the <PARAM> tag. <PARAM> tags are placed after the <APPLET> tag and before any of the "alternate HTML" statements and the </APPLET> tag. The <PARAM> tag looks like this:

```
<PARAM NAME=appletAttribute VALUE=value>
```

where NAME identifies the particular attribute and VALUE identifies its value. If you have more than one parameter, you use more than one <PARAM> tag. Inside the applet code, you access the values passed in with <PARAM> with the getParameter() function.

Java with Class

Java and JavaScript share many things, one of which being "objects" or things that give you access to different parts of a Web page. Java extends this by allowing you to create your own types of objects, as well as offering up a larger collection of "canned" objects. Predefined objects in Java are bundled together in "classes" or collections of objects that share a common purpose.

Classes are at the heart of what makes Java an object-oriented language. A class is like a library of objects, all of which inherit certain characteristics from the class itself. "Class" is a hierarchical concept—one class could be a subset of a higher-level class. In Java there is a term "abstract class," which is a parental class containing many child classes. In this case, though, the abstract class is never directly used—it is defined solely to provide the "genes" for its children classes.

If any of this seems confusing, that's because it is. That is why there are entire books written about object-oriented programming and Java in particular. Now, though, at least you have a taste for what object-orientedness is about—modules that are part of larger modules, which are part of yet larger modules.

C++ is a very common object-oriented programming language that also revolves around these class concepts. One major difference between C++ and Java, in terms of how they deal with classes, is that Java programs can more easily withstand changes in class definitions without breaking any programs based on the previous definitions. In C++, on the other hand, if you change any class definitions, every program written using the previous definitions needs to be recompiled. For this reason, Sun calls Java "dynamic."

Hello World!

Let's close with a quick look at making your own Java applet. As with JavaScript, you'll use the traditional "Hello World" program. The Java program looks like this:

```
/* HelloWorld.java: Hello World...Java Style */
public class HelloWorld
{
    public static void main(String args[])
    {
        System.out.println("Hello World!");
    }
}
```

Remember to save this file as **HelloWorld.java**. Now, once you type that in, you need to compile the applet. Get yourself to a DOS prompt (you'll need to open a DOS window to do this) and type:

```
javac HelloWorld.java
```

Finally, you can run your new applet right from DOS by typing:

```
java HelloWorld
```

Congratulations! You've just taken another big step: Java programming!

Command Line? I'm Running a Mac!

If you're running a Macintosh (or a PowerPC), you're probably a bit confused by the reference to a "command line": the Mac operating system doesn't have one. Does this mean that Mac users are out of luck when it comes to creating Java applets?

Sadly, at this moment, the answer is, "Yes, unless you're willing to spend some money." There are no environments or library sets (source code) for Java compiling on the Mac available for free off the Internet. Several companies (Symantec at http://www.symantec.com/ and Metrowerks at http://www.metrowerks.com/ to name two) have announced that they will be integrating Java applet creation into their compilers...but their products aren't available yet.

Natural Intelligence, however, does market a package called *Roaster* that gives Mac users the ability to compile and develop Java applets on the Mac from inside the Mac OS. For more information, check out Natural's web page at http://www.natural.com/.

Keep in mind, however, that even if you were to start writing your own Java applets, there still isn't a Web browser available for the Mac that supports Java (that, too, is "coming soon"), which is another good reason to stick with JavaScript: it runs on Mac, IBM, and UNIX right now!

The Least You Need To Know

You learned that Java is a programming language, similar to C++ or Delphi that is built around *objects*. Java is similar to JavaScript, but Java also allows you to create your own object and class types, *extending* the language to do what you need it to.

Java programs are called *applets*. Once a program (applet) has been written, it must be *compiled* before it can be incorporated into an HTML document. After compiling the applet, it's linked into a Web page through the <APPLET> tag.

JavaScript: The Complete Overview

For those of you who want everything in one place, here's a complete reference to what makes up JavaScript. All JavaScript objects, object properties and methods are accessed via:

```
object.xxxxx;
```

where *object* is the particular object and *xxxxx* is the property or method.

The <SCRIPT> Tag

Indicates that the enclosed text is JavaScript. Additionally, it is good practice to hide the JavaScript statements within a <COMMENT> tag.

Syntax

```
<SCRIPT LANGUAGE="JavaScript">
<!-- hide from non-Java browsers -->

<!-- JavaScript statements and functions go here -->

//-->
</SCRIPT>
```

Attributes

LANGUAGE   Defines the scripting language—in this case, "JavaScript." This attribute *must* be included, unless the SRC attribute is used *and* the extension of the URL defined by SRC is .js.

SRC   Defines a URL (alternate file) where the JavaScript statements are located. JavaScript files should end with .js.

The window Object

The top-level object for each HTML document.

Properties

frames[ ]   Array of child frames. Frames are stored in the order defined in the source document.

frames.length   Number of defined child frames.

self   The current window.

parent   The parent window (if the current window is a subwindow in a <FRAMESET>).

top   The top-most window, which owns *all* visible frames. Top-most windows are their own parents.

status   The message appearing in the browser status window.

defaultStatus   The default message appearing in the browser status window, when the status property is not in effect.

name   The internal name, if any, defined for the window when opened with a window.open() method.

Methods

alert("message")   Displays a "JavaScript Alert" dialog box with the specified message.

confirm("message")   Displays a "Confirm" dialog box (one with OK and Cancel buttons) with the specified message. Returns TRUE if the user clicks the OK button, FALSE if the Cancel button is clicked.

prompt("message")   Displays a "prompt" dialog box, which queries the user to input data in response to a displayed message.

open("URL," "name")   Opens a new client window, give it the specified name (equivalent to the NAME attribute of a <FRAME> tag), and load the specified URL.

close( )   Closes the window.

The frame Object

Recall that a frame is a subwindow of the entire browser window. As such, the frame object contains almost all the same properties and methods as the window object.

The frame object lacks only the status, defaultStatus, and name properties of the window object.

The location Object

Contains information on the current URL.

Properties

href   The entire URL as a JavaScript string.

protocol   A string consisting of the first part of the URL (including the first colon), for example **http:**.

host   A string consisting of the hostname:port part of the URL, for example **\\www.winternet.com\~sjwalter**.

hostname   A string consisting of the hostname part of the URL, for example **www.winternet.com**.

port   A string consisting of the port (if any) from the URL. The port is a numerical value that (if it exists) is located after the hostname and is preceded by a colon. If there is no specified port, this string is empty.

pathname   A string consisting of everything in the URL after the third slash, for example **~sjwalter\javascript\index.html**.

hash   A string consisting of any text after the # (CGI parameters).

search   A string consisting of any text after the ? (CGI parameters).

The document Object

Contains information on the current document.

249

Properties

title   Current document title. If no title defined, `title` contains `"Untitled"`.

location   Full URL of the document.

lastModified   A `Date` object-compatible string containing the date the document was last modified.

referrer   Contains the URL of the calling document; that is, the page from which the user linked to the current page.

bgColor   Background color, expressed as a hexadecimal RGB value compatible with HTML syntax (for example, `"#FFFFFF"` for white). Equivalent to the `BGCOLOR` attribute of the `<BODY>` tag.

fgColor   Foreground (text) color, expressed as a hexadecimal RGB value compatible with HTML syntax. Equivalent to the `TEXT` attribute of the `<BODY>` tag.

linkColor   Hyperlink color, expressed as a hexadecimal RGB value compatible with HTML syntax. Equivalent to the `LINK` attribute of the `<BODY>` tag.

vlinkColor   Visited hyperlink color, expressed as a hexadecimal RGB value compatible with HTML syntax. Equivalent to the `VLINK` attribute of the `<BODY>` tag.

alinkColor   Activated (after button press, before button release) hyperlink color, expressed as a hexadecimal RGB value compatible with HTML syntax. Equivalent to the `ALINK` attribute of the `<BODY>` tag.

forms[ ]   Array of `form` objects in the document, in the order specified in the source. Each form has its own `form` object.

forms.length   The number of `form` objects within the document.

links[ ]   Array objects corresponding to all HREF links in the document, in the order specified in the source.

links.length   The number of HREF links in the document.

anchors[ ]   Array of all "named" anchors (`<A NAME="">...</A>` tags) within the document, in the order specified in the source.

anchors.length   The number of named anchors in the document.

Methods

write("string")   Writes *string* to the current window. *string* may include HTML tags.

writeln("string")   Performs the same as `write()`, but adds a carriage return. This affects only preformatted text (inside a `<PRE>` or `<XMP>` tag).

clear( )   Clears the window.

close( )   Closes the window.

The form Object

Corresponds to a `<FORM>` tag set defined in a document. Each `<FORM>` tag has its own `forms` object.

Properties

name   String value of the NAME attribute of `<FORM>`.

method   Numeric value of the METHOD attribute of `<FORM>`: `"0"` = GET; `"1"` = POST.

action   String value of the ACTION attribute of `<FORM>`.

target   Window targeted for form response after the form has been submitted, as specified in the `<FORM>` tag.

elements[index]   The `elements` property is an object that contains as its properties, the object of each element in the form. Thus, if your form has three elements—a text input box, a submit button, and a checkbox—then `form.elements` is an object that contains three properties, each one a respective object (a text object, a submit button object, and a checkbox object).

length   Contains the number of elements in the form.

Methods

submit( )   Submits the form.

Event Handlers

onSubmit( )   Identifies code to run (either JavaScript statements or functions) when the form is submitted (when the user clicks a defined Submit button).

251

The text and textarea Objects

The text (specified by the <TEXT> tag) and textarea (specified by the <TEXTAREA> tag) elements share the same object components.

Properties

name   String value of the NAME attribute.

value   String value of the contents of the field.

defaultValue   String value of the initial contents of the field.

Methods

focus( )   Sets input focus to the object.

blur( )   Removes input focus from the object.

select( )   Selects the object's input field.

Event Handlers

onFocus   Executes when input focus enters field (by tabbing in or by clicking but not selecting in the field).

onBlur   Executes when input focus leaves the field.

onSelect   Executes when the field is input-focused by selecting some of its text.

onChange   Executes when input focus exits the field, and the value of the field has changed from when onFocus occurred.

The checkbox object

Corresponds to the <INPUT TYPE="checkbox"...> tag.

Properties

name   String value of the NAME attribute.

value   String value of the contents of the checkbox. If checked, value="on"; if unchecked, value="off".

checked   Boolean value of the contents of the checkbox. If checked, status=TRUE; if unchecked, status=FALSE.

defaultChecked   Boolean value that reflects the CHECKED attribute (the default state).

Methods

click( )   Selects the checkbox, causing it to be "on" (or TRUE).

Event Handlers

onClick   Executes when the user checks or unchecks the box.

The radio Object

Corresponds to the `<INPUT TYPE="radio"...>` tag. The form `radio[index]` is used to refer to a single radio button of the `radio` object (that is, one of its multiple choices).

Properties

name   String value of the NAME attribute.

length   The number of radio buttons in the `radio` object.

value   String value of the VALUE attribute.

checked   Boolean value. True if pressed; false if not pressed.

defaultChecked   Boolean property that reflects the value of the CHECKED attribute.

Methods

click( )   Selects the radio button.

Event Handlers

onClick   Executes when the radio button is selected.

The select Object

Corresponds to the `<SELECT>` tag. The JavaScript object consists of an array of `option` objects, each of which has the following components:

Properties

length   Contains the number of objects in the `select` object.

name   The internal name of the `select` object as defined by the NAME= attribute.

selectedIndex   The index number of the currently selected option of the `select` object.

options   This property is an object reflecting the contents of the <OPTION> tag used when defining a select object in HTML. It contains the following properties:

text   String containing the text after the <OPTION> tag.

value   Reflection of the VALUE attribute. This is sent to the server when the Submit button is pressed.

defaultSelected   Boolean that reflects the SELECTED attribute of the <OPTION> tag.

selected   Boolean that indicates the current selected state of the option.

Event Handlers

onFocus   Executes when input focus enters the field.

onBlur   Executes when input focus leaves the field.

onChange   Executes when input focus exits the field, and the field value has changed since the onFocus event.

The button Object

There are three types of buttons in a FORM, defined by the TYPE attribute of the <INPUT> tag:

➤ Submit (TYPE="SUBMIT")

➤ Reset (TYPE="RESET")

➤ Custom (TYPE="BUTTON")

All button objects (regardless of type) have the following components:

Properties

value   String containing the VALUE attribute.

name   String containing the NAME attribute.

Methods

click( )   Selects the button.

Event Handlers

onClick   Executes when a button is clicked.

The submit and reset Objects

The submit object relates to the button defined by the `<INPUT TYPE="submit">` tag, whereas the reset object refers to the `<INPUT TYPE="reset">` tag. Both contain the same properties, methods, and event handlers. Note that the submit button does *not* contain the onSubmit event handler; that event handler belongs to the form object.

Properties

name   The contents of the NAME= attribute.

value   The contents of the VALUE= attribute, which in the case of a submit button is the text displayed on the button face.

Methods

click( )   Selects the button.

Event Handlers

onClick   Triggers when the button is clicked.

The password Object

A password form element is a text-entry box that hides the user input by masking typing with asterisks. It is defined with the `<INPUT TYPE="password">` tag. The password object relates to the characteristics of this element.

Properties

defaultValue   Contains the contents of the VALUE= attribute.

name   The contents of the NAME= attribute.

value   The current data entered into the password field.

Methods

focus( )   Brings focus onto the password element.

blur( )   Removes focus from the password element.

select( )   Selects the current data in the password element, ready to be modified.

The navigator Object

This object is used to determine which version of Netscape Navigator a visitor to your page is using.

Properties

appCodeName   Reflects the "codename" of the user's browser. For example, the codename for Navigator is "mozilla" (I don't know why, either).

appName   Reflects the real name of the user's browser.

appVersion   Reflects the version number of the user's browser.

userAgent   This property reflects the full information on the user's browser, including its codename, version number, and platform (such as Win95).

The string Object

The string object provides a wealth of methods for manipulating the contents of a string.

Properties

length   The length of the string—that is, how many characters long it is.

Methods

big( ), **blink( )**, **bold( )**, **fixed( )**, **italics( )**, **small( )**, **sub( )**, **strike( )**, **sup( )**   All of the above methods add their respective HTML tags to the string. For example, if the variable `message` currently contains the string `"Hello"`, then

`message.big()` would yield the string `"<BIG>Hello</BIG>"`

`message.italics()` would yield the string `"<I>Hello</I>"`

And so forth, for the HTML tags appropriate for the method names above.

fontColor(color), fontSize(size)   Adds respective HTML tags to a string, assigning font color or font size as specified in the parameter passed to the method.

charAt(index)   Returns the character located at position *index* within the string.

indexOf (searchValue, [fromIndex])   Searches the string for the first instance of the string *searchValue*. If *fromIndex* is specified, it begins the search from that position within the string. Returns value of index of first letter where the string is first found.

lastIndexOf (searchValue, [fromIndex])   Searches for *searchValue* beginning at the end (rightmost) of the string and working backward. Reports first instance found searching backward from end, or *fromIndex* if specified.

substring (indexA, indexB)   Extracts the substring starting from position *indexA* to position *indexB*.

toLowerCase( ), toUpperCase( )   Convert string to all lowercase, or all uppercase, letters.

The Date Object

To use the Date object, you must first create a new instance of a Date object. Do this by assigning a variable of your choosing to new Date(), as follows:

```
variablename = new Date();
```

The object contains no properties, and a plethora of methods, which can be used to extract or set various characteristics of the date.

Methods

getDay( ), getDate( ), getHours( ), getMinutes( ), getMonth( ), getSeconds( ), getTime( ), getTimeZoneOffset( ), getYear( )   Each of these methods returns a value respective to the method name; for example, getMinutes() returns the current number of minutes into the current hour.

setDate( ), setHours( ), setMinutes( ), setMonth( ), setSeconds( ), setTime( ), setYear( )   These methods can be used to set the respective values.

toGMTString( )   Returns current date in GMT format, which is exemplified by:

```
Sun, 11 Feb 1996 13:18:21 GMT
```

toLocaleString( )   Returns the current date in "locale" format, which looks like:

```
02/11/96 13:18:21
```

257

parse(date)   This method is commonly used in combination with the `setTime()` method. The `setTime()` method requires its parameter in the number of milliseconds since January 1, 1970 at 00:00:00 hours. The parse method can convert a traditional date string (such as `"May 23, 1972"`) into millisecond format for use with the `setTime()` method.

The Math Object

This object contains properties and methods that allow access to common mathematical constants and calculations.

Properties

The following properties represent the following constant values:

LN10	(natural log of 10)	2.302
LN2	(natural log of 2)	0.693
PI		3.1415
SQRT1_2	(the square root of $^1/_2$)	0.707
SQRT2	(the square root of 2)	1.414

Methods

abs (x)	Returns absolute value of x
acos (x)	Returns arc cosine of x
asin (x)	Returns arc sine of x
atan (x)	Returns arc tangent of x
ceil (x)	Returns the least integer greater than or equal to x
cos (x)	Returns the cosine of x
exp (x)	Returns e (Euler's constant) to the power x
floor (x)	Returns the greatest integer less than or equal to x
log (x)	Returns the natural log of x
max (x, y)	Returns the greater of x and y
min (x, y)	Returns the smaller of x and y
pow (x, y)	Returns x to the yth power
round (x)	Returns x rounded to the nearest integer (.5 cutoff)
sin (x)	Returns sine of x

sqrt (*x*)	Returns square root of *x*
tan (*x*)	Returns tangent of *x*

Reserved Words

The following words are *reserved words*, which means that you cannot give your variables, functions, methods, or objects any of these names. Some of these words are already used for different purposes in JavaScript, and others are reserved for future use, such as further expansion of the JavaScript language.

abstract	else	instance of	static
boolean	extends	int	super
break	false	interface	switch
byte	final	long	synchronized
case	finally	native	this
catch	float	new	throw
char	for	null	throws
class	function	package	transient
const	goto	private	true
continue	if	protected	try
default	implements	public	var
do	import	return	void
double	in	short	while
			with

Predefined JavaScript Colors

Here is a list of JavaScript's built-in color names. Instead of using a hexadecimal triplet to specify the colors on your page, you can assign a string literal to specify one of the following built-in color names (see Chapter 13 for details on how to do this):

Color	Red	Green	Blue	Hexadecimal Triplet
aliceblue	240	248	255	f0f8ff
antiquewhite	250	235	215	faebd7
aqua	0	255	255	00ffff

continues

continued

Color	Red	Green	Blue	Hexadecimal Triplet
aquamarine	127	255	212	7fffd4
azure	240	255	255	f0ffff
beige	245	245	220	f5f5dc
bisque	255	228	196	ffe4c4
black	0	0	0	000000
blanchedalmond	255	235	205	ffebcd
blue	0	0	255	0000ff
blueviolet	138	43	226	8a2be2
brown	165	42	42	a52a2a
burlywood	222	184	135	deb887
cadetblue	95	158	160	5f9ea0
chartreuse	127	255	0	7fff00
chocolate	210	105	30	d2691e
coral	255	127	80	ff7f50
cornflowerblue	100	149	237	6495ed
cornsilk	255	248	220	fff8dc
crimson	220	20	60	dc143c
cyan	0	255	255	00ffff
darkblue	0	0	139	00008b
darkcyan	0	139	139	008b8b
darkgoldenrod	184	134	11	b8860b
darkgray	169	169	169	a9a9a9
darkgreen	0	100	0	006400
darkkhaki	189	183	107	bdb76b
darkmagenta	139	0	139	8b008b
darkolivegreen	85	107	47	55662f
darkorange	255	140	0	ff8c00
darkorchid	153	50	204	9932cc
darkred	139	0	0	8b0000

Color	Red	Green	Blue	Hexadecimal Triplet
darksalmon	233	150	122	e9967a
darkseagreen	143	188	143	8fbc8f
darkslateblue	72	61	139	483d8b
darkslategray	47	79	79	2f4f4f
darkturquoise	0	206	209	00ced1
darkviolet	148	0	211	9400d3
deeppink	255	20	147	ff1493
deepskyblue	0	191	255	00bfff
dimgray	105	105	105	696969
dodgerblue	30	144	255	1e90ff
firebrick	178	34	34	b22222
floralwhite	255	250	240	fffaf0
forestgreen	34	139	34	228b22
fuchsia	255	0	255	ff00ff
gainsboro	220	220	220	dcdcdc
ghostwhite	248	248	255	f8f8ff
gold	255	215	0	ffd700
goldenrod	218	165	32	daa520
gray	128	128	128	808080
green	0	128	0	008000
greenyellow	173	255	47	adff2f
honeydew	240	255	240	f0fff0
hotpink	255	105	180	ff69b4
indianred	205	92	92	cd5c5c
indigo	75	0	130	4b0082
ivory	255	255	240	fffff0
khaki	240	230	140	f0e68c
lavender	230	230	250	e6e6fa
lavenderblush	255	240	245	fff0f5

continues

261

continued

Color	Red	Green	Blue	Hexadecimal Triplet
lawngreen	124	252	0	7cfc00
lemonchiffon	255	250	205	fffacd
lightblue	173	216	230	add8e6
lightcoral	240	128	128	f08080
lightcyan	224	255	255	e0ffff
lightgoldenrod-yellow	250	250	210	fafad2
lightgreen	144	238	144	90ee90
lightgrey	211	211	211	d3d3d3
lightpink	255	182	193	ffb6c1
lightsalmon	255	160	122	ffa07a
lightseagreen	32	178	170	20b2aa
lightskyblue	135	206	250	87cefa
lightslategray	119	136	153	778899
lightsteelblue	176	196	222	b0c4de
lightyellow	255	255	224	ffffe0
lime	0	255	0	00ff00
limegreen	50	205	50	32cd32
linen	250	240	230	faf0e6
magenta	255	0	255	ff00ff
maroon	128	0	0	800000
mediumaquamarine	102	205	170	66cdaa
mediumblue	0	0	205	0000cd
mediumorchid	186	85	211	ba55d3
mediumpurple	147	112	219	9370db
mediumseagreen	60	179	113	3cb371
mediumslateblue	123	104	238	7b68ee
mediumspringgreen	0	250	154	00fa9a
mediumturquoise	72	209	204	48d1cc

Color	Red	Green	Blue	Hexadecimal Triplet
mediumvioletred	199	21	133	c71585
midnightblue	25	25	112	191970
mintcream	245	255	250	f5fffa
mistyrose	255	228	225	ffe4e1
moccasin	255	228	181	ffe4b5
navajowhite	255	222	173	ffdead
navy	0	0	128	000080
oldlace	253	245	230	fdf5e6
olive	128	128	0	808000
olivedrab	107	142	35	6b8e23
orange	255	165	0	ffa500
orangered	255	69	0	ff4500
orchid	218	112	214	da70d6
palegoldenrod	238	232	170	eee8aa
palegreen	152	251	152	98fb98
paleturquoise	175	238	238	afeeee
palevioletred	219	112	147	db7093
papayawhip	255	239	213	ffefd5
peachpuff	255	218	185	ffda69
peru	205	133	63	cd853f
pink	255	192	203	ffc0cb
plum	221	160	221	dda0dd
powderblue	176	224	230	b0e0e6
purple	128	0	128	800080
red	255	0	0	ff0000
rosybrown	188	143	143	bc8f8f
royalblue	65	105	225	4169e1
saddlebrown	139	69	19	8b4513
salmon	250	128	114	fa8072

continues

continued

Color	Red	Green	Blue	Hexadecimal Triplet
sandybrown	244	164	96	f4a460
seagreen	46	139	87	2e8b57
seashell	255	245	238	fff5ee
sienna	160	82	45	a0522d
silver	192	192	192	c0c0c0
skyblue	135	206	235	87ceeb
slateblue	106	90	205	6a5acd
slategray	112	128	144	708090
snow	255	250	250	fffafa
springgreen	0	255	127	00ff7f
steelblue	70	130	180	4682b4
tan	210	180	140	d2b48c
teal	0	128	128	008080
thistle	216	191	216	d8bfd8
tomato	255	99	71	006347
turquoise	64	224	208	40e0d0
violet	238	130	238	ee82ee
wheat	245	222	179	f5deb3
white	255	255	255	ffffff
whitesmoke	245	245	245	f5f5f5
yellow	255	255	0	ffff00
yellowgreen	154	205	50	9acd32

Speak Like a Geek: The Complete Archive

address   Usually refers to an Internet machine name; for example, www.machine.com.

absolute address   A URL that includes the full Internet address of the machine on which the HTML file resides; for example, http://www.machine.com/~username/index.html.

alert   Pop-up window that displays a message to the user. The user must click the "OK" button to proceed.

anchor   A location within an HTML document that is invisibly "marked" with HTML tags. Links can point to this anchor, and take the user to specific locations within one HTML document.

applet   Another name for a Java miniprogram. Applets are the Java elements that are run through Java-enabled browsers. In JavaScript, these are called "scripts" rather than applets.

arithmetic operator   Any of the following symbols: * (multiply), +, –, / (divide), % (modulus), ++ (increment), –– (decrement), or – (negation). Arithmetic operators are used with variables or numeric values in an expression, to yield a mathematical result.

array   An object with a list of properties. In an array, the properties are named in numerical sequence, as in: arrayname[0], arrayname[1], and so on.

assign   Refer a value to a variable name.

assignment   The act of referring a value to a variable name; for example, purchases = 10.

assignment operator   One of the following symbols: =, +=, –=, *=, /=, or %=. All but = will perform the indicated arithmetic on the current variable value and its assigned value.

assignment statement   The whole syntactical construction of assignment: purchases+=(mugs*orders);

attribute   An HTML structure that sets a particular parameter value for a given HTML tag.

binary   Numerical representation in base-2; for example, 10001100. This is the "alphabet" that the computer ultimately understands.

Boolean   An element of logic: **true**, **false**, **and (&&)**, **or (||)**.

browser   A program that allows you to navigate the *World Wide Web*. Browsers can be either text-based or graphical. Some examples of browsers are Netscape Navigator, HotJava, and Microsoft Internet Explorer.

bug   An error in a computer program. See *debugging*.

C   A common programming language, which JavaScript is partially based on.

C++   An object-oriented programming language, the closest relative to JavaScript.

call   The act of telling JavaScript to execute a function.

case-insensitive   In a case-insensitive language or operating system, the computer makes no distinction between lower-and uppercase letters, considering them equivalent. Thus, "cat" is the same word as "Cat."

case-sensitive   In a case-sensitive language or operating system, the computer distinguishes between lower- and uppercase letters, considering them different characters. Thus, "cat" is a different word from "Cat."

CGI   *Common Gateway Interface*, the programming interface that allows Web servers to perform special functions. CGI programs are commonly written in *Perl* and can perform such tasks as complex database searches, custom Web page construction, or secure Web access control. CGI is regarded as complex, and JavaScript is a simpler alternative for performing similar programming feats.

clause   A portion of a full JavaScript statement. For example, within the `if...else` statement, either just the `if` portion or just the `else` portion is a clause.

command   Any "word" that tells the computer to do something.

comment-out   Insert proper comment symbols into code, telling JavaScript not to attempt to execute the words that follow.

comments   Author-entered descriptions in program code meant for human programmers to read, not JavaScript interpretation.

comparison operator   One of the following symbols: ==, <, >, <=, >=, or !=. Returns true if the comparison is valid, otherwise, it returns false.

compiler   A program that converts a collection of programming language statements from "near-human-readable" form (which is what the programmer writes) to "computer-readable" form so that the computer can run them.

compressed files   Computer files that have been reduced in size by a *compression program*. Compression programs are available for all computer systems. For instance, PKZIP is used on DOS machines, WinZip is used with Windows, *tar* and *compress* are used with UNIX, and StuffIt is used on Macintosh computers.

concatenate   Combine any number of strings into one longer string. For example, `"my"` + `"dog"` + `"loves"` + `"me"` yields `"my dog loves me"`.

conditional statement   A JavaScript statement that directs program flow based on the validity or invalidity of a comparison. Examples include `if...else` and `while`.

constant   A variable that is assigned a value that is never meant to change.

cyberspace   The "area" or space in which computer users travel when "navigating" or *surfing* around on a network or the Internet.

debug   The irritating act of attempting to track down errors or design flaws in a program.

debugger   A program designed to help track down *bugs* in other programs. See *bug*.

decompress   To convert compressed, unreadable data into uncompressed, readable data.

define   In JavaScript, to describe the name, parameters, and statements of a function.

definition   In JavaScript, the name, parameters, and statements that make up a function.

document object   The JavaScript object that contains properties and methods relevant to the HTML document. These include colors, anchors, links, and form elements.

download   The process of transferring information from one computer to another. You *download* a file from another computer to yours. The reverse process (transferring a file from your computer to another) is called *uploading*.

element   A screen element is any widget on the computer screen. A form element is one portion of an HTML form, such as a text box, a checkbox, a radio button, a submit button, or a selection box.

e-mail   Slang for *electronic mail*, this is the system that lets people send and receive messages with their computers.

embed   Simply means to insert into a text file. JavaScript programs are "embedded" into an HTML file.

empty string   A string variable that contains no value. You can create an empty string with the assignment `stringname=""`.

error An illegal statement in the JavaScript program that JavaScript cannot understand.

error handler A programming statement that changes program flow in case an error is encountered.

evaluate The act of performing the specified calculation or comparison. JavaScript "evaluates" expressions, such as arithmetic operators or comparisons.

event When a user performs some action that JavaScript recognizes, such as a mouse click in a certain location.

event handler A JavaScript structure that responds to (handles) a particular event or response by the user of the browser. Event handlers are identified by special HTML *attributes*.

event watching When JavaScript keeps an "eye out" for an event to happen. Defining an event handler for an event tells JavaScript to event watch.

execute To perform the actions specified in the program code.

explicit code Rather than calling a function, writing out the code to execute the function directly. Used in relation to defining an event handler.

expression Virtually any "phrase" of JavaScript code, such as an assignment, arithmetic, comparisons, and so on.

eZine An "electronic magazine."

false The value returned from a comparison operation, if the comparison is invalid.

FAQ Shorthand for *Frequently Asked Questions*, a *FAQ* is a document that contains a collection of the most commonly asked questions (and their answers) on a particular subject.

focus When a user clicks on a form element and it becomes "active" for interaction, it is said to "have the focus."

form Any number of user-interactive features in a Web page, including text entry boxes, checkboxes, radio buttons, selection boxes, and any other buttons.

frame A subwindow within the browser window.

FTP *File Transfer Protocol*. A *protocol* that defines how files are transferred from one computer to another. Also, the name of a program that uses this protocol to move files between computers. Sometimes, you'll find **ftp** used as a verb: "Ftp to ftp.netscape.com …".

function A collection of JavaScript statements that perform a particular operation. Also called a *method*.

function call When JavaScript is told to execute a named and defined function. Occurs in the form `functionname(parameters)`.

Gamelan   The premier Web site of Java applets and Java/JavaScript-related information and links: http://www.gamelan.com.

Gopher   A hierarchical information-retrieval protocol popular on the Internet before the Web (which uses the http protocol).

hash mark   The symbol #. In a URL, the hash mark is used to specify an anchor to start user at; for example, http://www.machine.com/~userid/index.html#anchorname.

helper application   An independent program used to process files that the Web browser does not know how to process.

history list   The list of URLs that have been visited during the current Web browsing session.

hostname   The Internet address (or "name") of a machine that holds a particular HTML document; for example, www.machine.com.

HotJava   The browser developed by Sun Microsystems that runs Java applets. HotJava itself is written in Java. HotJava does not yet support JavaScript programs.

HTML   *HyperText Markup Language*, the formatting language supported by the World Wide Web. Web documents are written using various HTML *tags*, which control how the information in the document is presented through the browser.

http   *HyperText Transfer Protocol*, the *protocol* used by the World Wide Web to transfer HTML documents.

hypertext   A system in which documents contain links that, when clicked, allow readers to move between areas of the document or between documents, following subjects of interest in a variety of different paths. The World Wide Web is a hypertext system.

image map   A Web page graphic that the user can click on and be directed to various places depending where in the image he clicked.

increment   To increase the value of a variable, usually by 1.

index number   The number referring to one of the properties in an object. Alternate terminology would refer to a list element of an array (both are the same in JavaScript).

initialize   To assign a starting value to a variable. Often this is 0, but it doesn't have to be.

input   When a user enters data requested by the program; also the name of an HTML tag <INPUT> that defines a form element.

instance   A particular object created from an object definition. An object definition defines the skeleton structure of an object, whereas an instance refers to an actual object based on that skeleton.

instantiate   The act of creating an instance of an object. Done by assigning an object definition (a function) to a new variable, using the new keyword: `instanceobject = new Objectdefn();`

internet   Spelled with a lowercase *i,* the term refers to computer networks that are connected together (or *interconnected*).

Internet   Spelled with a capital *I,* the term refers to the collective of interconnected networks that are globally accessible.

Internet provider   Another term for *service provider.* The company that gets you connected to the Internet.

interpreter   A program that translates computer language statements into computer-readable form and executes them at the same time (at "run time"). This is in contrast to a compiler, which interprets and converts the statements into computer-readable form and then saves the result into a separate file, which can be executed later.

iterate   To repeatedly move through a program loop.

iteration   One sweep through a program loop.

Java   A programming language that extends the Web to handle the distribution of *interactive content*: video, audio, multimedia, and so on. Java programs are called *applets* and run from within a Java-enabled browser, such as HotJava or Netscape Navigator 2.0.

JavaScript   An English-like *scripting language* that supports much of Java's capabilities but doesn't require extended programming knowledge.

JDK   The *Java Developer's Kit,* created by Sun Microsystems to assist Java programmers in creating Java applets.

.js extension   If you are including a file of JavaScript code via the SRC= attribute of the <SCRIPT> tag, then this file's name must contain the extension `.js`.

keyword   Any one word that JavaScript recognizes as having meaning to it, such as if, then, var, new, and so on.

link   Text or an image in a Web page that, if clicked, will bring the user to another Web page, or another location within the current Web page (an anchor).

literal   An actual numeric value or string value; for example, `"5"` or `"cats"`. String literals must be enclosed in single- or double-quotation marks.

LiveScript   The scripting language developed by Netscape that was the predecessor to *JavaScript.*

load   To retrieve an HTML file and display it in the Web browser.

loading   Retrieving data into Web browser, either from the local hard drive or from across the Internet.

logging off   The opposite of *logging on*, where the computer service is informed that you want to terminate the connection. The process usually involves typing a command such as **exit**, **logout**, **logoff**, or **bye**.

logging on   Slang for the process of connecting to a central computer network or service from a local computer (sometimes referred to as *logging in*). The process usually involves entering a *username* and *password*, ensuring that only authorized individuals can use the computer service.

logical operator   Any of the following: && (AND), || (OR), ! (NOT). Used in conditional expressions; returns true or false.

login   The procedure of *logging on*.

loop   A section of program code that is executed over and over in repetition, until some condition changes.

loop counter   A variable that changes through each iteration of the loop, in correlation with how many times the loop has been executed. The loop counter is often used in the condition that continues or ceases the loop.

Lycos   A popular Web search engine, which locates information anywhere on the World Wide Web: http://www.lycos.com.

MB   The abbreviation for *megabyte*, roughly one million bytes.

megabyte   A measure of the quantity of data, disk space, or computer memory (*RAM*). One million bytes.

method   A function that is a property of a JavaScript object.

Microsoft Internet Explorer   A new-ish Web browser from Microsoft, intended to compete directly with Netscape Navigator. Does not support Java or JavaScript at this writing, but will.

module   A miniprogram, essentially equivalent to a function.

modulo   The % operator.

modulus   The result of the modulo (%) operator, which returns the remainder of a division operation. Thus, 10%3 results in 1.

multimedia   Any computer program that uses one or more of the following: text, graphics, sound, and video.

nest(ed)   When a statement is used as part of another statement. For example, were the if clause of a statement another if...else statement, these would be nested. Also, when bookending symbols such as brackets { } or parentheses ( ) are used within one another.

Netscape   Short for Netscape Communications Corporation, the company that produces the highly popular Netscape Navigator Web browser.

Netscape Navigator   The Web browser product available from Netscape (http://home.netscape.com). Supports Java and JavaScript, and virtually every other Web capability.

newline character   The symbol that represents a linefeed to the computer. The JavaScript method `document.writeln()` sends a newline character at the end of the output, whereas `document.write()` does not.

null   Literally, "nothing." No value—not 0, which *is* a value. Just *nothing*.

numeric variable   A variable that contains a numeric value, such as 5.

object   A very important feature of JavaScript. An object is a variable that is, in fact, a set of subvariables known as *properties*.

operand   A variable or value used in an operator expression. For example, in the expression `orders*10`, both `orders` and `10` are operands.

output   Any data that is sent to the screen (or, perhaps, to the printer).

parameter   Additional information that is passed to a Java applet or a JavaScript function. Parameters supply applets and functions with information they need to complete their task.

parameter passing   The act of sending values to a function or applet. Done either in a function call or `<APPLET>` tag.

parent object   If object A contains a property B, where property B is also an object, then A is the parent object to B.

parse   The act of pulling desired data from a larger set of data. Often used in reference to a string, where one uses a method to pull specified parts of the string out of the whole one.

Pascal   Another programming language, somewhat similar to C.

pass   The act of sending data or values into a function or applet.

Perl   A popular UNIX-based scripting language. Often used in partnership with CGI.

pixel   One dot of light on the computer screen. Common computer screens contain 640 horizontal × 480 vertical pixels. Depending on the video configuration and monitor size, other computers may have screen sizes of 800 × 600 pixels, 1024 × 768 pixels, or even 1200 × 1024 pixels (on a 21" monitor, lest the user go blind).

placeholder   A book convention wherein you insert some text that refers to actual variables or values you would put in its place were you actually writing the code. For example, `lunch(parameters)` means to call the function `lunch()` with some parameters appropriate to the particular situation.

port   In the context of the Internet, a *port* is similar to a CB radio channel. Different Internet applications (*FTP*, the *World Wide Web*, *Telnet*, and so on) communicate on different ports throughout the Internet.

program flow   The order in which program commands and statements are executed. Normally, they are executed in sequence (from top to bottom), but conditional statements and function calls are frequently used to alter program flow.

programming language   Any set of keywords and syntax that you can combine to instruct the computer to perform some tasks.

property   A subvariable of an object. An object is a set of related variables known as properties, and each property is a variable or function in and of itself. The construction `object.property` is how they are referred to in JavaScript. For example, `status` is a property of the object `window`, and it can be assigned a string to display in the browser status line.

protocol   A set of rules that defines how computers transmit information to each other, allowing different types of computer hardware and software to communicate with each other. Each type of Internet application (*FTP*, *Telnet*, and so on) has its own protocol.

public domain software   Software that is not owned by anyone and is freely available for use and redistribution.

relative address   A URL without the machine name specified, it assumes starting at the same directory as the current document. For example, extras/more.html is a relative address referring to the specified subdirectory and file name, assuming the same starting path as the current document.

reserved word   One of the words that JavaScript recognizes for its own uses, and thus cannot be used as a variable name. Reserved words include all keywords that are part of JavaScript statements.

return   A keyword that is used to return a value at the conclusion of a JavaScript function. This value is assigned to a variable if the function was called in an assignment; for example, `result=functionname();`

REXX   A somewhat popular scripting language, similar to PERL. Commonly used in OS/2 and a variation of which is used on the Amiga (AREXX).

run   The act of executing a computer program.

script   A series of program statements that instruct the computer on how to accomplish a task.

scripting language   The set of rules and keywords that comprise a functional script. Same as a programming language, except that scripting languages are traditionally less strict and simpler to learn.

self   A synonym for a `window` object; `self.status` is equivalent to `window.status`. Can be used to avoid conflicts with other labels in the JavaScript program.

self-extracting archive   A compressed file that can be run like a regular program, except that the "program" that runs is the decompressor, and the result is a reconstructed collection of programs or files.

server   A program or computer that "services" another program or computer (referred to as the *client*). For example, within the World Wide Web, your *browser* is the *client* and the computer you connect to is the *server*.

service provider   A company that provides a connection to the Internet for a fee. Different providers charge different fees—so shop around for the best deal before you subscribe to a particular provider.

source code   The actual text that comprises the program itself.

statement   A JavaScript construction that usually winds up affecting program flow. Loops and conditionals, such as `for` and `if...else` are statements.

status line   The small message window at the bottom of the browser window. The status line can be programmed to display specified messages using the `window.status` property.

string   A value that consists of a series of alphanumeric characters, enclosed in quotation marks.

submit   To send the user-entered form data to a specified action, either another URL or some data processing function in JavaScript.

subvariable   A variable that is a property of an object.

Sun Microsystems   The company which, besides manufacturing very fast, very expensive UNIX computers, also created the Java language and the HotJava browser. Sun partnered with Netscape to create JavaScript.

supervariable   An object. This is a variable that consists of a set of variables.

support   In software lingo, refers to the capability of an application to handle some task. A browser that "supports" JavaScript is capable of running JavaScript programs.

surf   The act of viewing Web pages. Often implies moving from one to another to another via links. Surfing is supposed to make you cool.

syntax   The grammatical rules of a programming language.

table   An HTML design element that formats and displays data in an on-screen table structure.

tag   An HTML "code" that defines how a portion of a Web document is to be formatted by the browser for display.

Telnet   An Internet facility by which you can connect ("log in") to another machine any-where on the Internet.

template   A skeleton design. Serves to define an outline.

The Web   More Internet shorthand for the World Wide Web.

this   A JavaScript object that is used as shorthand to refer to the current object in question. Used in relation to forms and method definitions.

trigger   An onEvent definition, which tells JavaScript "what to do" when a specified event occurs.

true   A logical (Boolean) value, returned from a comparison.

unary   An operator that takes only a single operand; for example ++ (increment), −− (decre-ment), and − (negate).

UNIX   A computer operating system; one that the majority of *hosts* connected to the Internet run. There are several different versions of UNIX available today, fondly referred to as *flavors*.

upload   The process of transferring information from one computer to another, specifically from your computer to someone else's (either another user's computer or a server).

URL   *Uniform Resource Locator*, an "address" that defines the exact location (and *protocol*) of a computer or document on the Internet.

UseNet   The world's largest public "bulletin board," where folks post and reply to messages from others. Divided into many thousands of subtopics of interest (known as "newsgroups").

user   Whoever is visiting your Web page, and, therefore, "using" and interacting with your JavaScript program.

value   Some form of data. A numeric value is a number. A string value is a string. Either can be assigned to a variable. A literal value is a specific number of string explicitly stated, not assigned to a variable.

validation   The practice of evaluating data to see whether it meets some criteria.

variable   A "label" that refers to some value. Often, the value may change, allowing the programmer to use named labels to keep track of various quantities or other forms of change-able data.

W3   Internet shorthand for the World Wide Web.

WebCrawler   Another Web search engine, somewhat old: http://www.webcrawler.com.

widget   A prewritten JavaScript program that creates a small user-interaction doohickey, such as a scroll bar.

window   The on-screen area in which the browser displays a Web page's contents related to the current browser window.

window object   The JavaScript object that contains properties related to the current browser window.

World Wide Web   A *hypertext* system that allows users to "travel through" (or *surf*) *linked* documents, following any chosen route. World Wide Web documents contain a variety of topics; selecting various *links* leads you from one document to the next. The nature of the system allows links to span computers, literally taking you from one part of the world to the next with the click of a mouse.

WWW   Yet more Internet shorthand for the World Wide Web.

Yahoo   The premier subject catalog for the World Wide Web, with search facilities: http://www.yahoo.com.

Index

W-Z

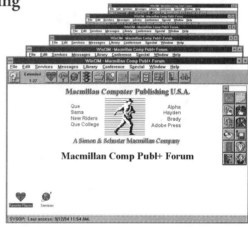